TIME OFF

A Practical Guide to Building Your Rest Ethic and Finding Success Without the Stress

JOHN FITCH AND
MAX FRENZEL

W0018961

RUPA

Published by
Rupa Publications India Pvt. Ltd 2025
7/16, Ansari Road, Daryaganj
New Delhi 110002

Sales centres:
Bengaluru Chennai
Hyderabad Jaipur Kathmandu
Kolkata Mumbai Prayagraj

P-ISBN: 978-93-5702-827-1
E-ISBN: 978-93-5702-750-2

First impression 2025

10 9 8 7 6 5 4 3 2 1

The moral right of the authors has been asserted.

Printed in India

To all the brave leaders, free spirits, creatives, full-time parents, entrepreneurs, early retirees, dreamers, and other time off evangelists—past and present—who had the courage to break away from the grind, the hustle, and the busyness, and show through their example and rest ethic how much can be achieved when time off is taken seriously.

TIME OFF

John Fitch is a business coach, angel investor, and writer. He is a recovering workaholic who wrote this book for a former version of himself. John studied Business and Media at the University of Texas at Austin. He has built a career designing digital products and as an active angel investor in technologies that are automating the mundane work that most people don't enjoy. He cultivates great ideas and inspiration by hosting a dinner party, training Jiu Jitsu, taking a short trip to somewhere new, farming watermelons, playing music, and dancing with his significant other. You can find John at www.john-fitch.com.

Max Frenzel is an AI researcher, writer, and digital creative. After receiving his PhD in Quantum Information Theory from Imperial College London and working as a postdoctoral research fellow at Tokyo University, Max has been involved in several tech startups, focusing on the intersection of AI research and product design. Most recently, he has been interested in the applications of AI and deep learning to creativity, design, and music. Some of the AI art Max has been involved in was exhibited at places like the Barbican Centre in London, and he is a regular public speaker on topics such as AI and creativity. In his time off, Max enjoys good coffee, tries to perfect his bread baking skills, and produces electronic music and performs around Tokyo. You can find him online at www.maxfrenzel.com.

Mariya Suzuki was born in Nara and studied illustration in Long Beach, California. She currently works as an illustrator/artist in Tokyo. She has contributed her work for many musicians, food professionals, and books and magazines from around the world. Aside from work, she enjoys going around town to draw subjects whose shape or story catches her attention, as well as what surrounds her in her everyday life. Find her at www.mariyasketch.com.

What is
without
periods of
rest will
not endure."

—OVID

Contents

WHAT IS TIME OFF?

Picture this:

- You go on a long walk in the woods or the park near your home with no intended destination or purpose. Then, toward the end of your stroll, you suddenly have an "aha!" moment about a prominent project you've been working on. You know exactly what idea to pursue next.
- You need to focus, so you put your phone on do-not-disturb mode or press the sleep button on your tablet. As the notifications disappear, your creativity soars.
- You unwind after a solid day of effort, sigh as you hit the comfy mattress, and close your eyes before fading into eight hours of deep sleep. You wake up refreshed and greet the day with enthusiasm.
- Having completed an exciting chapter of your career, you decide not to jump straight into the next big thing but instead book a mini sabbatical. You travel to Italy to learn how to make pasta, or maybe go camping in New Zealand for a few weeks. Your only goal is to discover what's next for your life story.
- Three beautiful hours fly by on a Wednesday afternoon thanks to the flow state you found yourself in while taking a break from your desk to get lost in a hobby.
- The sound of a long-time friend's deep laugh has you cracking up, while you both linger over a two-hour dinner. For once, you aren't talking about work but rather how crazy you both were as kids.
- You end a long phone call with your parents. You are grateful you made the time to connect because you are not sure how many more of those conversations you have left.

Did visualizing these moments bring you any feelings of peace? When was the last time you experienced moments like this? How often do you allow yourself to break away from being busy? And is your busyness even achieving all that much in the first place?

We commonly think of rest as the opposite of work. We either rest, or we are productive. Hear the words "time off," and it's easy to default to thinking about the weekend or the vacation time granted to you at work. You might picture yourself sitting on the couch playing video games or lying on the beach sipping cocktails. But this book isn't about vacations, at least not primarily. This book is also not a call to be lazy, nor is it an instruction manual for slacking off. Far from it! *Time Off* is about the practices that keep us from feeling overwhelmed and overworked; practices that allow us to live happier, richer, more fulfilled lives; practices that, somewhat counterintuitively (although we hope that it will seem very obvious by the end of this book), allow us to be our most productive and creative selves. And we need them now more than ever.

In 2019, the World Health Organization included "burnout" in their International Classification of Diseases as an "occupational phenomenon." Stress, anxiety, and disillusionment are more prevalent than ever before, especially among millennials. Overwhelm and overwork are stifling our creativity and crippling our society.

As much as we may like to think of ourselves as robots who can run effectively around the clock, we need distance from the daily hustle. Even if we could work at full capacity, day in and day out, we shouldn't. A lot of the wonderful parts of the human experience center on rest, reflection, and recovery. Our minds and bodies need a reprieve from the constant pressure and demands on our time and brainpower. If we want to accomplish the big things we've set out to do—to create, lead, contribute, and make an impact—we need a rest ethic as strong as our work ethic.

FINDING YOUR REST ETHIC

Take in a deep breath and hold it.

Keep holding. How long can you hold your inhale until it gets uncomfortable? Thirty seconds? A few minutes? It doesn't take long until we all, eventually, need to exhale.

Think of your work ethic as the inhale (it is, in a way, as essential to your career as air is to your body). With a good work ethic, we make, execute, coordinate, manage, fulfill, and get things done. Task list—inhale. Project execution—inhale. Making our ideas come to life—inhale.

But we can't keep inhaling forever. Eventually we have to exhale. This exhale is your rest ethic, and it is just as essential.

A solid rest ethic gifts us inspiration, ideas, and recovery. It allows us to build up our enthusiasm and sustain our passion. Gaining a fresh perspective—exhale. Project ideation and "aha" moments—exhale. Letting big ideas incubate in your mind—exhale. And just as a deep exhale prepares you for a better inhale, your rest ethic enables you to have a better work ethic.

Before we explore the idea of rest ethic any further, let's first define what makes a good work ethic, since this is all too often confused with simply working hard. Jason Fried and David Heinemeier Hansson provide a great definition in their book *It Doesn't Have to Be Crazy at Work*:

> A great work ethic isn't about working whenever you're called upon. It's about doing what you say you're going to do, putting in a fair day's work, respecting the work, respecting the customer, respecting coworkers, not wasting time, not creating unnecessary work for other people, and not being a bottleneck.

We couldn't have said it better ourselves. Excessive hours don't guarantee quality work. And quality work, not quantity or busywork, is what a good work ethic is all about. Now, there are plenty of fantastic books out there about improving and refining your work ethic. Titles like *7 Habits of Highly Effective People*, *Relentless*, *Mastery*, and *Turning Pro* have got you covered. Our focus here will be on your rest ethic, leisure, and the wellspring of creativity and impactful ideas your time off can produce.

So, what might a well-designed rest ethic look like?

This book will teach you that it involves much more than taking a vacation or a day off. A great rest ethic is not just about working less. It's about becoming conscious of how you spend your time, recognizing that busyness is often the opposite of productivity, admitting and respecting your need for downtime and detachment, establishing clear boundaries and saying "no" more often, giving your ideas time and space to incubate, evaluating what success means to you, and ultimately finding and unlocking your deepest creative and human potential.

A rest ethic and a work ethic—we need both. They are two sides of the same coin. But today, it seems like too many of us are running around holding our breath for way too long. How effective is our work ethic without enthusiasm and creativity? How can we be effective leaders and come up with the big, innovative, impactful ideas our world needs if we're stressed and burned out?

The team behind this book experienced the need to exhale firsthand. John reached a breaking point in his life and discovered a novel concept of time while on a life-changing sabbatical. Max was drowning in busyness without feeling productive, and during some quiet days in the mountains started thinking back to his leisurely but highly productive PhD days. Our illustrator, Mariya, was falling out of love with drawing because she had taken on too many projects and had to relearn to emphasize quality of work—and enjoyment— over quantity of projects. All three of us had a bumpy and winding road discovering the importance of having a rest ethic. We wrote this book to make your road a bit easier.

TIME OFF IS TIMELESS AND UNIVERSAL

Did you know that Albert Einstein would regularly sail the seas with his wooden boat to find serenity? Or that Beethoven developed his body of work all while spending his afternoons embarking on lengthy walks, stopping at a tavern to read the newspaper? Throughout the pages of this book, we will introduce you to a wonderful and diverse cast of real people—innovators, game changers, Nobel Prize winners, thought leaders, billionaires, prolific artists, and Greek gods, as well as the guy and girl next door—who all practice time off through a variety of refreshing habits, mental models, and actionable principles. You will be surprised by how many of them found their own version of success without being overwhelmed or burned out. They created quality work not in spite of taking time off, but because of it.

We are not claiming that these methods will fit everyone. In fact, some of the advice you'll find throughout this book might even be contradictory. Time off is highly personal. Some people may find theirs in solitude, others among friends. Some prefer activity, while others find energy in complete rest. If done right, even work can fall under our definition of time off. We want to present you with an extensive collection of tools, tactics, and habits that worked for a variety of very successful people, past and present. Using this as inspiration, we encourage you to mix and match, try them for yourself, make them your own, keep what is useful, and ignore the rest.

Is it possible to grow a successful company in an internet-driven era without raising millions of dollars and working around the clock to stand a chance for survival? Absolutely. And we can benefit from exploring the stories of those who have done it, such as Stephan Aarstol and Brunello Cucinelli.

Do you have to sacrifice your various passions and specialize in a single narrow domain in order to stay competitive? Not at all! In fact, as artificial intelligence becomes better at specialized tasks, range and a broad set of interests might be the best way to stay relevant, and people like software engineer (and rapper) Brandon Tory and journalist Tim Harford can show us how.

Can you appreciate leisure if you are in a complex leadership position with tens of thousands of people depending on you? You must, if you want to be an effective and empathetic leader. Roman emperor Marcus Aurelius firmly believed this two millennia ago, and business magnate Richard Branson still does today.

Can you be world class in your chosen field without sacrificing rest and your private life? Hell yes! Top athletes like LeBron James and Firas Zahabi know this. And so do renowned chefs Alice Waters and Magnus Nilsson, as well as actress Lupita Nyong'o.

Even if you do not sit at the very top of the corporate hierarchy, happen to be a Roman emperor, run your own business as a freelancer, or aim to be a pro athlete or top chef, there are many ways in which you can incorporate time off into your daily routine at the office, or while away from it, as the examples of Sarah Arai, Pete Adeney, and others show.

What connects all of these people is their refusal to subscribe to the idea that busyness and full speed are the only paths to success. "Get the outwork myth out of your head," urge Jason Fried and David Heinemeier Hansson. "Stop equating work ethic with excessive work hours. Neither is going to get you ahead or help you find calm." But a good rest ethic can.

As we will see shortly, the greatest minds in history understood the need for time off. But this is not an outdated concept. Even though most of us seem to devalue it today, time off is as applicable—and essential—now as it ever was, more so even. Those of us who recognize this ancient wisdom and put it into practice are reaping tremendous benefits.

Throughout this book we will explore the many facets of time off by diving deeper into specific topics such as creativity, sleep, and play—all backed up by scientific arguments, a wealth of inspiring stories, and concrete actionable advice for cultivating your own rest ethic. Toward the end of the book, we will share with you our vision of a not-too-distant future in which, thanks to developments in automation technologies and AI, creativity, innovation, and, yes, even human-ness—those things machines can't replicate—will be in the highest demand. And to access (and excel in) that future, we'll need a solid rest ethic and a deep appreciation of leisure more than ever before. We'll need time off.

But before we get into all this, we want to start with a question: Just what exactly went wrong and how did we end up forgetting about time off?

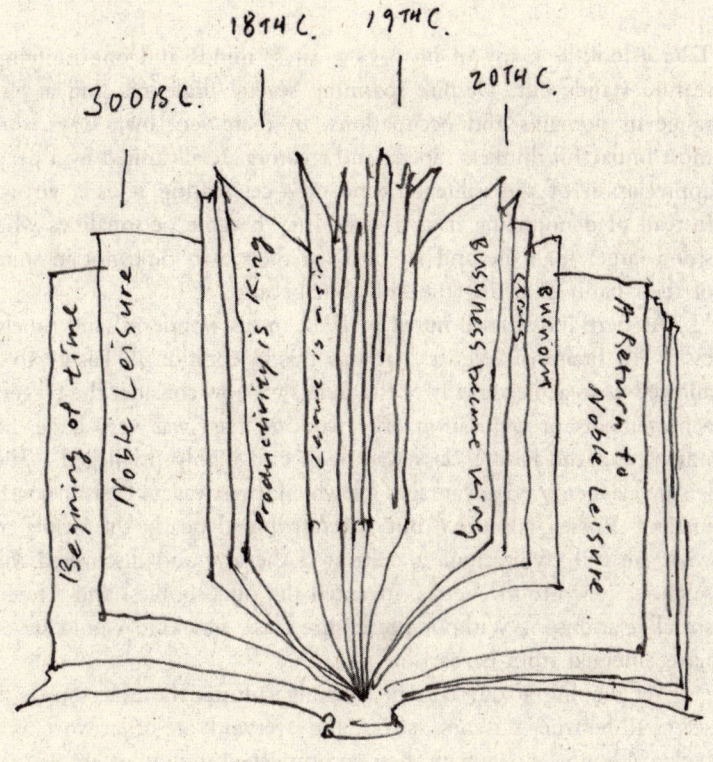

TIME OFF THROUGHOUT HISTORY
–What Went Wrong?

Take a look at many of history's greatest minds and one unifying feature stands out. Despite spanning several millennia and a vast range of domains and occupations, in their very own ways, our most impactful thinkers, doers, and creators are all united by a deep appreciation of the value of time off—celebrating it as a virtue, instead of denouncing it as a vice. They became personalities who stood larger than life and far outlived their own time not in spite of their habit of taking time off, but because of it.

As Bertrand Russell noted in 1932 in his wonderful and timely essay "In Praise of Idleness," it was this celebration of leisure that allowed us to achieve many of the things we now consider the biggest achievements of civilization. The working class was very large, he noted, and the leisure class was small and highly privileged. "The leisure class enjoyed advantages for which there was no basis in social justice," Russell admitted, but it "contributed nearly the whole of what we call civilization. It cultivated the arts and discovered the sciences; it wrote the books, invented the philosophies, and refined social relations…. Without the leisure class, mankind would never have emerged from barbarism."

Yet looking at our current working culture, the exact opposite seems to be true. Busyness, stress, and overwork are often worn as a badge of honor, showing just how accomplished and important we are. Someone who leaves work on time and takes ample breaks during the day can't possibly be as productive as someone who grinds out long hours of overwork day after day and rarely leaves their desk, right?

Well, unless all the historical examples are freakish outliers (which they are not), and unless Bertrand Russell was just some random dreamer with some funny ideas about what really shaped civilization (which he was not), something seems to be misaligned. Somewhere along the line, something went wrong, and we ended up forgetting the value of rest. As Nassim Taleb noted, "only in recent history has 'working hard' signaled pride rather than shame." With this false pride, our culture has descended into a crisis of mental health issues, burnout, and widespread unhappiness. Even the one thing we so desperately seem to be seeking—productivity—is suffering as a result.

For most of history, people knew that in order to be fully present and focused when working, they had to balance busyness with high-quality rest and switch off from work mode. Today, however, many of us hover around 50 percent—we are never fully present and focused at work (because we don't know how to be), nor are we fully detached from work during rest. Neither fully on nor fully off. The problem is that effort is not cumulative. Two hours at 50 percent doesn't even get close to one hour near 100 percent in terms of productivity, and this is especially true if the task involves a creative component—which more and more tasks do; the days of repetitive factory work are all but numbered, as we will explore.

Luckily, a select few have kept the knowledge of time off alive. They are running ventures and influencing society just as the wonderful people of days past. And more and more people are rediscovering the value of this practice (and hopefully, this book will convince some of you to join this movement).

Before we get to this, let's first explore what went wrong. How did we end up with such distorted—and as we shall see counterproductive—priorities? How did most of us forget that rest and time off are essential? To understand what happened, let us first take a brief look at the role of work and leisure throughout history.

AT THE BEGINNING OF TIME

Once upon a time, time wasn't really time as we know it. For our hunter-gatherer ancestors, natural cycles and the simple needs of the present moment were what mattered most. You were hungry, so you went to hunt. It got dark and you became tired, so you went to sleep. The concept of work as we think of it today did not exist either.

Work was simply "providing"— providing shelter so you wouldn't be left to the elements or providing food so you wouldn't starve.

Living in a largely unpopulated world full of natural abundance, these foragers found food so easily that a few hours of light work could, in many cases, sustain them for three days. It's estimated that the average "workday" of foragers took fewer than three hours, leaving them with ample time to spend on whatever they felt like doing. The lifestyle of foragers offered plenty of sleep and leisure and had very little chronic stress (while providing occasional doses of healthy acute stresses, in the form of large predatory animals). Burnout and other related diseases, as well as the concept of busyness, had yet to be invented by modern civilization.

This all changed about 10,000 years ago. The Neolithic Revolution took place, and with it came permanent settlements and the advent of agriculture. Rather than simply responding to our immediate needs, we now had to start thinking long term, metaphorically and literally sowing the seeds for future harvests. Agriculture required humans to put in immense amounts of effort to tend to their crops and livestock and to plan ahead for potential payoffs in a future far more distant than anything a hunter or gatherer ever had to consider. There wasn't time, and then there was.

The new concept of personal property in settled societies also meant that people started competing with each other. For the foragers, putting in any work beyond covering the tribe's basic necessities was not only useless, but actually wasteful. However, the settled societies suddenly started developing concepts of personal wealth that led people to try to outwork each other. For the first time we established a direct link between putting in more time and work and getting more out in return for the effort.

At least initially, humanity made the most of the newfound stability and larger community size. The Mesopotamians invented the wheel and established mathematics, the Chinese mastered silk weaving and manufactured paper, and the Egyptians built the pyramids and developed elaborate religious traditions. Culture flourished. In Ancient Greece and Rome, as well as in the cultural centers of the East, big and impactful ideas emerged at a speed never seen before. In short succession, we witnessed the birth of democracy, philosophy, astronomy, math, theater, and literature—ideas that fundamentally shaped our world.

Yet, despite all of this, modern society would take a look at a day in the life of most ancient Greeks and Romans (at least those fortunate enough to be neither poor nor slaves) and label them as lazy bums. Those who actually made the biggest contributions deliberately aspired to not have to work—in their eyes, if you had to work, you were not successful. And it was exactly this leisure-focused life, and the time it provided for philosophy, games, literature, family, and sports, that allowed culture to blossom. Leisure, as Bertrand Russell would later write, was "essential to civilization." And according to one of the Ancient Greeks, Aristotle, leisure was not only essential, it was the highest ideal anyone could aspire to. Work was a necessity. But leisure was noble.

ARISTOTLE

Greek Philosopher (384—322 BC)

"As I must repeat once again, the first principle of all action is leisure."

"All of life can be divided into work and leisure, and war and peace; and of actions, some aim at what is necessary and useful, while others aim at what is noble.... Just as war is for the sake of peace, so work is for the sake of leisure and what is necessary and useful is for the sake of what is noble."

Athens, Greece, around 330 BC. Aristotle is hard at work at the Lyceum, the location of the Peripatetic school of philosophy he founded. He is deep in thought and discussion about logic, metaphysics, mathematics, biology, botany, ethics, and politics. But what we might today classify as knowledge work, was largely leisure to Aristotle. And not just any form of leisure—it was *noble leisure*.

The key distinction Aristotle saw between mere work and noble leisure was essentially the question of why we do it. Work is done for a purpose, a utilitarian goal. Leisure, on the other hand, is done purely for its own sake, in search of meaning rather than purpose. For this reason, Aristotle also did not consider rest as a form of leisure. Rest, in the way he defined it, always asks the question, "Rest from what?" (with the answer, "To do more work!"). In Aristotle's hierarchy, we rest for the sake of work, and we work for the sake of leisure. But leisure is defined entirely through itself. It stands at the top of the hierarchy.

So while today we might think of Aristotle's pursuits as "work," to him they were largely leisure. Most of his thoughts were pure contemplation, which he considered as an "activity that is appreciated for its own sake.... Nothing is gained from it except the act of contemplation." He was "pursuing science in order to know, and not for any utilitarian end." Something "useless" can be "beyond usefulness" and a true good in itself. Unfortunately, even among the most "pure" knowledge workers today, such as academics, this form of thinking removed from purpose rarely exists anymore. We no longer understand the concept of noble leisure.

This has a huge impact on our lives, both at the individual level and as a society. Paraphrasing Aristotle, if we are always too busy with work, or are given over to pure relaxation to recover for more work, we have neither the time nor inspiration to live virtuous lives and contribute to society and culture. We become a society without leisure. And without leisure, we become a society without big ideas.

True leisure, noble leisure, is not passivity or relaxation. It is an activity in which we can find our greatest fulfillment as humans. As the Noble Leisure Project blog puts it: "To be at leisure is to be free to pursue studies and activities aimed at the cultivation of virtue (such as music, poetry, and philosophy). These are properly the ends of noble leisure." Think for a moment: What activities bring you the most fulfillment outside of work? Have you been ignoring them?

While we might have largely forgotten Aristotle's idea of leisure, many of his thoughts lived on through the ages by inspiring countless thinkers that came after him. And we are not only hopeful that we, once again, find ourselves at the beginning of a renaissance in noble leisure, but we are actively making the case for noble leisure with this book. We hope that you will join us in this movement.

"One should act with a view to what is necessary and useful, but, more so, with a view to what is noble," Aristotle reminds us. "Nature itself aims not only at the correct use of work but also at the capacity for noble leisured activity. Since such activity equates to flourishing, it is the starting point for everything else." So let us all supplement our work with noble leisure, done for its own sake, rather than in order to rest for more work. What exactly this looks like has to be discovered by each of us personally, but it forms the starting point for everything else.

PRACTICE:

Learn to practice noble leisure

Noble leisure is the ultimate goal, the shining beacon that we hope will guide you through the remainder of this book. If we can return to noble leisure, we have truly mastered the art of time off. But to master time off, we must first recognize its value. Then, we can move on to what Aristotle called "the principal point: with what kind of activity is man to occupy his leisure?" While Aristotle had an answer to this question, we think that today each of us has to find our own answer. We hope that the following chapters will help you define this principal point for yourself, and find your personal way back to noble leisure.

VALUABLE TIME, NECESSARY WORK, NOBLE LEISURE

In Aristotle's time, society was centered on leisure. As Catholic philosopher Josef Pieper points out in his book, *Leisure: The Basis of Culture*, it was the ancient Greek word for leisure, "σχολή" (*skole*), that provided the origin from which the Latin *scola*, and our modern English "*school*" were derived. In its original sense, school prepared people for a life of culture and leisure.[1] In fact, it is telling that neither ancient Greek nor Latin even had words for work, only the negation of leisure (*a-scolia* in Greek and *neg-otium* in Latin).

While such a shift in perspective seems unthinkable today–given that we live in what Pieper calls a world of "total work" where the idea that we "live to work" is often taken for granted and the opposite is seen as crazy—we can still learn a lot from the Ancients. And we should.

The entire notion of the "intellectual worker" is decidedly modern and shows just how much our thinking and perception of work have changed. Traditionally, intellectual pursuits were always reserved for the leisure class, far removed from work. The Ancients thought of knowledge as mostly receptive—we passively receive it through observing the world. Knowledge needs space to breathe and time for contemplation. Ancient Greek philosopher Heraclitus described it as "listening to the essence of things."

In many ways, noble leisure forms the basis of knowledge work, but Aristotle and his contemporaries would hardly recognize this modern concept. On a societal level, we have lost track of the main

---

[1]Today, one could argue, most education systems are cultivating lives of industry and conformity to the busyness lifestyle. We could certainly benefit from remembering the origins of the word, and, as Pieper suggests, once again focus on "education as opposed to training, culture as opposed to instruction." Pieper urges us to return to the roots of leisure: "We must begin by setting aside the prejudice—our prejudice—that comes from overvaluing the sphere of work."

point—we have confused the roles of work and leisure, and started equating the latter with laziness and sloth. Over time, hard work started to equal moral good. And, as we will see, this gradual fusion of work and morality still haunts us to this day. The key driver behind this shift was our evolving perception of time.

VISIBLE TIME: PRODUCTIVITY IS KING

For much of human history, work was largely unsupervised and people were free to go about their craft—and life—in any way they wanted, as long as there were results. The idea that you could buy a person's time, rather than their product, would have been seen as absurd. Our notion of time itself was rather different. We measured time in natural cycles or by how long it took to accomplish certain tasks.

In an article titled "Time, Work-Discipline, and Industrial Capitalism," historian E. P. Thompson tells the story of "primitive people" who follow the "cattle clock," measuring time by how long it took them to take care of their livestock or to tend to their social relations. When the oxen have gone to the grazing ground, that marks one time. A later time might be defined by when the sheep have been unfastened. And the same was true for time intervals. In Madagascar, "a rice-cooking" was a valid duration (roughly 30 minutes).

This task-oriented notion of time is the most natural. Cows must be milked when they are ready, not when it's "milk o'clock," and the boats have to go out with the tides. This concept of time is also the easiest to comprehend for humans, and, according to Thompson, leads to the "least demarcation between 'work' and 'life.' … The working-day lengthens or contracts according to the task and there is no great sense of conflict between labour and 'passing the time of day.'" We simply did what needed to be done, without worrying too much about time itself.

But as the complexity of our operations grew and multiple people had to work together, sometimes over large geographical regions, there came a natural shift to timing our labor. The task-oriented framework broke down and timed labor became the norm: now you had to synchronize your schedule with that of others and show up to work "on time."

Suddenly, anyone who didn't stick to this new framework appeared "wasteful and lacking in urgency," writes Thompson. A clear distinction between "employer's time" and "own time" emerged. As he puts it: "Not the task but the value of time when reduced to money is dominant: Time is now currency: it is not passed but spent." In other words, your time has become valuable to someone else and can be exchanged and given away for value. It no longer belongs solely to you. It's a commodity.

This shift marked a turning point not only for time, but also for leisure. When time became a valuable currency that could be traded for money, leisure's value declined. Worse, leisure became genuinely wasteful, the equivalent of burning money. If you didn't produce anything with your time—if there was no output—you wasted it. Productivity becomes the name of the game. After all, people aren't paying you to sit around and do nothing (at least not yet, but we'll get to that); they're paying for what they get from your time. How much you produce is a clear and visible indicator of how you used your valuable time.

Output was not the only way in which we made time visible. From the 14th century onward, we started to put clocks in public centers and church towers in larger cities and market towns. Sound was easier to transmit than visual signal, so we used church bells and factory whistles to inform people of the time and remind them to use it wisely (Are you using your time to worship? You better be! Are you using it to work? If not, stop wasting your valuable time—and your employer's money—and be productive!). A long lineage of noisy timekeepers was born. Its current culmination, the personal alarm clock (now, most likely your smartphone), wakes most of us on a daily basis, starting our day by screaming: "Hurry up! Let's go! Time is wasting!"

Time was now inextricably linked with value, and leisure came to be seen as wasting this value. But another, more insidious force would soon come into play. And under its influence, the value we associate with time and what we do with it became a question of our value as a person. But before we dive into that, we want to remind you that there's more than one way to think about time.

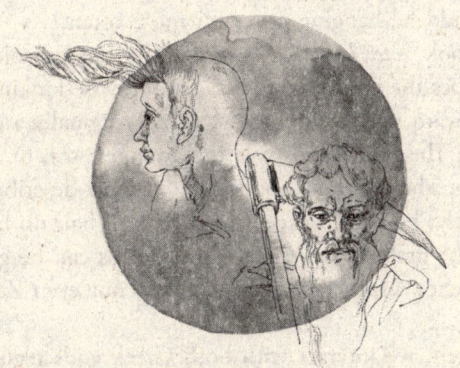

KAIROS & CHRONOS

Greek Gods

"Every kairos is a chronos, but not every chronos is a kairos."

—Hippocrates

You may not realize this, but we look at the ancient Greek god Chronos frequently. Everywhere from our wrists to our smartphone lock screens, and even on stovetops, we find "the time." We constantly check it in an attempt to always precisely coordinate our schedules and keep from being late. And we are often stressed out because we aren't sure if we will be "right on time." Chronos, who is often depicted as Father Time, symbolizes measured time—minutes, seconds, Google Calendar invites, and the alarm clocks that startle us to wake up and start the daily dash of appointments.

In modern times, many only worship Chronos. He has his utility, and most of modern civilization would not be possible without him. But there is yet another version of time that looks much different from Chronos. Kairos is another Greek god who symbolizes a separate and powerful concept of time that doesn't get as much spotlight as it deserves. If Chronos is father time, then Kairos is the cool uncle that you should be hanging out with more often.

In his book *Your Life in Rhythm*, author and theologian Bruce Miller describes the god Chronos as "an old, wise-looking man with a long gray beard whose curved scythe was originally a curve of the zodiac circle. The god Kairos was the youngest son of Zeus. He is believed to be the spirit of opportunity. Aesop describes Kairos as running swiftly; he is bald except for a lock of hair on his forehead, which must be grabbed from the front. Kairos can be grasped only as he approaches. Once he has passed you, not even Zeus can pull him back."

Figuratively, we interact with both Greek gods regularly. Miller describes the differences between the two types of time in everyday experiences we have: "When you are on a three-hour date with the one you love, time flies. When you are in a boring, three-hour lecture, time crawls. The chronos time is the same: three hours. The kairos time is very different, flying versus crawling. While chronos involves the quantity of time an activity takes, kairos looks at the quality of that time."

The ancient Greeks operated in harmony with the different rhythms and profound wisdom delivered by these two gods. It is not that one is better than the other, but knowing which one to pay attention to allows you to be more balanced and present in everyday life. By overplanning and being fixated on clock time, we can miss the right moment for something. If you are feeling inundated with tasks, and overworked, there is a good chance that you're fixating on Chronos and could benefit from more of a Kairos perspective.

Kairos is quality time rather than quantity. Have you ever had a day where you worked for hours and still didn't have any quality work to show for it? Yet on other days you worked for a fraction of the time but produced some of your proudest work? Kairos surrounds those kinds of flow states. Kairos time is happening during the light-bulb moments when we have a breakthrough in the shower or on a walk. We don't know when Kairos will manifest, but being too rigid with your clock time can leave you blind to seeing when it is right there in front of you. During our time off, we are welcoming opportunities that are hard to access otherwise.

It is easy to obsess about Chronos almost all of the time. At some point, we have all complained that there never seems to be *enough* time. We're trying to squeeze more hours into our days because we are afraid of running out of it. But when we were younger, we were not this way.

We seemed to experience more Kairos time when we were children. We somehow miraculously coordinated a long day of adventure and wonder with our friends out of intuition and spontaneity. Nobody was late or early, but everyone was indeed present and fixated on the moments rather than the time of day. Those days seemed like they stretched way longer than our adult days. We didn't have much of an agenda but transitioned from one spontaneous activity to the next. But then, most of us grew out of it because adults need to live in the "real" world.

It doesn't have to be this way. When we take time off from obsessing about Chronos time, we can slow down and exercise our *"what's possible?"* mindset. We have a chance to access a different way of experiencing time. Rather than focusing on its passing, we can concentrate on the density of every single moment.

Another meeting at work, with no agenda, that you can barely tolerate has a low density of precious moments. A unique day on which you had a picnic with friends and got lost in deep conversations that sparked new insights has a high density of those moments. We can't take credit for coming up with this way of looking at time; John acquired this wisdom in Greece.

Over a meal, a wise woman from the Greek island of Ikaria told him all about Kairos. Ikaria, also known as the islands of people who forget to die, is renowned for the longevity of its inhabitants, and John wanted to understand what was driving the health of everyone on the island. This woman believed that the reason people live so long on this particular island is that they live most of their lives thinking about Kairos time rather than Chronos time. She calmly elaborated that fixating on Chronos stresses us out because we can't control the timing of everything. We get attached to it and then worry about something we can't control. Worrying is a by-product of paying too much attention to Chronos. The people of Ikaria have lower levels of stress because they are intentional about not being slaves to clocks and watches. They create an open space to invite the gift of quality moments into their lives.

PRACTICE:

Enjoy a No Chronos day

Pick a day where you are going to intentionally not pay attention to your watches or clocks. Time off and time on are rhythmic decisions that we can make in our work and other activities. Think about how you will stay healthy in body and mind throughout the year by deliberately oscillating between intensity and renewal. As much as you operate by Chronos time, try to cultivate Kairos time as well. It is less about balance and more about being able to transition between them with a smooth rhythm.

WHEN TIME BECAME SACRED, WORK BECAME NOBLE, AND LEISURE BECAME A SIN

As Chronos took over and an absolute and universal notion of time became more prevalent, another related concept started to emerge. Around the turn of the 18th century, the idea of "time discipline" developed. Fewer and fewer people followed a traditional path of devotedly learning a craft through apprenticeships and later opening their own small workshops or businesses. Instead most worked fixed (albeit long) hours in factories with little concern about work or other things to keep them occupied in their off-hours. It didn't take long for the (mostly Puritan) middle and upper class to worry about what the poor would do with their spare time. Essentially, a bunch of concerned prudes with too much time on their hands started paying a lot of attention to how others were spending their hours.

As a result, the elites pushed for the virtuousness of work (*The poor should be occupied and employed all the time since otherwise they just loiter around or get drunk!*). They worried that those without the proper "mental cultivation" would not use their leisure time in a respectable way. So they thought the lower class would be better off working. Thompson quotes a pamphlet from 1755, stating that "the necessity of early rising would reduce the poor to a necessity of going to Bed betime; and thereby prevent the Danger of Midnight revels." He goes on to quote from the pamphlet that early rising would also "introduce an exact Regularity into their Families, a wonderful Order in to their Oeconomy." Yes, it helps the elite to control the lower classes, but it's really for the poor people's own sake.

To convince everyone of this new idea—the virtuousness of work—the Protestant upper class invoked religion to give work a divine justification and meaning. In what sociologist Max Weber would come to coin as the "Protestant Work Ethic," work was elevated to one of the highest moral goods, something God had created us to do. According to this new way of thinking, God had intentionally left the world unfinished to allow us humans to complete his work through our labor. As Thomas Carlyle, one of the strongest proponents of this new gospel, put it, "All work, even cotton spinning, is noble; work is alone noble…. Blessed is he who has found his work; let him ask no other blessedness. He has a work, a life-purpose…. All true Work is sacred; in all true Work … there is something of divineness. Labor, wide as the Earth, has its summit in Heaven."

We couldn't have diverged any further from Aristotle and his belief that leisure is necessary, useful, and noble. Carlyle wanted nothing to do with it, condemning leisure and proclaiming that "work is alone noble." Many other clerical leaders of the time agreed with Carlyle and chimed in too. In the previously mentioned article,

Thompson cites the English Puritan leader, Richard Baxter, on the use of time: "Use every minute of it as a most precious thing, and spend it wholly in the way of duty." Oliver Heywood, another Puritan, even went so far as to say you end up in hell if you slack during life: "O Sirs, sleep now, and awake in hell, whence there is no redemption." Time, especially time busying ourselves with labor, suddenly became the most precious and fleeting thing God had given us, so we mustn't waste it. Not only was noble leisure forgotten, leisure had actually become a sin.

With this, the groundwork for the worship of busyness and work that persists to this day had been laid. By linking work to morality over and over, the Protestant work ethic sneakily wormed its way into our culture, and worse, our sense of ourselves—and it persists even long after the religious association disappeared. How you spend your time became conflated with who you are. Are you productive (good)? Or idle (bad)? We fully internalized the idea that work is morally good, which makes it extremely hard to shake off, even—or maybe especially—in a knowledge economy.

As anthropologist David Graeber points out in his book *Bullshit Jobs: A Theory*, "There seems to be a broad consensus not so much even that work is good, but that not working is very bad; that anyone who is not slaving away harder than he'd like at something he doesn't especially enjoy is a bad person, a scrounger, a skiver, a contemptible parasite unworthy of sympathy or public relief." Someone hardworking *must* be admirable, and someone who avoids work *must* be contemptible.

We might not really know its origin, but we all know this nagging feeling that we need to pretend to be busy, stressed, and overworked to deserve our pay, and that it can't possibly be the enjoyable parts of our jobs that we are being paid for. We're caught up in a bizarre situation where many define their dignity and self-worth through their work, but at the same time, many of us hate our jobs. Graeber calls this "the paradox of modern work," but from the Puritan point of view there is no paradox—it all makes perfect sense. If we see work as a character-forming tool, then the more we hate work, the better. We feel dignity and self-worth because we hate our jobs. Busyness, stress, and overwork have become our modern form of divine self-sacrifice.

GOD, YOUR BOSS, AND EVERYONE ELSE WHO OWNS YOUR TIME

When the Industrial Revolution gathered steam (pun intended) around the turn of the 19th century, the Protestant work ethic was already deeply ingrained in the culture and in our psyche. To work and be productive was unquestionably one of the highest moral goods. Many workers came to see their hard work as elevating them above those employing them. "Work was a sacred duty and a claim to moral and political superiority over the idle rich," write anthropologists Dimitra Doukas and Paul Durrenberger in their article, "Gospel of Wealth, Gospel of Work."

But as religion gradually lost its omnipotent grip, the perception of why work was good, or rather the opposite so bad, started to change amongst the elite. Rather than a sin against God, the newly emerging class of industrialists started to equate idleness with another moral vice: theft. They paid for their employees' time, so they felt like they owned it.

This had clear consequences for how work was done—though not always the ones desired by the employer. Whereas originally you had to first turn your time into output before you could trade it for money, the intermediary step was now essentially removed. Instead of being rewarded or praised for doing your work quickly, if you're paid hourly, you're often punished with pointless busywork. Even if you finish your work, you better keep your butt in that chair, because your boss paid for it to be there.

Adapting to these changes, workers' demands also started to change. They now included better hourly wages, overtime pay, and shorter workdays—all concepts that only make sense in the context of selling your time. And many of the demands were more than justified, given that the average workers labored 10-to-16-hour shifts, six days a week. The recognition that time should belong to us—and that we should have more of it to spend on leisure—started to emerge. Workers started fighting for time off. Today, the May Day holiday, also known as Labor Day or International Workers' Day, is still celebrated by labor advocates all over the world in memory of a (violent) resistance that took place in 1886, demanding "time for 'what we will'" and asking for eight hours of work, eight hours of sleep, and eight hours of leisure.

It took several decades, but their demands were eventually met. In 1926, Henry Ford introduced the eight-hour workday and the five-day workweek (while simultaneously significantly raising salaries above industry standards). Why did Ford do this? It wasn't just because he was a nice guy. He might have been, but his reasons for doing this were much more practical and business driven. First of all, he recognized that if he offered better working conditions than anyone else, he could easily attract the best talent. And this is exactly what happened. The most skilled workers left his competitors and lined up to work at his factories.

Second, he figured that if people have no free time or are too exhausted to use their free time, they won't spend much money. In Ford's words, "people who have more leisure must have more clothes. They eat a greater variety of food. They require more transportation in vehicles…. Leisure is an indispensable ingredient in a growing consumer market because working people need to have enough free time to find uses for consumer products, including automobiles." Just as the culture flourished in the leisure-focused ancient Greece and Rome, Ford believed that the same would be true in modern times, although with a slightly more capitalist twist. More free time would boost the economy. Instead of noble leisure, Ford preached profitable leisure.

Finally, and maybe most aligned with the message of this book, Ford realized that his workers would be able to do a better job if they worked fewer hours. The restrictions on time would lead to more innovation and better methods. People would think about *how* to work rather than just grinding things out. He was convinced that "we can get at least as great production in five days as we can in six, and we shall probably get a greater, for the pressure will bring better methods." Besides, more rested workers are, in general, more effective, are motivated, and make fewer costly mistakes. Ford saw that even for manual labor, equating busyness with productivity only worked up to a certain point.

For his very own reasons, Ford was an early proponent for the return to a culture of leisure, essentially the first industrialist to recognize the importance of having a rest ethic. "There is a profound difference between leisure and idleness," he notes. "We must not confound leisure with shiftlessness…. The result of more leisure will be the exact opposite of what most people might suppose it to be." He even made a bold prediction for the future: "The five-day week is not the ultimate, and neither is the eight-hour day…. Probably the next move will be in the direction of shortening the day."

With Ford's push toward more leisure, and the success he could show as a result, others were quick to follow his example and optimism. In 1938, the US signed the Fair Labor Standards Act limiting working hours to a maximum of 40 hours per week. As Jon Staff and Pete Davis write in a *Fast Company* article, "Americans were so bullish on leisure that many experts thought the workweek would wither away. The economist John Maynard Keynes thought technological advancement would lead to a 15-hour workweek by the 2020s. A 1965 Senate subcommittee predicted a 14-hour workweek by the year 2000."

But this bullishness on leisure did not last too long. The morality of work had been so deeply established that we have all but forgotten how to use leisure, even if it's there for the taking. We have to visit one more deep valley—the busyness of the burned-out knowledge worker—before we can start to see glimpses of the promised land of noble leisure on the horizon. But before we enter this valley of darkness, we want to introduce you to a contemporary of Ford who maybe understood the true meaning and importance of noble leisure better than anyone else in his time.

BERTRAND RUSSELL

British Mathematician and Philosopher
(18 May 1872—2 February 1970)

"I want to say, in all seriousness, that a great deal of harm is being done in the modern world by the belief in the virtuousness of work, and that the road to happiness and prosperity lies in an organized diminution of work."

"Leisure is essential to civilization, and in former times leisure for the few was rendered possible only by the labors of the many. But their labors were valuable, not because work is good, but because leisure is good. And with modern technic it would be possible to distribute leisure justly without injury to civilization."

At the time of writing this book, Bertrand Russell's Wikipedia entry describes him as a "philosopher, logician, mathematician, historian, writer, essayist, social critic, political activist, and Nobel laureate." As a mathematician, his aim was no less than to create a logical foundation for all of mathematics, and his work on this, together with

Alfred North Whitehead, culminated in the *Principia Mathematica*, a monumental three-part series (several hundred pages of which are taken up by the proof that $1 + 1 = 2$) that played an important role in the history of mathematics. As a philosopher, Russell is generally considered one of the founders of analytic philosophy. His Nobel Prize was awarded in Literature "in recognition of his varied and significant writings in which he champions humanitarian ideals and freedom of thought." A full list of Russell's achievements and awards would fill pages—not exactly a life we would associate with idleness.

Yet, despite all this, Russell was a champion of leisure and idleness. Nowhere is this more manifest than in his aforementioned essay "In Praise of Idleness," published in *Harper's Magazine* in 1932, which is still as relevant today as when it was first published—if not more so. He opens the article with the problem we have already encountered, the common belief in the immorality of idleness. But, he continues, "I think that there is far too much work done in the world, that immense harm is caused by the belief that work is virtuous, and that what needs to be preached in modern industrial countries is quite different from what always has been preached." The world has changed. With modern technology, a worker can produce far more than she and her family need to survive. But our thinking has not evolved at the same pace. In fact, it hasn't changed at all.

This leads to several problems. One of them is inequality, which Russell illustrates with an example:

> Someone makes an invention by which the same number of men can make twice as many pins as before.... In a sensible world everybody concerned in the manufacture of pins would take to working four hours instead of eight, and everything else would go on as before. But in the actual world, this would be thought demoralizing. The men still work eight hours, there are too many pins, some employers go bankrupt, and half the men previously concerned in making pins are thrown out of work. There is, in the end, just as much leisure as on the other plan, but half the men are totally idle while half are still overworked. In this way, it is ensured that the unavoidable

leisure shall cause misery all round instead of being a universal source of happiness. Can anything more insane be imagined?

Russell was deeply aware of how a false sense of morality had hijacked and distorted our perception of work. "The morality of work is the morality of slaves," he writes, "and the modern world has no need of slavery." But the opposite, the idea of embracing and distributing idleness, goes against the common notion. As he argues:

> This idea shocks the well-to-do, because they are convinced that the poor would not know how to use so much leisure. In America men often work long hours even when they are already well-off; such men, naturally, are indignant at the idea of leisure for wage-earners except as the grim punishment of unemployment.

Just like the Ancients, Russell understood that idleness was crucial for civilization and culture to flourish: "There was formerly a capacity for light-heartedness and play which has been to some extent inhibited by the cult of efficiency. The modern man thinks that everything ought to be done for the sake of something else, and never for its own sake." Because of this, we have lost the energy to contribute to civilization and culture in the little free time we have. As he writes: "The pleasures of urban populations have become mainly passive.... This results from the fact that their active energies are fully taken up with work; if they had more leisure they would again enjoy pleasures in which they took an active part." Active engagement rather than passive consumption.

Russell made a bold suggestion: working hours could and should be reduced to four hours per day. But he was quick to add, "I am not meaning to imply that all the remaining time should necessarily be spent in pure frivolity." Instead, the extra time and energy should be reinvested into education and contributing to our culture. But, he believed that this would be a natural consequence of the reduction of work hours: "In a world where no one is compelled to work more than four hours a day every person possessed of scientific curiosity will be able to indulge it, and every painter will be able

to paint without starving, however excellent his pictures may be."
Russell concluded his essay with the thought that in a world of more
idleness, "above all, there will be happiness and joy of life, instead
of frayed nerves [and] weariness."

PRACTICE:

Save some energy for your time off

Do you spend your leisure time in an active or passive way? If passive,
is it because you are too tired and don't have any energy left to make
the most of your time? Reflect on how you can set aside time from
work (even just 30 minutes) and reinvest this energy into your curiosity,
creativity, and learning. Don't try to wishfully fit it in. Plan it out like
you would any work task.

VISIBLE TIME 2.0: BUSYNESS IS KING

Given that many leading industrialists and thinkers were supporting
and promoting leisure in the early 20th century, we should now
be living in a culture which, similar to ancient Greece and Rome,
values leisure and embraces time off. Henry Ford thought so too.
He believed in 1926 that his move from 10-plus-hour days to eight-
hour days was only the first step in a series of many more that
would ultimately lead to shorter and shorter workdays. He was,
unfortunately, dead wrong.

The trend toward shorter workdays and weeks not only stopped
but reversed. According to a 2014 Gallup poll, the average person
in the US works for 47 hours a week, almost a full day longer than
Ford's factory workers back in 1926. And that's only the average. A
full 18 percent of the US population report that they are working
over 60 hours a week. We are essentially back to late 19th- or early
20th-century standards.

We had the opportunity to come back to noble leisure (or at
least to a reasonable work-life balance), we could see it within reach,

but our broken moral compass took us in the wrong direction. We worship busyness more than ever. We are stressed out, burned out, and busy—but not productive. We find ourselves in a culture that, all too often, correlates busyness, stress, and overwork with accomplishment. If we continue on this path, we are either going to work ourselves to death or be replaced by robots.

The shift from manual work to knowledge work is probably part of what led us into this situation. A knowledge worker doesn't have eight Ford Model T engines to show for his day's efforts. The output of intellectual work is much harder to quantify; ideas are too intangible. In his book *Deep Work: Rules for Focused Success in a Distracted World*, author and computer science professor, Cal Newport, calls this problem the "Metric Blackhole." He argues that productivity and deep work, the work that leads to genuine creative and innovative breakthroughs, are tough to quantify for most modern knowledge workers. So instead we use "busyness as a proxy of productivity." It's a much simpler metric than true productivity or creativity, and an easy way to experience a quick sense of accomplishment without actually getting much done at all. And, unfortunately, it is often the most immediate way to get recognition and approval by our peers and superiors.

Busyness—essentially productivity without the output—has become the new version of visible time, and it reigns supreme. For entrepreneurs and creatives, this is particularly problematic. Like addicts seeking the next quick fix, we are hooked on busyness. Without any tangible progress indicators, or a boss constantly reminding us that he owns our time, our internalized sense that time equals value and morality becomes even stronger. Those who could choose to once again live Aristotle's idea of noble leisure are often furthest away from it.

But we need noble leisure more than ever. Genuinely productive knowledge work is the opposite of busyness and requires a harder, more thoughtful approach. It requires taking time off seriously. In addition to a solid work ethic, it requires an equally well-established rest ethic. Good knowledge work is, like the work of a craftsman, based on mastery and quality, rather than the sheer quantity of simple and repeatable tasks—which will soon be done by robots and AI anyway.

We need to acknowledge that productivity in creative work is much more multifaceted than the one-dimensional productivity of a manual laborer churning out widgets. Graeber writes that "for some reason, we as a society have collectively decided it's better to have millions of human beings spending years of their lives pretending to type into spreadsheets or preparing mind maps for PR meetings than freeing them to knit sweaters, play with their dogs, start a garage band, experiment with new recipes, or sit in cafes arguing about politics, and gossiping about their friends' complex polyamorous love affairs."

Entrepreneur and author, Stephan Aarstol, agrees when he muses that "if you were done with work by 1 pm every day, it's easy to see how you, depending on your interests could become a different type of productive. Productive in exercise, learning, parenting, social causes, community and more. Productivity that advances society, and creates a better world around you, goes far beyond merely being productive at your job." This is productivity in the ancient sense, which puts a focus on culture and the simple joy of life just as much as, if not more than, it does on sheer economy. Productivity that fills our lives with meaning, rather than productivity for the sake of being "productive." Productivity based on noble leisure.

We can see the shining Acropolis on the hill promising the return to noble leisure, but the valley we are in is worn down too deep and the cliffs feel too steep for us to climb. We cannot shake that which has been so ingrained in us over centuries, even if we have long forgotten its origin or justification. So, for now, we remain in the valley. And at times, because we don't know any better, we keep digging even deeper down.

One person who has seen just how deep this valley can be (but also found her way out of it) is Arianna Huffington.

ARIANNA HUFFINGTON

American Media Entrepreneur and Author

"Think about it: If employees are experiencing any of the symptoms in the World Health Organization's new definition of burnout—depletion and exhaustion, negativism and cynicism, reduced professional efficacy—are they going to put in their best performance? Or are they more likely to cut corners or to leave?"

Taking vacation wasn't enough to save Arianna Huffington, the founder of the *Huffington Post*. Her news and blog site quickly became one of the most widely read, linked to, and frequently cited media brands on the internet. From the outside, Huffington was as successful as anyone could aim to be. She is on *Time Magazine*'s list of the world's 100 most influential people and the *Forbes Most Powerful Women* list. In 2007, Huffington had been running the *Huffington Post* for two years and was working 18-hour days. But a humbling wake-up call occurred when, one day, she woke up under her desk in a pool of her blood with a broken cheekbone.

"I was successful by all standards, but I was clearly not successful if I was lying in a pool of blood on the floor of my office," Huffington recalls in an interview with Caroline Modarressy Tehrani. She went through rounds of doctors' appointments in an effort to identify what medical condition she had. "I thought I might have a brain tumor," she remembered. But then she discovered that "what was wrong with me was the way I was leading my life. And what was wrong with me is what's wrong with a lot of people."

The cause of her fainting was much simpler than brain cancer—it was exhaustion from working too much. Knowing that she wasn't alone, her entrepreneurial spirit now had a new problem to fix. She put her brutal wake-up call into action and launched Thrive Global, a corporate and consumer well-being and productivity platform with the mission of changing the way we work and live by ending the collective delusion that burnout is the price we must pay for success.

Huffington has since been empowering other people and companies to take care of themselves and prevent what had happened to her. With the momentum of Thrive Global, workplace burnout is becoming less of a stigma. Huffington is optimistic that "moving burnout from the 'I know it when I see it' column—where it was in 2007, when I collapsed from sleep deprivation and exhaustion and broke my cheekbone—to a fleshed-out workplace problem means we are now in a position to more effectively combat it. Only when we begin to understand our biggest problems can we also begin to effectively address them."

When most managers think of implementing time off from work, they put in a generic vacation clause in the company's policies and consider it done. Huffington has found that vacation is not enough, so she developed a time off concept called "Thrive Time" at her company. She explains that "Thrive Time, or intentional recovery, is about looking both backward and forward—renewing what was depleted by what had to be done to meet a deadline and giving yourself the resources to meet upcoming deadlines. It's the last stage of one project and the first stage of the next. That's why we don't think of it as a break, but as an essential thread of the day-to-day fabric of the workweek."

Thrive Global is like many companies in the market today, a young upstart company that has a lot to achieve with limited resources. Of course, they have to get results, and they aren't immune to meeting deadlines. Sometimes their team ramps up work hours to ship a product on time or go the extra mile for a client. But rather than that behavior becoming a new expectation that feeds burnout, they make sure to reward an intense period of work with intentional rest. As Huffington writes: "Thrive Time is what allows us to sustain that. It means taking time off to recover and recharge after you've met the deadline, shipped the product, or worked over the weekend. It could be a few hours, a morning, a whole day or even more."

It's also important to note that their Thrive Time doesn't count toward vacation, sick time, or other paid time off. Huffington emphasizes, "It helps make very clear to employees that recovery isn't separate from work. It's an essential part of work. Taking Thrive Time isn't a reward, it's a responsibility. That's why it also often comes at the suggestion of a manager, part of whose job is maintaining team performance and being vigilant to guard against burnout."

Preventing burnout and overwork is, luckily, becoming an important consideration for more and more business leaders. We are fortunate that people like Huffington are paving the way for other leaders and managers to rethink their relationship to time off and how it can be a strategic part of their business plan: "Now, with burnout in the spotlight, companies have a fresh opportunity to step up, for the sake of their people and for the health of the bottom line. Focusing on people's actual experience at work is no longer a nice-to-have, it's a must-have for anyone who wants to succeed in the long run. To find the cure to 'civilization's disease,' it's going to take a commitment to getting to the root causes of burnout."

Unlearning the bad habits of always working is not going to be comfortable, and a lot of people fail because they try to change too much too soon. "Most of us start off too big. We're deciding to launch into a whole new lifestyle all at once. Or we think we're just going to get there by the sheer exercise of willpower. But that ignores the science of how willpower works," says Huffington. So that is why Huffington and the Thrive Global team believe in "microsteps."

Huffington was inspired by the work of B. J. Fogg, a behavior change researcher and the director of the Persuasive Tech Lab at Stanford

University. Huffington explains, "It's about making the 'minimum viable effort'—going as small as you can." Or, as Fogg puts it, "To create a new habit, you must first simplify the behavior. Make it tiny, even ridiculous. A good tiny behavior is easy to do—and fast."

You may not be able to take an extended sabbatical next week to recover from too many long hours, but Huffington has a few microstep ideas for incrementally preventing burnout: To get better sleep, pick a time at night where you turn off your devices or set an alarm for 30 minutes before your bedtime. For more movement, suggest a walking meeting with a colleague. To be more creative, turn down an unfamiliar street to discover new people, sights, and sensations. To help with recharging, declare an end to the day, even if you haven't completed your to-do list.

PRACTICE:

Take a small step toward time off NOW

Don't wait for a vacation to implement your rest ethic. Consider all the actionable advice in this book, and for any aspects that speak to you, think about what microstep you could commit to and be successful at after your first go. You could do it tomorrow. Or right now!

STRESS, BURNOUT, AND THE NEED FOR A RETURN TO NOBLE LEISURE

In the 2019 edition of their *International Classification of Diseases*, the World Health Organization (WHO) included burnout as "a syndrome conceptualized as resulting from chronic workplace stress that has not been successfully managed." The official WHO report states that burnout is characterized by three key components: "feelings of energy depletion or exhaustion; increased mental distance from one's job, or feelings of negativism or cynicism related to one's job; and reduced professional efficacy." Sound familiar?

"An eight-hour workday, for a knowledge worker, is like a 16-hour day for the industrial labourer," remarks Stephan Aarstol. "The eight-hour workday was set up for the body, not the mind." Just as a century ago people were overworked beyond healthy sustainable physical capabilities, we are now experiencing something similar with our mental abilities. Where early industrial factory workers were physically drained and exhausted, modern workers in the knowledge factories of the world suffer the same fate on a mental level.

Millennials appear to be particularly affected by burnout. Part of this is likely the fact that we tie so much of our self-worth to our jobs, and then chase one short-term achievement after another, all the while comparing our own success to the success of others we see through their highly groomed social media personas. Often, we feel that even our hobbies and leisure time have to be turned into side hustles and business opportunities, or we're wasting our time.

In the *BuzzFeed* article "How Millennials Became the Burnout Generation" journalist Anne Helen Petersen recounts her own struggle with burnout, which manifested in a failure to get even the simplest stuff done—daily errands like appointments, replying to emails, or bringing something to the post office. She calls this phenomenon "errand paralysis." Petersen laments that many of us have become high-functioning workaholics. While we might still get the big stuff done, the most mundane and simple tasks have become difficult and a source of anxiety.

Reflecting on her own experience, she writes that "things that should've felt good (leisure, not working) felt bad because I felt guilty for not working; things that should've felt 'bad' (working all the time) felt good because I was doing what I thought I should and needed to be doing in order to succeed." Carlyle and his fellow proponents of the Protestant work ethic would be beaming with pride if they could read this, seeing the lasting impact of their work centuries after starting their crusade. Petersen cites Josh Cohen, a psychoanalyst who specializes in burnout, saying, "You feel burnout when you've exhausted all your internal resources, yet cannot free yourself of the nervous compulsion to go on regardless."

That nervous compulsion is the Protestant work ethic internalized. And time off is its antidote.

This book exists because we are extremely optimistic that our culture can find its way back to noble leisure, one little step at a time. But we want to reiterate, if it's not already abundantly clear, that we're not advocating a culture of laziness, sloth, or stagnation. It is a culture in which productivity and the joy of life go hand in hand, a culture of productivity in a much broader sense, rather than just economic output. A culture of creative, scientific, spiritual, and humanitarian progress. A culture of noble leisure.

In the chapters to come, you will discover different aspects of time off that you can incorporate into your rest ethic. You will meet some of the individuals and companies who have—very successfully—used these ideas to impact our world and shape it for the better. We hope that these examples can inspire you on your own path to noble leisure and enable you to be the creative, impactful, and well-rested person Aristotle would have been proud of.

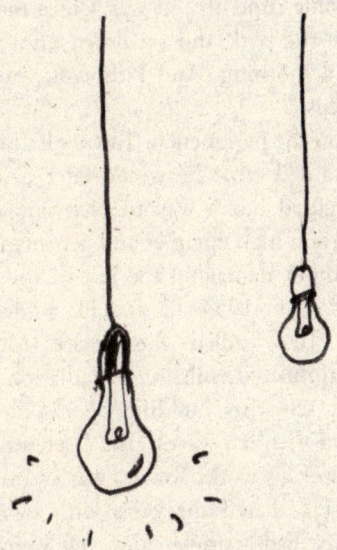

CREATIVITY

By the middle of the 20th century, optics, or the study of light, was considered a more or less solved problem. Most scientists believed that all the interesting discoveries in the field had been made and so focused their attention on other topics. But one scientist, driven by a deep curiosity to better understand how molecules interact with light, kept going.

Charles H. Townes was interested in how he could stimulate molecules in such a way that they would emit an intense beam of light at a single frequency (unlike most other sources, such as light bulbs, which emit a large spectrum of frequencies in diffuse directions). The key challenge was how to achieve the required energies without the device overheating and blowing up in the process. One spring morning in 1951, Townes, then a professor at Columbia University, took some time off: "It was a nice morning, so I got up and I went out in the park and sat down on a park bench by the azaleas; a beautiful morning. And I thought, now why haven't we been able to do this?"

Sitting there on the park bench, Townes let his thoughts wander. And eventually, he had what he would later describe as a "sudden revelation." He figured out a way to pick out and stimulate only molecules with certain high energies and get them to emit an intense burst of light, without damaging the rest of the device.

Three years later, in 1954, he and his students had a working prototype ready. They called the device MASER: microwave amplification by stimulated emission of radiation. Shortly thereafter, Townes and other scientists building on his idea managed to use visible light instead of microwaves. The laser was born.

In recognition of his work, Townes was awarded the 1964 Nobel Prize in Physics. He shared the prize with two Russian scientists who, independently, had a similar idea, but were beaten by Townes to actually building a working maser. Ironically, Townes later noted that his breakthrough revelation was partly inspired by a 1927 Russian science fiction novel, *The Garin Death Ray*, by Alexei Tolstoi. So, a Russian novel on a death-ray device helped an American scientist develop the laser, beating the Russians to it. And all of that in the early days of the Cold War. This itself reads like the plot of a novel.

Today, the results of Townes's work can be found everywhere, from supermarket barcode scanners to consumer electronics, from medicine to the military. But Townes was really only driven by curiosity: "I wasn't looking for an application. I wasn't thinking of a laser beam that would be a bright light or something. I wanted to find out more about molecules and I wanted to get shorter waves to study the molecules. Just basic work, not applied at all. But now look what's come out of it."

This is noble leisure in action: a creative breakthrough, reached in a moment of time off, achieved solely in search of meaning rather than purpose, but eventually advancing civilization in previously unimaginable ways. Townes, who died in 2015 at age 99, still visited his office at the University of California, Berkeley daily until 2014. We are speculating, but it is likely that to him this time did not feel like work. It was all leisure.

Had Townes been focused purely on applications, he might have followed the path of his colleagues and abandoned optics. All our lives would likely be entirely different if he had. But he followed his creative interests, and gave his mind the space to wander and explore. As Townes remarked, "There are always unturned stones along even well-trod paths. Discovery awaits those who spot and take the trouble to turn those stones." Time off, as this and many other examples show, allows us to spot those unturned stones and take the time to turn them, finding the creative discoveries hidden in plain sight that others are too busy to notice.

THE CREATIVE PROCESS AND TIME OFF

Graham Wallas was born in 1858 in Sunderland, a small city in the north of England. After studying at Oxford University he worked as a schoolmaster for a while before becoming a founding member of the London School of Economics, serving as its first professor of political science from 1914. But perhaps his most prominent and lasting contribution to the world was a book titled *The Art of Thought*, which he published in 1926 toward the end of his life. Inspired by the working habits of scientists like Hermann von Helmholtz and Henri Poincaré (whom we will meet later), Wallas outlined the first complete model of how the creative process works. Despite being almost a century old, Wallas's idea is still a significant influence on creativity researchers today, and his book is widely cited in academic literature.

At the heart of Wallas's theory is the breakdown of the creative process into four distinct stages:

- Preparation, or sitting down and doing the hard work.
- Incubation, or allowing our conscious mind to rest (or focus on other tasks).
- Illumination, or the much sought-after aha moment.
- Verification, or doing more work to see if your revelation has merit.

This process might seem pretty intuitive, but we rarely pause to think about it.

First, we have to actually sit down and do the hard work, examining the problem at hand from every angle and getting completely familiar with it. This is where the idea of "Deep Work" comes in, which Cal Newport defines, in his book of the same title, as "professional activities performed in a state of distraction-free concentration that push your cognitive capabilities to their limit. These efforts create new value, improve your skill, and are hard to replicate." Good preparation is itself a form of time off—time off from distractions in order to give undivided attention to the problem at hand. It's an essential step. But, in many cases, it won't get us to the desired solution. It is, after all, only preparation. That's where incubation comes in.

When we set the work down and allow our conscious mind to rest or focus on something else, our subconscious kicks in and gets to work—but in a very different way: making loose associations between different concepts and previous experiences. We get a feeling that a solution is getting closer. At this point, Wallas warned, we should not force it or the insight might disappear. Instead, we should have faith in our subconscious to do its job.

Subconscious incubation happens whenever we fully immerse ourselves in something other than the actual problem itself, whether that immersion is in high-quality leisure like a hike in nature, or deep work on another unrelated problem. But the key here is full immersion, not absent minded distraction and constant task switching. If we make time for incubation and trust in the power of our subconscious mind, magic happens.

Finally, we reach the stage of illumination, a moment of sudden inspiration or revelation. The stereotypical light-bulb moment where our mind goes "Eureka!" and everything suddenly makes sense. Wallas describes this moment as a "flash" or "click." This is also the time when our conscious mind takes over the process again. As Wallas writes, "It never happens that unconscious work supplies ready-made the result of a lengthy calculation.... All that we can hope from these inspirations, which are the fruit of unconscious work, is to obtain points of departure for such calculations." Time for more deep work to verify that our brilliant idea was in fact as brilliant as we thought.

This four-stage process is, of course, highly simplified, and in real situations, we often encounter several cycles of preparation and incubation before illumination finally strikes, or work on several problems in parallel. Someone engaged in the creative process "may at the same time be 'incubating' on a problem which he proposed to himself a few days ago, be accumulating knowledge in 'preparation' for a second problem, and be 'verifying' his conclusions on a third problem." And even within a single problem, if it is complex enough, you might at the same time be incubating on one aspect while consciously working on another. So don't keep banging your head against the exact same issue if you get stuck. Take some time off, focus on other things, and let incubation do its hidden magic.

The creative stages of preparation, incubation, illumination, and verification have stood the test of time and are still as relevant as they were when proposed in 1926. This shows us that only half of the real creative work is what we usually consider "work." The other half, which is just as important, occurs while we are taking time off, not consciously engaged with the problem. Just because incubation and illumination are subconscious processes does not mean we do not have control over them. They should still be treated as a skill.

This book itself is a direct product of the four-stage process. First, we had to do the preparation: many hours spent in deep work reading, taking notes, arranging thoughts, doing interviews, and writing snippets and longer pieces. But these hours were interspersed with long stretches of rest that allowed our subconscious to process the information and give structure to it. Many of the words and ideas here were not generated by our conscious minds at the moment of writing, but instead spontaneously came to us on long walks or while drifting off into an afternoon slumber. They came to us in moments of time off as illuminating insights, gifts from our subconscious minds.

Creativity is a constant interplay of time on (preparation, verification) and time off (incubation, illumination). Finding the right balance and flowing effortlessly between these two states is key. Many of us just hope for incubation to happen when we find some time, but the truth is we often don't. We have to make time for it—and that's why a good rest ethic is so essential.

Two creatives who cultivated a strong balance between deep work and time off—both making deliberate time for daily incubation in the form of long walks—were two of history's greatest composers. We will meet them next.

LUDWIG VAN BEETHOVEN AND PYOTR ILYICH TCHAIKOVSKY

Ludwig van Beethoven, German Composer
(17 December 1770—26 March 1827)

"How happy I am to be able to wander among bushes and herbs, under trees and over rocks; no man can love the country as I love it. Woods, trees and rocks send back the echo that man desires."

"Whence I take my ideas... I cannot say with any degree of certainty; they come to me uninvited, directly, or indirectly. I could almost grasp them in my hands, out in nature's open, in the woods, during my promenades, in the silence of the night, at earliest dawn."

Pyotr Ilyich Tchaikovsky, Russian Composer
(7 May 1840—6 November 1893)

"What a bliss to know that no one will come to interfere with my work, my reading, my walks."

Walking through the woods, several decades apart, was where inspiration most reliably visited two of the greatest composers of all time.

Pyotr Tchaikovsky firmly believed that he had to walk for exactly two hours a day, or "great misfortunes" would fall upon him. These walks were a way for him to calm down his body and mind, which could be severely agitated from an inspired work session. "If that condition of mind and soul, which we call inspiration, lasted long without intermission," he believed, "no artist could survive it." Tchaikovsky's inspiration burned so brightly that it threatened to burn him out if he didn't take time off. While today we mostly associate burnout with stressful office jobs, Tchaikovsky knew that people who work on their own passion projects can suffer the same fate if they are not careful and do not make time for deliberate rest.

Echoing thoughts that are all too familiar to most modern office workers, he was also painfully aware of how distraction is detrimental to flow states: "In the midst of this magic process [of flow] it frequently happens that some external interruption wakes me from my somnambulistic state: a ring at the bell, the entrance of my servant, the striking of the clock.... Dreadful, indeed, are such interruptions. Sometimes they break the thread of inspiration for a considerable time, so that I have to seek it again—often in vain." His two-hour walks provided distance from such interruptions. While few of us are likely to be disturbed by the entrance of our servant these days, the fundamental problem is as common now as in Tchaikovsky's days. It might be a text from a friend or a colleague's innocent tap on our shoulder. And often it can be difficult to explain that "just five minutes" actually wastes much more time than just five minutes. If it breaks our flow, even a tiny disturbance can cost us hours. Dreadful indeed ...

Ludwig van Beethoven, similarly, cultivated energy and creativity through walks. He knew that being physically strong and healthy was the best way to support his creativity. As his biographer Romain Rolland noted, "He sustains this strength of his by means of vigorous ablutions with cold water, a scrupulous regard for personal cleanliness, and daily walks immediately after the midday meal, walks that lasted the entire afternoon and often extended into the night; then a sleep so sound and long that he thanklessly complained against it! His way of living is substantial but simple."

For each melody that Beethoven and Tchaikovsky developed, it's wonderful to think about how many of the notes were assembled during their time away from composing. More credit should be given to the collaborative partner each of these legendary composers found in the solitude of nature, the silence of time off. Thanks to nature's influence, we can now get lost in the emotional melodies of Beethoven's Symphony Number 7 and Tchaikovsky's *Swan Lake*.

Sitting at a desk can often be one of the worst ways to generate novel insights. Taking a break, going for a walk, or doing some light exercise is one of the best ways to keep yourself healthy and sustain (or reinvigorate) creativity. The absence of distractions is a bonus that allows your thoughts to go even deeper. Few of us will attempt to be professional music composers, but many of us are trying to create our own personal magnum opus. It's time for you to welcome nature and time off as collaborators on your most precious project. Don't rely solely on having your butt in a chair and your nose to the grindstone.

PRACTICE:

When you feel stuck and out of new ideas, walk away from your work—literally

Go for a long walk, ideally out in nature, and let your legs and your thoughts flow freely. Escape the distractions and, like Beethoven, always carry a pen and notebook along with you to record any inspiration that might spontaneously come to you in this blissful state.

EXPLORATION BEATS SPECIALIZATION

Most people know Aldous Huxley best for his works of fiction, novels such as *Brave New World* and *Island*, in which he presented his visions of dystopia and utopia. But recently, with the resurgence of interest in psychedelics, his classic works of nonfiction, such as *The Doors of Perception*, are also gaining more attention and popularity. In these, Huxley tried to explore some of the most fundamental questions of society and human existence. And one thing that concerned him was his contemporaries' lack of balance and "nothing but" mentality.

Not only did Huxley see over specialization and narrowness of opinion as big societal issues, he also considered them as some of the greatest problems of education. In his collection of essays *The Divine Within*, he writes: "Everything takes place in a pigeonhole.... but what we do need in academic institutions now is a few people who run about on the woodwork between the pigeonholes, and peep into all of them and see what can be done."

As we shall see, it is now, more than ever, a viable—and smart—option to be the person who peeps into all the pigeonholes, running about on the woodwork.

Incubation does not only happen when we relax. It can also take place while we work on other things. As Wallas remarks, "We can often get more results in the same way by beginning several problems in succession, and voluntarily leaving them unfinished while we turn to others than by finishing our work on each problem at one sitting." Taking time off from work to attend to another pursuit that isn't necessarily your job is a modern form of noble leisure. It is a common theme among people who consciously practice time off. Cooking a meal for your friends, for example, is still work, but it is meaningful and helps you detach from your work-work so that incubation can begin.

As the British writer Arnold Bennett points out in his 1908 book *How to Live on 24 Hours a Day*, variety itself is a form of time off and can be just as effective as rest (and we will see in the next chapter that it actually *is* a form of rest):

> What? You say that full energy given to those sixteen hours [spent away from work] will lessen the value of the business eight? Not so. On the contrary, it will assuredly increase the value of the business eight. One of the chief things which my typical man has to learn is that the mental faculties are capable of a continuous hard activity; they do not tire like an arm or a leg. All they want is change—not rest, except in sleep.

Counterintuitively, putting more energy into leisure can energize us overall.

The author Arthur Koestler also considered the importance of incubation in creativity in his book *Act of Creation*. The more complicated a problem, he explains, the more we need our subconscious mind to work on it. And he highlights that breaking things—going against the accepted and established—is essential in creative thought: "The creative act has a revolutionary or destructive side. The path of history is strewn with its victims: the discarded isms of art, the epicycles, and phlogistons of science." This willingness to break things, we believe, can only come through exploration. It requires constant unlearning. It requires playfulness. Koestler warns against being a too reasonable person. "The 'reasonable person,'" he argues, "is level-headed instead of multi-level-headed; adaptive and not destructive; an enlightened conservative, not a revolutionary; willing to learn under proper guidance, but unable to be guided by his dreams."

The contrasting experience of professional musicians in different genres is a good example of this dichotomy. In his book *Range: Why Generalists Triumph in a Specialized World*, journalist and author David Epstein points to studies showing that many classically trained musicians specialize from a very young age, and practice their skill for countless hours of formulaic training and repetition. They are the poster children of deliberate practice. They are Koestler's "reasonable person."

Most top-level jazz musicians on the other hand, Epstein found, receive remarkably little formal training in their early days. They often try many different instruments, experimenting with them in their own way, before settling on the one they like most. A fair number of them never even learn to read musical notation.

Not to belittle the tremendous skill required of classical performers, but for many of them, after years of rigorous training, improvisation becomes almost impossible. The transition from jazz (range) to classical (specialization) is much easier, and more common, than the other way around. It's much easier to go deep after you've gone broad and surveyed the terrain than trying to explore once you've dug yourself into a deep hole. Epstein cites Jack Cecchini, a virtuoso guitarist who started out as a jazz player and later on discovered his love for classical guitar: "The jazz musician is a creative artist, the classical musician is a re-creative artist."

Re-creating is much easier for an AI to accomplish than creating. In fact, Max is actively working at the intersection of AI and music, collaborating with artists as well as commercial partners to explore how computational techniques can help humans create, select, and perform music in novel ways. Looking at the current landscape of AI music experiments, almost all of the ones that try to mimic human performers or composers focus either on classical music or on electronic music genres like techno, because both—in their own ways—follow very strict rules and patterns, making them very suitable for machine learning. Jazz improvisation is still far out of reach for the machines.

Our current algorithms are getting pretty good at very narrow domains, but are still terrible at connecting ideas across domains–and we don't believe that this will change in the near future. Ask yourself: In your own life and career, where are you playing improvisational jazz and where are you following the strict patterns of classical music? You might want to put more emphasis on the former. In an AI-enabled future, the jack-of-all-trades is likely to beat the master of one.

If we choose the path of range over specialization, we have to make sure to integrate all our different experiences. And to do this, we need times of rest and silence. Aldous Huxley was a fan of classical music, and he saw the absence of sound as a crucial ingredient in this, which he explains in an essay entitled "The Rest Is Silence": "Silence is an integral part of all good music. Compared with Beethoven's or Mozart's, the ceaseless torrent of Wagner's music is very poor in silence. Perhaps that is one of the reasons why it seems so much less significant than theirs. It 'says' less because it is always speaking." We need to expose ourselves to all the beautiful breadth the world has to offer, then take a step back and let it all sink in. The work we do is all the more creative and significant if it is interspersed with the silence of high-quality time off.

The common belief that we have to specialize to be successful is plain wrong. And more and more, it might do more harm than good. Countless examples show that it's possible to be excellent at more than one thing. But not if we compartmentalize. Rather than pursuing our passions in isolation, we should freely let them interfere, find their commonalities, and focus on excellence in their overlap. It's a win-win situation. Not only does this way of working and living allow us to find new connections and live up to our full creative potential (and help us stay ahead of AI), it also has time off directly baked into it. By embracing all our interests, we can let them grow into something much bigger than the sum of their parts, and achieve excellence and success without burning out.

If you are not fully convinced yet, let us take a look at two people who found their success through creative exploration and accepting their varied interests, and who believe that others can and should follow their example.

TIM HARFORD

English Economist, Journalist, and Public Speaker

"The modern world seems to present us with a choice. If we're not going to fast-twitch from browser window to browser window, we have to live like a hermit, focus on one thing to the exclusion of everything else. I think that's a false dilemma. We can make multitasking work for us, unleashing our natural creativity. We just need to slow it down."

Think of your typical work setting. You might be sitting at your desk working on a proposal for a new project while listening to some music, or maybe even a podcast. A notification pops up that you have been mentioned on Slack. You glance at what it's all about and then switch back to your proposal. But it's been a while (well, probably just five minutes) since you last checked your emails, so you might as well do that. All right, done, back to the proposal again. Having written another sentence, you catch a banner appearing on your phone from the corner of your eye. Better check what it is, it might be important. Nope, it wasn't. Back to work. A minute later, your coworker stops by your desk to ask if you've seen the recent email from your client. Yeah, you have, and will get back to it later. Again, time for the proposal. You're making progress with it. Those distractions don't bother you. You are good at multitasking. Right?

Unfortunately, our metacognition, the way we perceive our own cognition, is terrible. And we highly overestimate how good we are at multitasking. In fact, from a neuroscience point of view, as Edward M. Hallowell points out in his book *CrazyBusy*, true multitasking isn't even possible; our brain can only actively handle one thing at a time. So what we end up doing is just constant task switching—and that comes at a high cost. But there might be some way to make multitasking work for us. We just have to change the timescale (and depth) through which we do it.

In a 2019 TED Talk titled "A Powerful Way to Unleash Your Natural Creativity," economist Tim Harford introduced his concept of "slow-motion multitasking." Harford, who, besides writing several economics books and a long-running column for the *Financial Times* titled *The Undercover Economist*, is also an honorary fellow of the Royal Statistical Society, suggests that working on multiple things at the same time can actually be beneficial: "I'd like to argue that for an important kind of activity, doing two things at once—or three or even four—is exactly what we should be aiming for." "But 'at once' doesn't mean literally *at once*." Harford only suggests that the projects should overlap in their time frames. We should keep undivided focus in our minutes, hours, and maybe even days, but seek variety in the weeks, months, and years. For example, you might want to list all your different projects and interests and try dedicating each week entirely to one of them, as much as possible focusing on a single thing but then switching to another one the following week (or month, or whatever timescale makes the most sense to you).

Each project deserves its time and attention. By slowing down, we speed up our progress. "Slow-motion multitasking feels like a counterintuitive idea," Harford admits. "What I'm describing here is having multiple projects on the go at the same time, and you move backwards and forwards between topics as the mood takes you, or as the situation demands. But the reason it seems counterintuitive is that we're used to lapsing into multitasking out of desperation. We're in a hurry, we want to do everything at once. If we were willing to slow multitasking down, we might find that it works quite brilliantly."

This kind of macroscale multitasking is very different from what most of us are likely already engaging in daily. Harford uses the example of Albert Einstein, who, like many famous scientists of his time, was active in multiple areas of science: "Working simultaneously on Brownian motion, special relativity and the photoelectric effect— it's not exactly the same kind of multitasking as Snapchatting while you're watching *Westworld*. Very different. And Einstein, yeah, well, … he's one of a kind, he's unique. But the pattern of behavior that Einstein was demonstrating, that's not unique at all. It's ubiquitous among highly creative people, both artists and scientists."

While it was much easier in Einstein's day to make significant contributions in multiple scientific fields, it's still true that the most successful scientists, those who stay creative and productive over a long time, tend to work on a broad range of subjects. In the middle of the 20th century, psychologist Bernice Eiduson was studying the question of what differentiates top scientists from the mediocre ones, and she identified working on different topics as one key factor. Again, exploration beats specialization, even in a domain as specialized as the forefront of science.

Interestingly, Eiduson also found that many of the top scientists required solitude as another critical factor: "Almost all these scientists experienced periods of isolation.... During these times they turned to their own resources for solace and amusement, experimented with their abilities and extended them. They became comfortable about being by themselves and interested in using these periods to indulge in fantasy, work on problems, read, and so forth." Finding time off in solitude, these scientists explored their own minds and learned to exercise creativity and playfulness.

This aspect of playfulness should also be a part of your multitasking: "Creative people have ... multiple projects in progress at the same time, and they're also far more likely than most of us to have serious hobbies," Harford points out. "Creativity often comes when you take an idea from its original context and you move it somewhere else." It comes when you practice exploration.

Multitasking, the slow kind, can be really beneficial. Often, we work frantically on a microscale, switching tasks every couple of minutes, but with little variation on the macro-scale. The goal of slow-motion multitasking is to reverse this, to find consistency in the hours and days but variety in the weeks and months. So, slow down, and let the creative flow take you from project to project in a slow and unhurried way.

PRACTICE:

Practice slow-motion multitasking

Are you overwhelmed by all the tasks you have to handle simultaneously? How about slowing down and giving each one its separate day or week in your calendar? Or are you completely focused on one thing but often feel stuck? How about diversifying and elevating one of your side projects or hobbies into something bigger that deserves its own dedicated time? Try to multitask on a slow-paced macro level, and the creative insights you get might amaze you.

BRANDON TORY

American Software Engineer and Rapper

"I think it's counterproductive to talk about life in a way that divides work from what you do outside work. I do not see this as side hustle, I see it as doing two things that I really love. I'm just trying to create and have fun."

"I believe that as human beings, we have the capacity to accomplish more than one dream in our lifetime."

A homeless kid in Brockton, Massachusetts, is dumpster diving for discarded electronic parts. He tries to understand how computers work, building and fixing stuff, attending his church's computer summer programs, and teaching himself how to code in C from a book he bought. Despite his love for computers, he doesn't really talk about it to anyone. "I didn't wanna be the nerd," he will later explain.

A senior software engineer sits in his office at the Apple headquarters in Cupertino, California. He is an expert in C++, Python, and Java, and well respected by his colleagues. Each weekend he goes on a 10-hour round-trip drive to Los Angeles. There he is pursuing his interest in music, organizing parties, writing and recording songs, and performing at underground events. None of his Apple colleagues know that he has a particular interest in music and spends his weekends in this way. They all just know him as a skilled engineer. He is afraid of what people might think of him.

As you might have guessed, the kid who was homeless between the ages of 15 and 18 and the Apple software engineer are both the same person, Brandon Tory. Despite his difficult situation growing up, Tory scored highly on both the MCAS and SATs and attended the University of Massachusetts on a John & Abigail Adams Scholarship. He received a degree in electrical engineering. But he felt like engineering wasn't cool. So, after graduating, he tried his luck at a career in music—and though he did have some early success, Tory still didn't make much money and ultimately went broke while living in Los Angeles.

In 2016, he decided to use his engineering skills, go to Silicon Valley, and become a software developer, eventually ending up at Apple. This is when his weekly commute, and the double life it represented, started. He traveled back and forth between his lives as an engineer and as a musician. But he was embarrassed and scared in each community of the other part of his life being found out. "Since I was a kid, I've struggled with self-identity. I've struggled with expectations for myself," Tory explains. "The cost of maintaining an image, in order to protect my own insecurities about being a computer nerd—resulted in moments of intense joy, decorated with moments of intense self-doubt." He grew increasingly stressed out by the charade.

Eventually, encouraged by his sister, Tory decided to work on a short documentary about his double life. But instead of completing and releasing the documentary to the public, he made the bold move to turn the footage into a one-minute mock commercial for Apple that highlighted a new generation of engineers and creatives that don't believe in the hard boundary between science and art. "I can be a kid from a rough neighborhood who loves to rap and is also a level five machine-learning engineer," he said in an interview in 2019. "And others can too. That was my message." He sent the footage to some Apple executives. And it paid off. One Apple exec, Jimmy Iovine, who was heading Apple Music (and is himself a producer), got in touch with Tory: "When I asked him if we could meet, and he said yes, I literally dropped to my knees and praised God."

Under the mentorship and guidance of Iovine, Tory developed his personal philosophy, an idea he calls *Multidream Theory*. He realized that keeping his two lives so separate and hidden from each other was not only creating tremendous anxiety, but was also hindering his progress in either of the two disciplines. "The engineer in me wants to focus on science," he writes in *Medium*, "while the musician in me wants to focus on my culture and my art. What I've realized is the conflict itself is the art. The lines have blurred, and I refuse to live two separate lives. I'm by no means a perfect engineer, nor am I a perfect rapper, or a perfect husband/father. I think the secret to life is allowing our dreams to flow and to shapeshift." If we give it time and space to unfold, this flow of dreams starts to reveal commonalities. The different dreams start to interfere with and feed on each other, and lead to a single multidream that we can chase without compromising on any of the parts.

One core theme that runs through most people's dreams is an element of creativity. And we fully agree with Tory about the exciting future of creativity thanks to "the advancements we're making in technology. The thing that's so special about human beings is our creativity, and that's becoming more obvious as we create more machine learning models and artificial intelligence to do repetitive tasks." Tory believes, and so do we, that future generations will no longer define their entire lives through narrow (and often dull) specializations, but will instead follow career paths that are much less linear—paths that fork, loop, cross over each other, recombine, and ultimately lead us to more fully explore our creativity.

Tory has since decided to get more serious about music again. He left Apple and moved back to LA, where he is now working as a senior AI software engineer at Google, while simultaneously focusing on his music career. He is fully living his multidream, having found inner peace with himself and his different passions.

PRACTICE:

Live your multidream

When was the last time you proudly talked about or showcased your dreams to people you work with? Sharing more about your passions outside of work can bring you closer to your coworkers. Recognize that you do not have to focus on a single dream and give up all the others, but that you can achieve them simultaneously. Let one fuel the other(s), and let your time off from one be time on with the other. The key here is to recognize that this does not encourage context switching. As Tory says, "If excellence requires literally giving our all, context switching will always be flawed." Instead, discover that your dreams are not orthogonal, but all linked. If you can spot and utilize these links, progress in one will also be progress in all the others.

GETTING UNSTUCK

Creativity is about connecting dots. Exploring a large range of interests gives us access to a wealth of dots. But no matter how many dots there are, if we try to force it or if we're too focused on it and stuck in preparation mode, all we ever do is connect neighboring dots, resulting in rigid thoughts and stale ideas. To really see the interesting connections, we need to get a new perspective and gain some distance.

This can happen at many different scales. On a microlevel, maybe all we need when we feel mentally drained or stuck with a problem is to get away from it for an hour or even just spend a few minutes engaged in an activity that allows us to disconnect, for example, taking a short walk in nature. Just detaching from the problem for a bit can help us to gain a new perspective once we return to it. At an intermediate level, we have periods of time off that last anywhere from a single day to a week or two. This allows us to get more distance from the problem and, as a result, make more distant connections between ideas. Finally, we can think of extended periods of time off, starting anywhere from several weeks upward. Especially when combined with extended travel—which (as we will explore later) is a great tool to get a new perspective and detach from our usual thought patterns—this can be a highly effective form of incubation and can lead to very innovative ideas.

But knowing the importance of time off is only the first step. Really implementing it, fully trusting in its significance and ignoring the stigma that's unfortunately associated with it, is a different matter and takes practice. It requires slowly unlearning centuries of moral misdirection. It's both something we need to get better at on a personal level, but also something that needs to change from a societal point of view.

In true workaholic fashion, we often give too much weight and credit to the active preparation and verification stages of the creative process, simply because they are active and "difficult," so we think they must be virtuous and good and we downplay or ignore the importance of the passive incubation and illumination phases. Being always engaged in work, trying to force solutions, and attempting to compensate for lack of ideas with pure quantity of work not only makes you miserable, but it's also counterproductive. Ironically, our zealous pursuit of productivity might, in many cases, be achieving the exact opposite effect we are aiming for. It keeps us from unlocking the deep insights we're chasing. Work, especially the creative kind most knowledge workers are paid to do, is not linear or additive. No matter how much time you put in, the breakthrough insight will not come.

Graham Wallas knew this when he developed his theory of creativity. And so did physicist Hermann von Helmholtz, whom Wallas quotes on this: "[Following] previous investigation of the problem in all directions ... happy ideas come unexpectedly without effort, like an inspiration. So far as I am concerned, they have never come to me when my mind was fatigued, or when I was at my working table.... They came particularly readily during the slow ascent of wooded hills on a sunny day." For incubation—and ultimately illumination—to happen properly, we need time off, detachment, and a fresh perspective. Rest is one of the fundamental factors in the creative process.

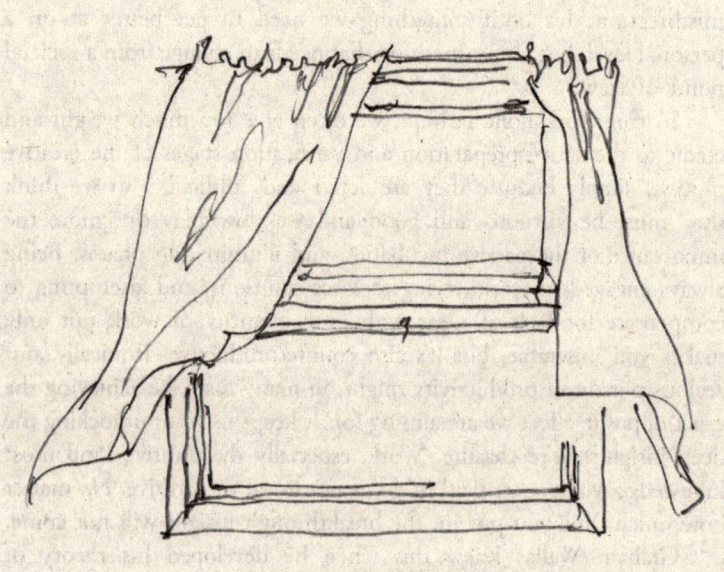

REST

Max had been struggling with his idea for months. He had spent hours buried in studies and an array of academic journals. And when he wasn't reading, he was thinking, turning the problem over and over in his mind. Max knew exactly what the issues were and what he wanted to achieve. He just couldn't figure out how to do it.

As an AI researcher, Max was trying to solve a problem related to how we represent data in many of the AI applications we encounter daily, such as finding similar-looking images, the song or movie recommendations made by streaming services, or photo tag suggestions. To accomplish these and related tasks, data scientists create "maps" (technically called latent spaces) of the data they are working with. The closer two things are on these maps, the more similar the data they represent. The problem is that given our current algorithms, the maps can be distorted and contain hidden "valleys" or "mountains," which impacts the results such systems provide. Imagine if Google Maps told you the closest route to your destination was only 100 meters, but didn't mention that you had to traverse a deep valley with steep cliffs to get there along this route. That's the issue data scientists can encounter with their data maps, and it was the issue Max was trying to improve upon.

Max knew how to figure out where these valleys and mountains were, but the tricky part was how to incorporate this information into the distances. He needed a way to distort the maps so that the distances became more meaningful (put mathematically: he was trying to flatten the metric of the underlying space). He'd been wrestling with it for months, with little progress to show for his efforts. Then Max went hiking.

Hakone is a region in central Japan known for its hot springs and scenic views of Mt. Fuji. It's a perfect spot for a weekend trip, and Max and his friend Ayako were making the most of it. Having spent most of the first day soaking in a beautiful outdoor bath surrounded by mountains and nature, on the second day, the two set out on a long hike. Max's mind was (seemingly) as far removed from work, math, and that pesky data-mapping problem as it could have been. He was fully present in their conversation and in the hike itself, paying careful attention so as not to trip over the many stones and tree roots dotting the steep and narrow paths. But at one point, an offhand remark sparked his thinking.

The two had been out in the mountains for a few hours and were considering how to make their way back to their hotel. So they consulted a bus map they had picked up at the local tourist information. The map was illustrated in a simple, hand-drawn style. It was not an exact to-scale representation of the terrain; instead, it was distorted to highlight the most important sights and routes. At that point, Ayako told Max how she had recently read a book on the history of cartography, and remarked, "Isn't it interesting that people used to draw maps so that things that were considered more important were drawn in a larger way?"

And that's when it hit him. The proverbial bolt of lightning, the metaphorical bag of bricks, the light at the end of the tunnel. It was right there: the solution to his problem.

Thematic maps called cartograms are drawn in such a way that the size of the area is scaled by some property of interest, for example, that region's GDP, its population, or its agricultural production. Max realized that he could use the same technique to solve his seemingly unrelated problem of data representations. If there is a "mountain ridge" in the data map, he could similarly blow up that mountainous area to make points separated by the ridge more distant. The more distance, the "higher" the mountain.

Upon his return to Tokyo, where he lived, it took Max only a couple of days to test his intuition and find that it worked reasonably well. After a few more experiments and some detailed analysis, he wrote a scientific paper on the new method with two of his colleagues. And all of it was based on that one sudden illuminating idea he had while hiking the hills of Hakone. He had needed to get away from work to make progress with work. Max just needed some rest.

10,000 HOURS? OR FOUR?

Charles Darwin worked for only three 90-minute periods a day and otherwise spent his time on long walks, taking naps, or lost in thought. Henri Poincaré, one of the most prolific and universal thinkers, spent his active work hours from 10am to noon and then 5 to 7pm—just enough time to wrap his head around a problem and then let his subconscious take over. Similarly, mathematician G. H. Hardy believed that four hours of conscious work was the maximum and filling the other time with too much "busy work" was hugely counterproductive.

As it turns out, Darwin, Poincaré, and Hardy were on to something. Four hours a day, if they are genuinely focused, spent on the right things, and supported by good rest, are really all we need to achieve great things. It's an idea that flies in the face of our busyness culture.

A much-cited study by Anders Ericsson and colleagues led to the famous "10,000-hour rule" for greatness, popularized by Malcolm Gladwell's book *Outliers*. This rule, claiming that it requires 10,000 hours of deliberate practice to reach expert level in any domain, found a welcome audience in a world that treats busyness, stress, and overwork as virtues rather than vices, and many adhere to it like dogma. But Ericsson's study also showed that deliberate practice must be limited per day to be effective—and four hours seemed to be the ideal number.

Even more interestingly (and a point often ignored), the study also illuminated the difference in the way top performers rested. Their leisure time was more structured and planned compared to average performers. So, they engaged not only in deliberate practice, but also in deliberate *rest*. They slept on average one hour more, too. In fact, many creatives and successful leaders use naps as powerful tools to incubate after getting their four hours of focus done.

In that way, sleep can be used to break up a block of deep work, effectively dividing a working day into two, allowing a "two-shift day." Some even went further to perfect their use of sleep, like Salvador Dalí with his "slumber with a key" method, accessing the hypnagogic state—the transition from wakefulness to sleep—for powerful creative insights. We'll discuss sleep more thoroughly later on. As you're about to see, rest goes way beyond mere sleep.

REST IS PRODUCTIVE

Rest is commonly thought of as the opposite of work. We either rest, or we are productive. But the strict separation between work and rest is a modern misconception. If we define "work" as the entire process of productivity and creativity, not just as the thing most of us are supposed to be doing from 9 to 5, then rest is as integral a part of work as the obvious busywork we are all performing daily.

For a long time, it was assumed that the brain powers mostly down when we rest. However, when neuroscientists, armed with ever-improving brain imaging technologies, were actually able to observe brain activity, they saw something quite different. The 18th-century poet William Cowper was on to something when he wrote, "Absence of occupation is not rest; / A mind quite vacant is a mind distressed." What researchers found was that a mind at rest is anything but vacant. Rather than an overall decrease in activity, the activity just shifts to different parts of the brain. These parts that activate during rest eventually became collectively known as the Default Mode Network (DMN).

With additional research, it soon became clear that the DMN is not only highly active, it is also crucially important. A study by the University of Southern California neuroscientist Mary Helen Immordino-Yang and her colleagues has found that DMN activity is highly correlated with intelligence, empathy, emotional judgment, and even overall sanity and mental health. Rest, it turns out, is critical to health, development, and, yes, to productivity.

Excellent work, particularly of the creative and innovative kind, needs rest and relaxation just as much as it requires time actively engaged in work. When we rest, our brain is busy consolidating memories, and quietly searching for solutions to problems we encounter. As the DMN kicks in, our intuition takes center stage and our creativity and problem-solving skills become more non linear, making more distant associations. If you have ever had a powerful daydream or epiphany while on a walk or in the shower, you can thank your DMN for that. In a moment that feels restful to you, your DMN is quietly seeking out big-picture strategies for the problems you're trying to solve or the creative breakthrough you might be seeking. But if your mind is occupied with distractions, this process gets hindered. In that way, effective, deliberate rest is very different from just zoning out in front of the TV, mindlessly swiping on Tinder, or clicking from cat video to cat video on YouTube.

It has been shown that the brains of creative people have a more strongly developed DMN, allowing them to keep working more effectively when they rest. Interestingly, there are also specific areas in the DMN of creative people that are suppressed compared to the average population. The left temporoparietal region, which is responsible for subconscious idea evaluation, seems to be less active, suppressing fewer ideas, letting them instead rise up to the conscious mind. And this ultimately leads to those elusive aha moments.

Spending more time resting and less time actively engaged in work not only boosts creativity and happiness, it also makes the time spent on work more efficient. Web development company Basecamp (formerly 37 Signals) experimented with shorter work weeks, adding an additional day to the weekend, and found that "just about the same amount of work gets done in four days vs. five days.... Three-day weekends mean people come back extra refreshed on Monday. Three-day weekends mean people come back happier on Monday. Three-day weekends mean people actually work harder and more efficiently during the four-day work week."

Once you commit to making more time for rest, your work directly benefits. The self-imposed time constraint makes you focus on what's essential. It makes you reevaluate the way you work and the methods you use. You become less likely to fall into the trap of visible busyness, actually getting stuff done rather than scheduling another pointless meeting or moving some images around in the presentation you are working on. You become more aware of the true value of your time, not just as a currency to exchange for money, but something valuable to you personally, something to be invested in any way you deem the most meaningful. And investing it in a variety of passions can be the key to making your creativity soar.

HENRI POINCARÉ

French Mathematician, Theoretical Physicist, and Polymath
(29 April 1854—17 July 1912)

"Often when one works at a hard question, nothing good is accomplished at the first attack. Then one takes a rest, longer or shorter, and sits down anew to the work…. All of a sudden the decisive idea presents itself to the mind. It might be said that the conscious work has been more fruitful because it has been interrupted and the rest has given back to the mind its force and freshness."

After struggling for two weeks to prove that a certain type of mathematical function, now called a Fuchsian function, could not exist, Henri Poincaré did what might be all too familiar to many of us: he drank too much coffee and, as a result, lay in bed restlessly staring at his ceiling. But suddenly, the ideas floating through his mind started making sense. Rather than proving the functions did not exist, he discovered the opposite. As he fell asleep, Poincaré felt confident that he could prove the existence of a certain subclass of Fuchsian functions. The next morning, he "had only to write out the results, which took but a few hours."

Shortly thereafter, while working on a follow-up problem, he had to leave for a geological expedition, noting that "the incidents of the travel made me forget my mathematical work," but several days into the trip, he recalled that while getting on a bus "at the moment when I put my foot on the step, the idea [that would eventually solve the problem] came to me, without anything in my former thoughts seeming to have paved the way for it."

After returning from his trip and verifying his new insight, Poincaré got stuck on yet another problem: "Disgusted with my failure, I went to spend a few days at the seaside and thought of something else. One morning, walking on the bluff, the idea came to me, with just the same characteristics of brevity, suddenness and immediate certainty."

Few people in the history of math and science have been as prolific and influential as Henri Poincaré. It is hard to even begin to describe the numerous and varied contributions he has made to mathematics and the sciences. Barely any field has been left untouched by his influence. His work on Fuchsian functions mentioned above ultimately led to the proof of Fermat's Last Theorem, which puzzled mathematicians for centuries. He himself was also the originator of another (in)famous problem, the Poincaré Conjecture, which was seen as so important that the Clay Mathematics Institute offered a $1 million prize for its solution, and which was finally proved by Grigori Perelman in 2006. Trying to list (and explain) all of Poincaré's work would fill several books.

At the same time, few have been stronger believers in the power of intuition and the subconscious mind. And he believed in the importance of rest and time off for fueling this power. They were some of his most reliable productivity tools.

Working only two two-hour slots per day, from 10am to noon, and again from 5 to 7pm, he deliberately used the time in between to allow his subconscious mind to work and for ideas to incubate and mature. His output speaks for itself, both in quantity and enduring importance.

On the longer time scale, using his own form of slow-motion multitasking, Poincaré's work habits have been compared to a bee flying from flower to flower, and the American mathematician Eric Temple Bell described him as "the last universalist." Working on different projects allowed Poincaré's subconscious mind to solve unrelated problems, while simultaneously gathering new inspiration and cross-pollinating his research.

Henri Poincaré recognized that the most fruitful form of time off "is on the one hand preceded and on the other hand followed by a period of conscious work." The correct balance is key. Both work and rest play an important part in productivity and creativity, and ultimately a fulfilling life.

PRACTICE:

Split your workday into several distinct parts: short bursts of high focus, with good types of rest in between

When was the last time you actually gave your undivided attention to one question for an hour or two? Jot down a significant problem you are trying to solve and spend two hours thinking through only that. No distractions allowed. But don't force it either. If you feel completely stuck with a problem, step away and let your subconscious work on it. We're not talking procrastination, but good rest. You might be surprised by the ease with which you can solve the previously unsolvable problem after you've allowed your unconscious mind to take the reins.

REST IS ACTIVE

"The best rest for doing one thing is doing another thing," writes Wilder Penfield in his essay "The Use of Idleness." "It is the vigorous use of idle time that will broaden your education, make you a more efficient specialist, a happier man, a more useful citizen. It will help you to understand the rest of the world and will make you more resourceful." Not a bad sales pitch.

It's a common misconception that mental faculties tire and need to be recharged. This is only partially true. What our mind really wants is for us to change things up. So having active leisure time will not negatively affect the next day's performance at work. It will boost our performance. When absorbed in a completely different challenge, your mind can fully unleash the subconscious on a previously encountered problem (the process of incubation), without being distracted by new inputs from the conscious mind.

Many influential scientists were avid musicians, artists, or sportsmen. Max has found the high-intensity exercise of CrossFit and the calm flow from baking bread or producing music to be the most effective. John enjoys practicing the martial art Jiu Jitsu or hosting elaborate dinner parties for creatives to mingle and inspire each other.

As you may have already noticed in some of the profiles, long walks have been a particularly common habit among history's great minds, and many profound insights came on walks. Other examples of these insights include Heisenberg's uncertainty principle, Hamilton's discovery of quaternions, and Rubik's design of the Rubik's Cube. "The moment my legs begin to move my thoughts begin to flow," said Henry David Thoreau, another walker.

Science backs up Thoreau's perspective. Exercise, which we will explore in much more detail later, induces profound structural brain plasticity and directly improves the brain, just like it improves muscles and the cardiovascular system. During exercise, the production of neurotrophins—proteins encouraging the formation and growth of neurons—is significantly increased. Moreover, endurance exercise releases the hormone irisin, which in turn triggers the production of brain-derived neurotrophic factor BDNF, one of the most active neurotrophins. In other words, breaking a sweat makes your brain grow and form new connections—connections that might help you solve that tricky problem you were stuck with and achieve the next creative breakthrough.

Additionally, exercise both relieves stress and helps build a higher tolerance against future stress. Our brains, and, as a consequence, our productivity and creativity, directly benefit from us being active—and though it may seem counterintuitive, such activity is precisely the sort of good rest our minds need to recover.

THE FOUR FACTORS OF RECOVERY

When you think of rest, what do you picture? A nap in a hammock under a shade tree? Sprawling out on your couch in front of a *Seinfeld* marathon? Rest is not *just* rest, and not all rest is *good* rest. Burning three hours on Reddit is not the same as taking a nap or going for a walk. We've established that we need good rest to get all the positive benefits on our productivity and well being, and that rest can be active. But what exactly defines good rest?

As Alex Soojung-Kim Pang points out in his book *Rest: Why You Get More Done When You Work Less*, research has shown that there are four major factors contributing to proper rest and recovery:

- Relaxation, or allowing our mind and body to wind down.
- Control, or deciding how to spend our time and attention.
- Mastery, or being challenged enough to get into a flow state.
- Detachment, or being so absorbed that we forget about work.

If your definition of rest is limited to relaxation, then you're ignoring three-quarters of the essential components of good rest.

Control: Many factors in our daily lives are beyond our control. Your boss makes a decision that completely uproots your work of the last three months, your client sends you new specifications right before the project deadline, or you get stuck abroad at the worst possible time because an unpronounceable Icelandic volcano decides to erupt and paralyze all air traffic over Europe (which actually happened to Max many years ago during university exam season). This can be stressful and distracting, and can drain your energy and creativity.

To balance this, it's good to have an element of control in your rest. Pursuits like painting, cooking, or making music are fully in our control. Even something as unpredictable as an adventure holiday still allows us to make our own decisions, unlike, say, a work situation where we have to act according to company policy. We decide how we spend our time, energy, and attention. And as a result, this form of rest recharges us for the times when things become chaotic again.

Mastery: Playing an instrument or writing poetry might be fully in our control, but that doesn't mean it's easy. But, somewhat paradoxically, this makes them particularly good rest activities. True rest is active and involves *mastery experiences*—experiences that are challenging and mentally absorbing enough to get us into a flow state (without being so difficult that we just quit in frustration).

In John's Jiu Jitsu classes, he spends hours working on just one specific technique to improve his mastery. When he spars with his training partners, he has to be fully present or his opponent will quickly wrap him into a submission. He feels refreshed from his training sessions because, for those hours, he is able to stop thinking about his projects. Mastery experiences are an integral component to rest. They are so engaging and demanding that they push everything else out of mind, leaving no space for rumination about work.

Detachment: And this brings us to the final, and maybe most important, component of good rest: the ability to put work (or whatever else we are taking a break from) entirely out of our mind and attend to other things, which is crucial for physical and mental recovery. In other words, can you "log off" for the day? As Sabine Sonnentag writes in a study on the importance of detachment:

"Empirical research has shown that employees who experience more detachment from work during off-hours are more satisfied with their lives and experience fewer symptoms of psychological strain, without being less engaged while at work…. [The research also] identified positive relations between detachment from work during off-hours and job performance."

One common trait among many top performers is the ability to rapidly, and at will, switch between two binary states, either being fully ON, focusing all their mental and physical energy on their particular craft, or fully OFF, in a state of calm and detached relaxation. Most of us, on the other hand, spend our lives in some analog state fluctuating around some mean of "half on" and "half off," never reaching either extreme and never experiencing the benefits that come from them.

Practicing full detachment, whether on evenings and weekends, or on extended vacations, is crucial in developing this skill, the ability to be fully engaged when it counts, and effectively recover when it doesn't. The most creative and productive workers are those who can unplug entirely from work.

Good rest is not mere relaxation. It is active and challenging. It demands our full attention. It stimulates us and gets us into flow states. It allows us to forget all our other concerns for a while, and be fully present in the moment, without the unspoken anxiety that's at the heart of boredom. One person's good rest can even look like someone else's work. Sometimes, all that is required for good rest is a healthy dose of variety.

SØREN KIERKEGAARD

Danish Philosopher (5 May, 1813—11 November, 1855)

"Of all ridiculous things the most ridiculous seems to me, to be busy—to be a man who is brisk about his food and his work."

"Far from idleness being the root of all evil, it is rather the only true good."

Every farmer worth his salt knows that you can't just keep growing the same crop year after year in the same place and expect a consistently high yield. If you do that, you completely deplete the soil of its nutrients and increase the risk of soil erosion and pest infestations. Instead, a smart farmer uses crop rotation, a system in which different crops are grown in consecutive seasons. This alternating pattern allows the soil to recover from one particular crop and leads to overall healthier farmland and higher yield. Even better than just letting the soil recover by itself, if the right crops are chosen in the consecutive cycles, one crop can actually fertilize the soil for the next one, releasing the exact nutrients into the earth that the ensuing one needs to thrive. This practice is so effective (and simple) that it has been used in one form or another since ancient times, at least since 600 BCE in the Middle East.

Søren Kierkegaard, the founding father of existentialist philosophy, believed that this principle of crop rotation applies not only to agriculture, but also to the pursuits of the human mind. Kierkegaard was born into an immensely wealthy family in Copenhagen (and spent the rest of his life living off his father's inheritance, so you might argue that it was particularly easy for him to practice time off). From early on in his life, this frail child was surrounded by death, with five of his six siblings dying before he even reached the age of 22. Maybe as a result, Kierkegaard became somewhat obsessed with the idea that he had to leave his mark on the world before his own death. And he chose philosophy as his way to achieve this.

Boredom was what Kierkegaard considered to be the real source of much of humanity's problems and went as far as calling it the root of all evil. But it is important to clarify here that Kierkegaard's notion of boredom was different from what we might think of when we hear the word. He wasn't talking about idleness, or stillness, or what we might call mindfulness today. In an essay titled "The Rotation of Crops," he writes: "Idleness, we are accustomed to say, is the root of all evil. To prevent this evil, work is recommended.... [But] idleness as such is by no means a root of evil; on the contrary, it is truly divine life, if one is not bored." We really have it backward when we think of idleness as evil. It is really boredom—the desire for activity, the craving of constant motion, and the fear of stillness—that is the problem.

"It is very curious that boredom, which itself has such a calm and sedate nature, can have such a capacity to initiate motion," remarks Kierkegaard. True idleness, he argued, has no desire to initiate motion because it is satisfied in itself. It doesn't worry about the future. It is simple presence in the current moment.

Someone who really embraces idleness can, like kids, find endless joy in the simplest of things, things that seem like nothing at all. Recalling his own time as a child, Kierkegaard reminisced, "What fun we had catching a fly, keeping it prisoner under a nutshell, and watching it run around with it!" When his anxiety hit him, he found temporary relief by reminding himself to be in the moment, just like a kid being fully absorbed while playing with a fly. "The fullness of time," he wrote in *The Concept of Anxiety*, "is the moment as the eternal."

It is this idleness that Kierkegaard saw at the heart of creative insight and imagination. But much of modern society seems to fear idleness (or what we now more often call boredom) as possibly one of the worst things in existence. In this way, Kierkegaard shared the sentiment of mathematician Blaise Pascal, who famously said that "all of humanity's problems stem from man's inability to sit quietly in a room alone."

It is quite conceivable that someone is overstimulated but still constantly bored. Probably all of us know this feeling. Our phone is buzzing with notifications and bottomless feeds that just beg to be scrolled and there is plenty of busywork that needs to be done, but we still feel unbelievably *bored*. It's really the absence of meaning, not the absence of activity or stimuli, that makes us feel this way.

Even in the 1800s, Kierkegaard already saw the proliferation of busyness as a problem. In *Either/Or: A Fragment of Life*, he writes:

> There is an indefatigable activity that shuts a person out of the world of spirit and places him in a class with the animals, which instinctively must always be in motion. Some people have an extraordinary talent for transforming everything into a business operation, whose whole life is a business operation, who fall in love and are married, hear a joke, and admire a work of art with the same businesslike zeal with which they work at the office. The Latin proverb *otium est pulvinar diaboli* [idleness is the devil's pillow] is quite correct, but the devil does not find time to lay his head on this pillow if one is not bored. But since people believe that it is man's destiny to work, the antithesis idleness/work is correct.

Despite having been written almost 200 years ago, these words ring more accurately now than ever before. We confuse idleness with boredom and elevate work to something almost sacred.

And this brings us back to mental crop rotation. Kierkegaard believed that we can find immense creativity—and avoid boredom—by rotating the mental activities and projects we engage in, just as a farmer rotates his crops. If we get stuck with one activity, if our mental soil runs out of nutrients, it's time to move on to the next one and let our mind recover. But Kierkegaard warned that this has to be done the right way. Otherwise, it just creates more boredom. If we use it as an excuse for constant multitasking and restlessness, we'll have completely missed the point.

The crop rotation he suggests is more methodical and thoughtful, driven by idleness rather than boredom (and the restlessness that it implies): "The method I propose does not consist in changing the soil but, like proper crop rotation, consists of changing the method of cultivation and the kinds of crops. Here at once is the principle of limitation, the sole saving principle in the world…. Here is the extreme boundary of that principle that seeks relief not through extensity but through intensity." In this way, Kierkegaard's idea of crop rotation is very similar to Tim Harford's notion of "slow-motion multitasking." We should look for relief from boredom not by doing a thousand things, but by doing a few things at full intensity and giving them the time they deserve before moving on to the next one.

PRACTICE:

Employ crop rotation

Limit yourself to a few or even a single key activity or task for any given time and truly immerse yourself in it, finding freedom and joy in this limitation and presentness. Then, once your progress slows, move on to the next task, again giving it your full attention. Instead of constant diffuse multitasking, apply Kierkegaard's focused sequential way of working. Think of your work on one thing as time off from all the other stuff, and fertilize your mental soil for when you get back to them.

PROTECT YOUR REST

Even when we recognize its importance, time for rest doesn't just magically materialize. Especially if our current modus operandi is busyness.

It is our responsibility to make time for it. Or, as Alex Soojung-Kim Pang notes, *defend* it: "Taking rest seriously requires recognizing its importance, claiming our right to rest, and carving out and defending space for rest in our lives." We have to remember to unsubscribe from the Protestant work ethic ideals.

Just as with our attention, rest can also very effectively be defended from the world's attempts to take it from us by establishing routines and habits surrounding it. This, somewhat counterintuitively, requires putting more thought into planning our leisure time and protecting it from encroaching work. Particularly people who work mostly for themselves, at home, or on projects they are really passionate about need to take this seriously and proactively schedule time for rest.

Deciding in advance on a time to stop working can be used as an effective productivity strategy. Ernest Hemingway is famous for leaving his work unfinished midsentence at the end of a day. When you already know what comes next, you can get a "hot start" the next day instead of starting from a blank page. It also provides fuel for your subconscious and default mode network to assist you in your creative process. Stopping at the right time requires some self-awareness, but it can give huge payoffs. Developing a little work shutdown ritual that clearly marks the transition from work time to rest time—for example, writing out your to-dos for the next day, watering your desk plant, or reflecting on the day in your journal—can also be effective, especially for remote workers who don't have the natural "ritual" of the commute back home.

Rest and time off are too important to be left to chance or the empty spaces in our calendar. We need to schedule and protect them. We need to make time for them just as we would for a meeting or deep work session. And while many see their work time as "the day," we should treat leisure time as a "day within a day" and make plenty of time for it. This is particularly true for one of the most important forms of rest: sleep.

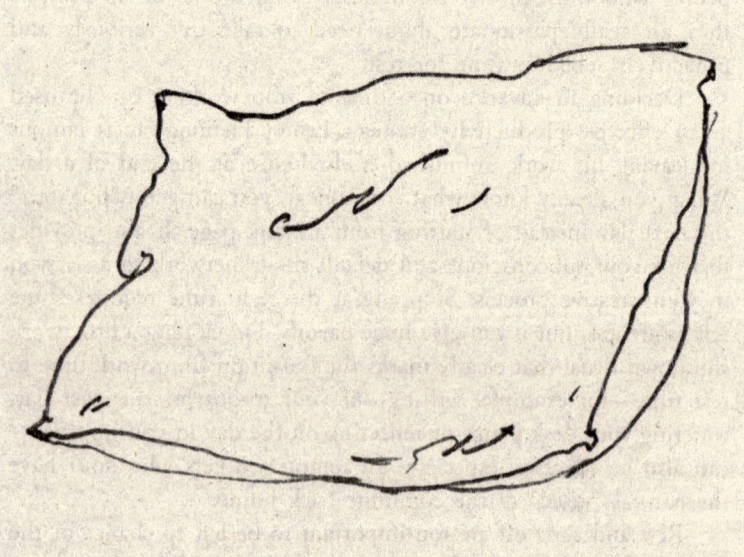

SLEEP

In recent years, both the American Centers for Disease Control and Prevention and the World Health Organization have declared sleep loss a public health epidemic. A shocking two-thirds of all people in developed countries do not get enough sleep—but how much is "not enough"? While the number varies a bit from person to person, the scientific community defines "habitual short sleep duration" as anything less than seven hours a night. Not that seven hours are ideal; it's just the absolute minimum. Seven hours!

You might now be thinking, "That's ridiculous. I never sleep for seven hours, and I'm doing perfectly fine." The problem is that we have terrible self-perception. Most people massively overestimate how well they perform on low sleep. Doing well on four to five hours is a myth ruled out by every scientific study so far, and people who claim they can do it are deluding themselves (which incidentally gets easier the less you sleep since your mental function is dramatically impaired). And sleep debt is additive. One week of six hours of sleep per night is just as bad as a single night with no sleep at all! Think about that for a second. How many sleepless nights have you accumulated over the last couple of months?

As we will explore shortly, sleep is critical for both health and productivity. If a pill could deliver the same benefits as a good night of sleep, it would be hailed as a miracle drug and we would all be taking it. Yet we happily sacrifice sleep and even brag about it. As Matthew Walker, author of the best-selling book *Why We Sleep: The New Science of Sleep and Dreams*, points out, we have an "arrogance in many business cultures focused on the uselessness of sleep." Walker, whom we will meet in more detail shortly, continues by saying that "this mentality has persisted, in part, because certain business leaders mistakenly believe that time on task equates with task completion and productivity." But this belief could not be further from the truth.

Our crusade against sleep, yet another misguided remnant of the Protestant work ethic and its successors, is not just negatively impacting our health, but also leading to an enormous productivity loss in the workplace. Walker cites studies that show that, on a national level, lack of sleep costs developed nations 1-3 percent of their GDP. Japan is leading this ranking with 2.9 percent of GDP lost (which is almost three times more than the country's entire defense budget, and close to the amount it spends on education). The US is not too far behind with 2.3 percent of its GDP. According to 2019 figures, the most recent as of this writing, that's about $493 *billion* wasted annually in the US alone because we believe that we only need a minimum amount of sleep!

Borrowing one of Walker's analogies, running on low sleep is like trying to boil a pot of water on low heat. If we just started our days well rested, we could achieve the same—or more—on "high heat" in a fraction of the time and with much less wasted energy. And we stand to gain much more than just less wasted energy if we take sleep seriously. Happier marriages, for example.

MATTHEW WALKER

British Sleep Scientist

"The shorter your sleep, the shorter your life span."

"If you don't snooze, you lose."

The sun is setting over San Francisco Bay, and Matthew Walker is starting to wind down from a day teaching and researching sleep science in his position as Professor of Neuroscience and Psychology at the University of California, Berkeley. Besides putting in a full day at his job, he's also been active in the gym and cycled to and from work. His last cup of (decaffeinated) coffee was hours ago. He is not buzzing from a hectic day, but relaxed. Comfortably tired, rather than hopelessly exhausted. Instead of sedating himself with a couple of drinks in front of a bright screen, Matthew might recline with an old-fashioned book before going to bed with his partner and spending some quality time cuddling and getting intimate. And then … one of them gets up to go to their own separate bedroom, and both get a good night of reinvigorating sleep.

If you now think something must be wrong with their relationship, you are probably not alone. Many people take it as a given that, in a healthy relationship, a couple sleeps together. But according to science, this might be a terrible idea. And Walker should know, since he is one of the most eminent sleep scientists and the founder and director of the Center for Human Sleep Science, having published over 100 scientific research studies on the topic and written the aforementioned best-selling book *Why We Sleep: The New Science of Sleep and Dreams*, which was a big inspiration for this entire chapter.

A year into their relationship, he and his long-term partner negotiated what Walker calls a "sleep divorce." From his research, he knew that if couples don't sleep well, they are less emotionally and physically intimate. One in ten relationships even ends as a result of sleep-related issues—tired and cranky people just have more emotional conflicts. So Walker and his partner decided to each get their own bedroom. And they are not regretting their choice: "It's worked out wonderfully; we both feel a lot more rested, and our relationship is better in every way. Your desire to be intimate increases the more you sleep. Getting better and longer quality sleep raises testosterone levels, vital for both men's and women's sex drives. I believe we must spread this message and fight the stigma surrounding sleeping in separate beds—for the good of our collective health as well as our relationships."

He stresses that this is not a one-size-fits-all approach, and some couples who sleep together genuinely do get enough good sleep. This idea that sleep is highly personal is a critical finding that also crops up in other places in Walker's research. Every one of us naturally falls into what is called a *chronotype*, essentially whether we are night owls or morning larks. Ideally, we would all know our chronotype and then match our schedules to that, sleeping and waking at the time that's most suited to our natural rhythm—whether that's 8pm to 4am or 2am to 11am. The problem is that our current society is not built for this. The standard 9-to-5 expects everyone to adapt themselves to a one-size-fits-all solution, despite the terrible effect this is having on a large part of the population. Those whose rhythms don't fit into this given schedule not only suffer adverse health and performance consequences, but are also denounced as lazy bums.

"We have stigmatized sleep with the label of laziness," Walker notes. "We want to seem busy, and one way we express that is by proclaiming how little sleep we're getting. It's a badge of honor." His assertion feels all the more poignant when we consider how such stigma manifests: "We chastise people for sleeping what are, after all, only sufficient amounts. We think of them as slothful.... We overvalue employees that undervalue sleep." Walker's observation hits home like a gut punch. Our thirst for visible busyness regularly makes us work ourselves well past the point of exhaustion, for the sole purpose that others see us doing so. As Walker points out, "Humans are the only species that deliberately deprive themselves of sleep for no apparent reason."

Walker himself strictly sticks to an eight-hour sleep window, with a consistent time every single day. His partner even takes nine hours to feel fully rested, going to bed half an hour before him and sleeping in half an hour longer. Another benefit of a sleep divorce.

"Sleep, unfortunately, is not an optional lifestyle luxury. Sleep is a non-negotiable biological necessity. It is your life-support system, and it is Mother Nature's best effort yet at immortality. And the decimation of sleep throughout industrialized nations is having a catastrophic impact on our health, our wellness, even the safety and the education of our children," Walker warns. "It's a silent sleep loss epidemic, and it's fast becoming one of the greatest public health challenges that we face in the 21st century."

Let's give up our "sleep machismo," bragging about how little sleep we get or need, and instead celebrate it as one of the most amazing things our body is able to do—from physical and mental healing all the way to supercharged idea incubation and gifting us creative breakthroughs. Sleep is maybe the single most essential and universal form of time off. Sweet dreams!

PRACTICE:

Set yourself a non negotiable "sleep opportunity window"

For most people, this should be at least eight hours. And it should be the same every day. Walker's personal window is 10:30 pm to 6:30 am, but you should set yours based on your own chronotype, whether you are a morning person or a night owl. If you sleep with a partner, consider getting a "sleep divorce" and sleep in separate bedrooms. Despite the stigma around this, data shows that relationships (and yes, also sex life) actually improve through this practice. Just make sure you still find time to cuddle before and after a great night's sleep.

THE POWER OF DREAMS

We all know what sleep looks like on the outside: closed eyes, relaxed muscles, no signs of communication or responsiveness, and maybe a bit of drooling, and sleep is also easily reversible (as opposed to a coma). We also know what sleep feels like when we experience it ourselves: an apparent loss of external awareness and a distortion of time in two distinct ways. We experience both *time voids*, where we wake up several hours later and have no recollection that any time has passed at all, as well as the unique feeling of *stretched time* in dreams, where (similar to psychedelic experiences) minutes can feel like hours. But to really understand and appreciate what sleep is and how it supports our health and creativity, we have to look at our brains.

Sleep is categorized into several different phases. A healthy person tends to go through several sleep cycles per night, each of which spans all the different phases and lasts for around 90 minutes. Simplifying things a little bit, the two primary phases of interest are deep sleep and rapid eye movement (REM) sleep. The former is largely responsible for physical healing and recovery, while the latter takes care of emotional healing and creativity.

While awake, the electrical activity of the brain can seem like utter chaos. We see lots of high-frequency activity, which is perfect for local information processing but doesn't connect the more distant regions of our brain. But as we enter deep "slow-wave" sleep, our brain's internal chatter slows down and different regions of the brain start to sync up and communicate with each other. This is crucial for moving stored information from one place in the brain to another, particularly from the short-term memory (in the hippocampus) to long-term memory (in the cortex). While we are awake, we capture new information, and when we are sleeping, we transfer and distill this information. Deep sleep is the diligent librarian that makes sure nothing gets lost, everything is filed in the right place, and memories get efficient tags and cross-references.

But slow-wave sleep is far from the whole story. The other main component of sleep, REM sleep, is maybe even more remarkable and makes full use of the information assembled and prepared by deep sleep. REM sleep is the phase during which dreaming occurs, and it's a creative powerhouse. While we are awake, we think in a very logical and hierarchical structure. As we enter REM sleep, this logical structure seems to dissolve, and we start making more and more crazy associations between distant memories—which can manifest in the wonderful and bizarre dreams we experience. Breaking free from the usual fairly conservative thought patterns of our waking consciousness in this safe environment is one of the most powerful tools for creative insights and problem-solving. It's idea incubation on steroids.

Additionally, REM sleep allows us to reinforce new memories and motor skills by replaying them in our dreams. Most musicians or athletes will know this very well. Let's say you decide to take a nap at the end of a tough practice session, during which you were trying to master a new chord progression on a classical guitar but couldn't quite nail it. Then, once you awaken from your slumber, you find your strumming of the guitar strings just flows smoothly, as if by magic. Such is the power of dreaming. It is really the backbone of learning. Sleep before learning moves existing memories out of the hippocampus into the cortex, freeing up space for new information, and sleep after learning consolidates the new material, effectively hitting the save button. Many top performers, one of whom we'll meet at the end of this chapter, have learned to use sleep as one of the critical tools in their training arsenal.

Interestingly, humans sleep considerably less than all other primates but have a much higher ratio of REM sleep. During REM sleep, our muscles completely relax, leaving us paralyzed to prevent us from acting out our dreams. If you have to sleep high up in a tree to be out of reach from predators, this kind of muscle relaxation is potentially awful news; you might just fall and break your neck while in the middle of a dream. But with the discovery of fire, our ancestors could move down from the trees and sleep on the ground in reasonable safety, allowing for a night of much deeper sleep—and more REM sleep.

Some scientists argue that this advantage was one of the critical factors that allowed humans to develop more complex communities and technologies, and ultimately led to us becoming such a dominant species. While we sleep less than our primate relatives, we make much better use of our sleep. We quite literally dreamt our way to modern civilization. Sleep is really the foundation of our ingenuity, and we should make full use of it.

Our nightly cycles of sleep are an extremely efficient mechanism that optimizes our mental stability and performance, and empowers us to be the great thinkers, innovators, and leaders we aspire to be. Unfortunately, many of us are going through our lives severely sleep deprived. And the consequences are much more terrifying than most people realize.

THE MIRACLE DRUG

The list of negative consequences from a lack of sleep is long. Very long. On too little sleep, our cardiovascular health takes a severe hit—hospitals are reporting an almost 25 percent spike in heart attacks the day after countries switch to daylight savings time and people sleep one hour less.[2] A lack of sleep directly leads to diminished concentration and bad judgment—staying up for 19 hours straight, the equivalent of being awake from 7am to 2am, is as bad for your cognitive abilities as being legally drunk (and drowsy drivers are responsible for a massive number of traffic deaths). Neglecting sleep suppresses our immune system—even just a single night of short sleep dramatically reduces the amount of cancer-fighting killer cells, and regularly sleeping only six hours increases cancer risk by 40 percent. And for a final figurative kick in the balls, less sleep is directly linked to reduced sex drive, and in men to a drop in sperm count and testosterone—if you didn't buy into Matthew Walker's suggestion to get a sleep divorce before, maybe now you do.

Those are only some of the many negative effects on your health if you don't take sleep seriously. But while this may sound scary, we should instead look at the flipside, and treat sleep as a free and abundantly available miracle drug that can prevent and cure a whole host of diseases and ailments. And it's a smart drug too! Getting plenty of sleep can boost our cognitive abilities, as well as our social skills, dramatically.

---

[2]Once again we can learn from the Greeks: a study from the University of Athens Medical School, "Siesta in Healthy Adults," shows that those who take frequent naps have a more than 37 percent lower risk of heart attacks, suggesting we should all follow the Greek example and embrace a siesta culture.

REM sleep isn't just a powerful force for creative incubation; it's a tremendous housekeeper. The emotional centers in our brain are highly active, while at the same time the brain is entirely free of the stress-triggering hormone noradrenaline. This allows us to safely replay stressful memories and emotions and resolve them, weeding out "bad" memories, processing negative emotions, and reducing addictive behavior. In this way, sleep very effectively heals emotional wounds through dreams.[3] Sleep, and particularly dreams, makes us more emotionally stable, and as a result, more empathetic and understanding of others.

Most of us have probably experienced a leader or manager who seems to have a very short temper and can't control their emotions, impacting their team in a negative way. Chances are, they're the same kind of person who prides themselves on how little sleep they need. But with little sleep, rational control from our prefrontal cortex dims down, and the amygdala takes over, leading to inappropriate emotional reactions like anger, reactivity, and fight-or-flight response. Overall, our emotions amplify, both the good and the bad, resulting in mood swings and risky behavior. So if you want to be an effective leader, guiding your team in a calm manner and staying cool in the face of difficult decisions, you can greatly benefit from the balancing power of sleep.

The amygdala taking over and running the show is not just bad for our emotional stability, but also for our stress levels. Our sympathetic nervous system is responsible for throwing the body into overdrive in extreme stress or dangerous situations. This is a good response if you are running away from a tiger, or need intense focus in a tough negotiation, but it was not designed to be on all the time. If we are sleep-deprived, our sympathetic nervous system

---

[3]Unfortunately, as Rosalind D. Cartwright observes in her book The Twenty-Four Hour Mind, this process can get disturbed, for example, in people with PTSD or certain forms of depression. Instead of having the dreams resolve their emotions and experiences in a stress-free environment, patients relive the terror of their experience again and again in recurring nightmares.

may be chronically active, leading to higher heart rate and blood pressure, anxiety attacks, and breathlessness. Overall, it causes lots of damage. It might sometimes be difficult to get good sleep when you are stressed and anxious, but this is exactly the time when you need it most, so you should allow yourself to make plenty of time for sleep in stressful situations.

Sleep is like housekeeping for the brain. It acts as its primary waste disposal system. During sleep, brain cells shrink by an incredible 60 percent, allowing cerebrospinal fluid to rush through and flush out toxins like amyloid beta, a sticky protein whose accumulation is the leading cause of Alzheimer's disease. By getting plenty of sleep, you're actively keeping your brain healthy and young, warding off the various neurodegenerative diseases that plague many people in their later years.

In short, you can't create big things, lead amazing teams, solve great challenges, or make transformative art if you are sick (or worse, dead), if your brain is foggy, or if you are cranky and riddled with stress. Luckily, there is an easy solution to all these problems: a good night's sleep. Every night. And to make sure you get the most out of your sack time, let's look at how to optimize your sleep.

HOW TO GET MORE SLEEP

By now, you have probably realized just how critical proper sleep is. It's perhaps the single most essential and universal form of time off, and a good sleep routine should be a core part of everyone's rest ethic. Professionals take their sleep seriously, and your goal should be to sleep like a pro. Amazon CEO Jeff Bezos believes that sleep is one of the most important things he can do for his shareholders, saying in an interview with Thrive Global that "if you shortchange your sleep, you might get a couple of extra 'productive' hours, but that productivity might be an illusion." If you want to be a pro, you have to sleep like one. Real professionals aren't sleep-deprived.

Unfortunately, as most of us regularly experience, getting enough sleep can be a challenge. There are two key processes responsible for making us feel sleepy and able to fall asleep. The first of them is our circadian rhythm, our internal clock with a roughly (but not quite, hence the "circa" in circadian) 24-hour cycle. This clock gets properly synchronized with our 24-hour cycle through external cues, particularly light, but also other environmental factors such as changes in temperature. This cycle is among other things responsible for making us feel alert in the morning through the release of cortisol, as well as getting us ready for sleep at night through melatonin.

The other factor responsible for making us sleepy is the buildup of "sleep pressure," or, more specifically, the molecule adenosine. The higher the concentration of adenosine in our body, the more tired we feel—with some caveats: caffeine docks to the same receptors as adenosine, effectively tricking our body into believing that not much sleep pressure has built up. Adenosine gets cleared during sleep, and when we feel fully refreshed in the morning, it means we got rid of all our adenosine. But unfortunately, more and more people build up so much sleep pressure and sleep so little that they still have residues the next day, leaving them feeling groggy, especially until they get the first cup of coffee, sweeping their adenosine buildup under an increasingly bulging rug.

One key to becoming a pro in any discipline is building good routines and habits. And this is just as true for sleep. A solid sleep routine is the best way to sync your circadian rhythm and sleep pressure, and to make sure you get that good snooze that allows you to show up in top form every single day. The most critical first step is simply to make enough time for sleep, scheduling at least an eight-hour window per night. This should be non negotiable except for true emergencies (or the seemingly continuous emergency that is raising a small child). And ideally it should be the same window every single day, so that our body learns when it's time to wind down and switch off, and also when to power back up in the morning.

But what if you are already giving yourself enough time to sleep at the same time every day but just can't fall asleep? Self-diagnosed insomnia is widespread. And while many people genuinely do suffer from real insomnia, many more are actually just causing their own sleep issues through very preventable behaviors.

Caffeine is by far the most widely used drug in the world (and don't get us wrong, lots of caffeine went into writing this book). But as noted, caffeine blocks adenosine and prevents it from signaling to our body that we are tired. This can be great when we want to focus in the morning, but it can keep us from falling asleep at night. The half-life of caffeine in our body varies a bit from person to person but is roughly five to six hours. That means if you have a cup as early as noon, a quarter of that caffeine (!) will still be in your blood at midnight. And most of us reach for several cups of coffee until late into the afternoon. Max once tracked his (reasonably average) caffeine consumption over several months and simulated the caffeine concentration in his blood based on the data. His results suggested that by his usual wake-up time of around 8am, he still had an average of 20 to 30 mg of caffeine in his body (that's about half the amount in a single shot of espresso). It takes much longer for your body to get rid of the caffeine than you might think. So be conscious of how much you consume and when you have your last coffee.

Alcohol is another somewhat misunderstood substance when it comes to sleep. A common misperception is that alcohol helps with sleep. But just like sleeping pills, while we might perceive a faster onset, the quality of the sleep is actually much worse. Sedation and sleep are far from equivalent. Alcohol also strongly fragments our sleep, leading to frequent wake-ups (which we might not remember the next morning) and suppresses REM sleep. Even just a small amount of alcohol negatively impacts all the positive effects of sleep. We don't want to be killjoys (and we certainly like a glass or five from time to time), but if you're going to optimize your sleep, avoid alcohol as much as possible, especially close to bedtime. Maybe we can take another example from Mediterranean culture and enjoy a glass of wine with lunch instead of dinner. Or maybe, like some Germans, have a beer for breakfast?

Perhaps the most under appreciated factor in high-quality sleep is temperature. We used to sleep in caves, which were dark, quiet, and cold. But now, most of us sleep in rooms that are way too warm. To easily initiate sleep, our core body temperature actually needs to drop by 1°C. Sleeping in a warm bedroom covered with thick blankets makes it hard for that to happen. Experts recommend keeping the bedroom between 59 and 66°F (15 and 19°C). This will probably seem extremely chilly to most, but once you get used to it, you might find that it'll help you sleep like a bear in hibernation. Somewhat counterintuitively, a warm shower or bath before sleeping can also help cool you down. While you might feel heated up from it, the warm water draws blood to the surface of your body and allows your core to cool down, allowing for a faster and more refreshing slumber.

Finally, there is light. Artificial light has allowed us to break free from the natural cycles of light and dark imposed on us by the sun. But this has wreaked havoc on our circadian rhythm. Rather than bright sunlight during the day and darkness during the night, we envelop ourselves in the dim glow of indoor lighting for most of our waking day. This both prevents kickstarting our activity in the morning and prevents proper initiation of sleep in the evening. What you should do instead is try to get as much natural sunlight early in the day (leave those shades at home, they might look cool but are zapping your energy), and then dim down as much as possible closer to sleep time. Blue light, such as bright LEDs and backlit screens, should be avoided close to sleep since it signals the body that it's the middle of the day and prevents it from releasing the melatonin necessary to get yourself ready for sleep.

So tonight, maybe light some candles and spend some relaxing time away from any screens, before retreating to your cool cave and allowing yourself to sink into a deep and restorative slumber that will prepare you for the great things you are trying to achieve tomorrow, whether that's making a breakthrough in your research, landing that big client you've been pursuing for a while, or winning the NBA championship.

LEBRON JAMES AND MIKE MANCIAS

American Basketball Star and His Long-Time Personal Trainer

"I could do all the training. I could do all the ice bags and the NormaTecs and everything that we do that we have as far as our recovery package while I'm up. But when you get in that good sleep, you just wake up, and you feel fresh. You don't need an alarm clock. You just feel like, 'Okay. I can tackle this day at the highest level.'"

LeBron James is considered one of the greatest basketball players of all time. Since 2011, he has been ranked the best player in the NBA by ESPN and Sports Illustrated. His accomplishments include three NBA championships, four NBA Most Valuable Player Awards, three NBA Finals MVP Awards, and two Olympic gold medals. There is no doubt that he has put in his practice time on the basketball court. But it's his trainer, Mike Mancias, who ensures that James's performance, skills, and longevity are nurtured outside of the basketball arena.

"With any elite athlete," Mancias believes, "the one thing that we all, as trainers and therapists, have to keep in mind is that recovery never ends. Recovery never stops. If LeBron plays 40 minutes one night, if he plays 28 minutes one night, we're still going to keep recovery as our number one focus, whether that be in nutrition, whether that be in hydration, more flexibility exercises, stuff in the weight room. It's a never-ending process, really."

Mancias knows that the "always-recovering" mindset allows a player like James to be successful and provide longevity throughout his demanding, high-stakes career. One non-negotiable for James's routine is his sleep habits. James and Mancias look at his sleep quality as sharply as they do his free-throw shots. "He gets on me every single day," says James, "every single day about my sleep. 'How much sleep did you get last night? How much sleep? How much sleep? You get your eight hours? You get your nine hours?' all the time." Mancias believes that to deliver peak performance, whether that's athletic or otherwise, we need to be fully rested. Did you get your eight or nine hours of sleep last night? If not, is it possible that your productivity is suffering as a result?

Mancias's experience is backed up by science. A 2011 study published in the journal *Sleep* found that Stanford basketball players could increase their performance by getting more sleep. After a baseline was established, they were then asked to sleep for a full ten hours per night—significantly more than their usual six to nine hours—for five to seven weeks. At the end of this period, their accuracy had, on average, improved by 9 percent. They could sprint faster, and they reported overall better performance during practice and in games. Imagine what many people would give for 10 percent more performance in their field? But maybe all they have to do is sleep in a bit every day.

At the risk of pointing out the obvious here: James is operating at a high level. Aside from the pure athletic intensity of a professional basketball match, he also has to coordinate with his teammates, their coach, the media, and his sponsors. Managing all of this in one day is taxing. In order to pick back up and do it again, Mancias and James know that his body needs to heal itself while he's asleep. Mancias also emphasizes that while this is definitely true for a basketball star, it is the proper approach for any person operating at a high level. "You can be a businessman, a doctor, lawyer, etc., you need your sleep, guys," Mancias says. "And you must sleep in order to recover from whatever it is, either playing an NBA game or a big day in the courtroom, in a hospital room or whatever. Sleeping is when the body heals itself. So it's very, very important."

If you ever catch yourself thinking that you don't have time for eight hours of sleep because you have a business to build or that it makes sense to catch up on sleep on your next vacation, know that you will not show up in your prime shape the next day. Sleep is where you will get your energy and focus. Sleep is where you can develop your competitive edge as a professional. And if you want to play at the highest level, whatever you do, make sure you take sleep as seriously as James and his trainer, Mancias.

PRACTICE:

Sleep like a professional

You likely won't become a basketball star overnight, but you can still have the sleep routine of a champion. James's bedtime routine includes setting the room temperature to an optimal range and making the room dark by shutting all the shutters and curtains, and turning off all the light sources. To relax and wind down, he ensures no electronics 30–45 minutes before going to sleep. By consciously controlling your sleep environment, you can get the same sleep quality as one of the greatest performers in the world.

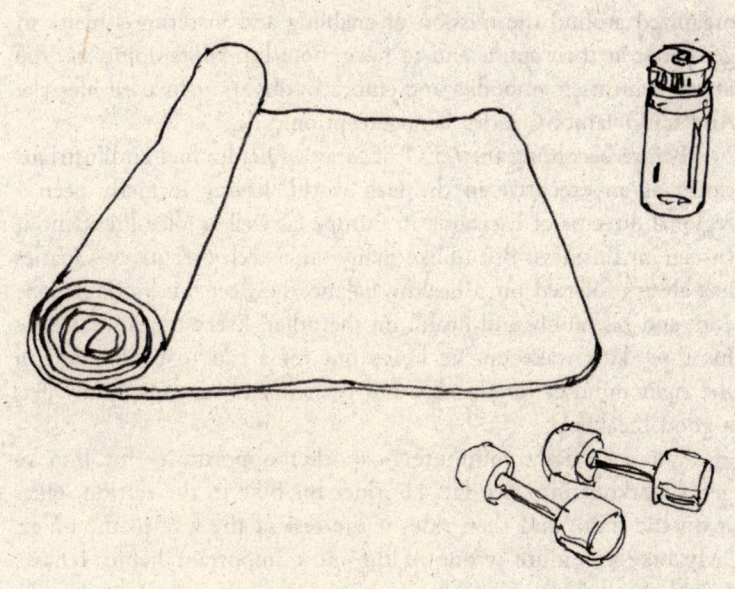

EXERCISE

Since its founding in 2009, Strava (Swedish for "strive") has quickly become one of the world's largest communities of athletes, particularly cyclists and runners, who use the service to track and log their workouts and share them with friends. The entire company is organized around the mission of enabling and inspiring athletes to get better at their sport, and to have more fun while doing so. The Strava team itself embodies and embraces this sport-focused lifestyle. And CEO James Quarles is no exception.

Before becoming the CEO of Strava, Quarles had an illustrious career as an executive in the tech world, having formerly been a regional director of Facebook in Europe, as well as Vice President at Instagram Business. But unlike many other tech executives, Quarles has always focused on a healthy balance between his work on one end, and his family and health on the other. Every morning, before his three kids wake up, he heads out for a run to get himself in the right mindset for the day and then makes sure his family gets a good breakfast.

Quarles's daily commute is another opportunity for him to get a workout into his day. He rides his bike to the station, takes it on the train, and then rides it the rest of the way to the office: "My bike commute is one of the most important habits I have: I ride even when it's raining (I have great rain pants), and I like breathing in the fresh air." Once he gets to work, he has a tight schedule until the evening, like most executives, but this simple routine allows Quarles to get in two workouts before the workday has even started.

Wednesdays are an exception to Quarles's busy schedule. Here, he manages to get in yet another workout in the middle of the day. In fact, the entire company is encouraged to work out together, with a time slot blocked out on everyone's calendar for the "Strava workout of the week." This is not only a great team-building routine but also helps reset and boost everyone's mind when they get back to work in the afternoon (after a shower and healthy lunch, of course).

No matter how packed Quarles's schedule is, he tries to always catch the same 5:58pm train home and does not allow work to spill over into his private life. During the week, the family tends to get healthy dinners delivered, while on the weekends, when he has more time, Quarles likes to cook himself. Overall, his evenings sound like those of a dedicated family man rather than a busy CEO: "My evenings are everything you'd expect: story time, homework, reading, and trying to get everybody in bed. It's just changing jobs from my day job to my night job." Quarles's strong work ethic as Strava CEO is matched with an equally strong rest ethic in his time off.

Working well in a sustainable way, whether as tech exec or in any other role, requires a balance between these two aspects. Quarles has recognized this and made it a priority in his life: "For me, living a healthy life is about balance, energy, and awareness. By balance, I mean moderation and making sure different aspects of your life don't disproportionately affect others. Energy involves thinking about what gives me more capacity, like working out, boot camps, running, biking, stretching, and strength training. Energy is also about nutrition." It's easy to get lost in busyness and forget the importance of good nutrition and exercise on our health and ability to lead. To avoid this, we should build routines around them, making them integral parts of our rest ethic.

KEEP FIT, STAY SHARP

Exercise is good for us, and most of us know this (whether we act on it or not). We are designed to move, and sitting in chairs all day long is terrible for our health *and our creative projects*.

The science is clear on this, too. Exercise induces profound structural brain plasticity and directly improves the brain, just like it improves muscles and the cardiovascular system. During exercise, the production of neurotrophins, proteins encouraging the formation and growth of neurons, significantly increases. Moreover, endurance exercise releases the hormone irisin, which triggers the production of brain-derived neurotrophic factor BDNF, one of the most active neurotrophins. In case you aren't a neuroscientist and all this terminology is making you go cross-eyed, here's the take home: you are keeping your brain strong and forming new connections when you get out and move your body. Exercise is the constant renovation of the idea factory between your ears, equipping you to handle more complex challenges and projects. Our brains—and as a consequence, our productivity and creativity—directly benefit from us being active.

Alex Soojung-Kim Pang confirms in his book *Rest: Why You Get More Done When You Work Less*, that exercise strengthens not only the body but also our ability to stay strong in our work: "It's valuable for helping deal with the pressures and disappointments of professional life. It helps you live a longer, healthier life. And it helps you maintain your intellectual edge and creative powers for more of your life."

Pang reports in his book that heavy hitters like former US president Barack Obama, Supreme Court Judge Elena Kagan, computer pioneer Alan Turing, and UCLA chemist and Nobel laureate Donald Cram deliberately scheduled and prioritized exercise as a way to keep up with their demanding work. And even if we don't aspire to be as notable as these folks, everyone can benefit from regular physical activity. All of us face stress and difficult situations in our lives from time to time, and the predictable and controllable stress of vigorous physical exercise is a perfect way to fortify our body and mind to handle those situations with more grace.

Countless studies have shown that exercise can increase brain stamina, expand intelligence, and provide the endurance and psychological resilience necessary to do creative work. And this applies to people regardless of their age or athletic ability. Rather than reiterating the well-established benefits of exercise that most people are probably already aware of, we really want to stress its impact on your creative muscles.

Exercise is one of the best tools we have to pull our mind out of the daily grind, boost our brain's performance, and see things in a new light. Putting in time to work out is not wasted work time. As Pang notes, "We shouldn't be surprised that people manage to be physically active and do world-class work. We should recognize that they do world-class work because they are physically active." So to do world-class work and live up to your potential, take exercise as seriously as you do any other part of your work. It should not be something you do when you happen to find time, but something you actively make time for.

Many successful people swear by meditation to boost calm and creativity, but quietly sitting in a lotus pose and intensely focusing on breathing isn't everyone's cup of tea. If you feel this way, you can use exercise as an active form of meditation. You get many of the same benefits—such as a mental reset and change of perspective. The common advice of "don't sweat the details" could stand to be replaced with "Go sweat out the details." To move your projects forward, maybe you should consider moving your body first.

Exercise not only builds muscles, but it also builds character and grit, two things you need to survive in the marketplace. When you train for a challenge like a marathon or a martial arts competition, you relearn the art of goal setting and determination. Incubating and coming up with ideas are crucial to making the difference we want to see in the world, but those ideas are just hallucinations unless you are disciplined enough to act on them.

The more you make physical exercise a part of your rest ethic, the more you prove to yourself what you are capable of physically. And eventually this determination will translate over to your work ethic. A workout in the middle of the day is not a waste of time; it can give you the creative confidence boost you need to finish the day strong.

Finally, there is a less obvious but no less significant benefit to working with a coach on the field or a trainer in the gym, especially for creatives and entrepreneurs who are often guilty of thinking they need to do it all. Learning to let go of constant control and accepting that it's okay for someone else to help and direct you is a crucial step on the road to success. Your ability to collaborate with your trainer will make you a better teammate to your coworkers and clients.

None of this is to say that we have to aim for competition-level performance every single day to reap exercise's benefits to our body and mind. Just the opposite, in fact. Take your recovery seriously and save your full strength and best form for the days when it really counts. The same is true with creativity. Yes, showing up every day to do the work is great, but that work does not always have to be a polished masterpiece—nor can it be. Some days, doing nothing more than scribbling down a few bad lines or making some unintelligible doodles are exactly what we need to unblock us and stretch our mental muscles, and we shouldn't feel guilty or bad about these days. They are essential maintenance, a crucial part of our overall progress.

Elite athletes and their trainers—as well as top performers in any other discipline—know that you get the most out of your training if you are as fresh as possible each time. If you're so sore that you're moving funny, then your next workout day is going to be compromised. As Josh Waitzkin, who has won several world championship titles in both chess and the martial art of Tai Chi Push Hands, put it in his book *The Art of Learning*, "In virtually every discipline, one of the most telling features of a dominant performer is the routine use of recovery periods." The better we are at recovering, he notes, the greater our potential.

His advice applies to even the toughest of modern-day gladiators.

don't go through the recovery phase, you will not reap the benefits of your training." He wants his athletes' workouts to be challenging but manageable. What is manageable? Zahabi uses the simple exercise of a pullup to help us understand.

"Let's say I make you do pullups. The max you can do is ten. At eleven, you couldn't do it. Should I make you do ten on our workout? No. I am going to make you do five. So that the next day, you can do five. Eventually, we will get to six. When six becomes really easy, we are going to do seven." With Zahabi's approach to manageable training, you open yourself up to more consistency over time. And in any profession, consistency matters.

If you are constantly maxing out as a performer, you will need to take several days to recover and risk the chance for injury or a loss in motivation. Zahabi elaborates, "If you did ten pullups on Monday, you will be sore until Thursday. So now it is Thursday, and you have only done ten pull-ups from Monday to Thursday. But if I did five pull-ups every day, I am at 20-25 pullups by Thursday. I have more volume than you. Now, if you add up at the end of the year, who trained more? I have trained way more than you. The real question is, how much training can you pack into a week and enjoy it? How much volume can you expose yourself to?"

Working out should be enjoyable and addictive. It makes it easier to make yourself do a lot of it and develop a stable, healthy habit of movement consistency. A simple way to think about it is that once you get the "workout high" feeling, you are done. End your workout here and don't let yourself go into the phase where your body is beaten up and tired. He calls this awareness your "perceived exertion," and it is paramount in the sustainable and safe training of top athletes, as well as the continuous growth of any other world-class performers.

Zahabi connects his idea of being conscious of our perceived exertion to psychologist Mihaly Csikszentmihalyi's research on "flow" to describe this optimal zone of performance. The "flow channel" is the Goldilocks zone, just right, in between anxiety and boredom. If something is too laborious, you'll feel anxious. If something is too simple, you'll get bored. But if something is in that sweet flow zone where your skills match the difficulty, you'll find it delightful. Finding your flow in anything can help you to be happy and productive. But it's difficult to set ourselves up to experience it consistently if we do too much. Overtraining occurs in a lot of gym cultures because it is rare that everyone in attendance is at the same skill level. They all have a different flow channel. A lot of people drive themselves into anxiety when they go there, and they might not be aware of it if they are not training to the right level of perceived exertion. They push themselves to exhaustion and come to associate training with pain, and that is intimidating for someone trying to make a consistent habit of it. Zahabi's advice is to optimize your work for flow.

Your flow zone in any endeavor should be something you enjoy and at a pace that you can embrace. Design your work and your workouts in a way that's neither too hard nor too easy. That way, the experience will be so much fun that you'll naturally want to come back to it in short order. Zahabi advocates, "The concept of flow is pure genius. We have all been in a state of flow, the flow channel. Time flies by when you are in a flow. The worst workout feels like every minute is an hour. In your flow channel, you have the right amount of difficulty, so you aren't stressed but still enough so that you are not bored. Training should be addicting. Imagine if it was addicting. Everyone would be fit. Training should be a pulling force. You should want to do it. And if you don't do it consistently, you won't reach mastery."

Zahabi is not anti-intensity, of course. But he makes it clear that intensity should be applied thoughtfully. "Intensity should be done every once in a while when you get more conditioned, but the default should be volume and enjoyable," says Zahabi. This approach, focused primarily on flow, is what has allowed him and St. Pierre to achieve greatness in the octagon through a high volume of movement and practice. "This is why George has been so good," Zahabi says. "And why he has stayed so healthy. People line up to spar with him because he understands the flow."

Can you improve your flow state at work or in the gym? Was

yesterday boring? Try taking on a bit more of a creative challenge. Was yesterday brutal and you are dreading today's work? It might be time for some quality time off and thinking about what your limits and boundaries are. Cultivating and protecting our flow state helps us show up to our desk, office, or gym with enthusiasm and excitement. And in the long run, consistency wins over intensity. Always.

PRACTICE:

Become aware of your limits and stay within them in order to expand them

For your next workout or work session, pay attention to your "perceived exertion" and don't push yourself beyond the high. Each of us is at a different conditioning level, so gift yourself the awareness and honesty of where you are and stop before it hurts. Make your efforts a 7 out of 10 in terms of intensity and aim for frequency and consistency instead. Build your conditioning and, in time, that sweet flow zone where your skills match your intensity will level up. Your new 7 will far exceed your current 10. You will end up with more quality hours, and your practice will become more addictive. If you have trouble with shutting it down and packing it up early, just think about how you are storing up enthusiasm for the next day.

A 401(K) FOR YOUR BRAIN

"I want to be forever young," Bob Dylan once sang. And while exercise can't keep you always looking like you did in college, it's as close as we can get to Dylan's dream (at least for now). Moving your body not only keeps you physically in good shape, it also ensures that your brain stays healthy. This means you can keep creating, problem-solving, and stay agile well into your old age.

"The most transformative thing that exercise will do is its protective effects on your brain," argues Wendy Suzuki in her TED Talk "The Brain-Changing Benefits of Exercise." "You can think about the brain like a muscle," she says. "The more you're working out, the bigger and stronger your hippocampus and prefrontal cortex gets." And a bigger and stronger brain is not only good for the present moment, but also means that you are preparing your brain for the inevitable battle against neurodegenerative diseases and cognitive decline we all eventually face as we age. "You're not going to cure dementia or Alzheimer's disease," Suzuki argues, "but what you're going to do is you're going to create the strongest, biggest hippocampus and prefrontal cortex, so it takes longer for these diseases to actually have an effect. You can think of exercise, therefore, as a supercharged 401(k) for your brain, OK? And it's even better, because it's free." Well, sign us up!

Suzuki's 401(k) analogy is a powerful motivator for getting off the couch and getting in a sweat. Each rep, jog, move, weight, hike, or dance we do is compounding value and wealth for our brains. When you aren't feeling like working out, you can think about this financial analogy. Would you put your money into an account with negative interest rates? Probably not. So don't do it to your brain either.

Suzuki's findings apply not only to the young and spry, but even elders with signs of dementia can benefit from applying this knowledge. "The great news," says Suzuki, "is that studies have shown that even older adults, people 75 and older who have been diagnosed with Alzheimer's or dementia, can benefit from a three-month exercise regimen." Those patients who exercised more not only slowed their mental decline, but many of them actually reversed it. "That says to me," concludes Suzuki, "that you're never too old to benefit from exercise." No matter your age, if you are not already exercising, the best time to start is right now.

If exercise intimidates you or you can't find the motivation to get in a quick sweat, remember that your best bet for staying forever young, mentally and physically, is to get some movement in. It not only makes you feel better in the short term, but also provides long-term protection and insurance against mental decline, so you can stay creative—and sane—into old age.

And as you age with grace thanks to exercise, you can experiment with different modes of intensity to get different kinds of productivity-boosting effects.

TERRY RUDOLPH

Australian Quantum Physicist

"For work, I actually need very long uninterrupted stretches of time. It's almost a psychological issue. If I have something in my calendar, even if I have that uninterrupted time, just knowing that it's gonna come to a predetermined end is a problem."

"If you never realized what it's like to take time off, it's really difficult to appreciate its importance."

A small group of people is huddled together in a tiny hut on a remote mountain in Malawi, Africa. There is no electricity or running water. The flickering light of the fire burning in the corner of the hut is not enough to properly illuminate the quick writings of one of them on a tiny whiteboard, so the rest of the group stands close to the whiteboard with their phones out trying to provide enough light to decipher what's going on. Rather than a bunch of outcasts or fugitives trying to plan their escape, they're all quantum physicists, some of the best in the world brought together by Terry Rudolph for his "Quantum Malawi 2013" workshop.

As the workshop's website stated, its aim was "to encourage the presentation of new results and new research directions with only partial results, with plenty of time available for discussions." And there certainly was plenty of time for that. With only two talks per day, one in the morning and one in the evening, the scientists spent much of their time hiking, moving from one remote location to another in cars, boats, or planes, or sitting around campfires and roasting whatever the local fauna had to offer. Also, as Terry on a call recounts to us with a laugh, "Most of the day was simply spent trying to survive." But he, as well as the other participants of the workshop, still looks back at it with very fond memories. "A lot of physics got done. I certainly learned a bunch of things!" He remembers another participant saying one night, "I sit here, and I think half those people are potential Nobel Prize winners." Terry goes on joking, "I don't know if that was because he had too much weird African alcohol, but it definitely had that kind of feel to it."

When Terry is not adventuring through the hinterlands of Africa, he is usually trying to untangle some of the deepest mysteries behind the foundations of quantum mechanics in his role as Professor of Quantum Physics at Imperial College London, where he was also Max's PhD supervisor. Tracking him down was always tricky; you could never be quite sure in what country or even what continent you'd find him, and he'd only sporadically reply to emails. But luckily, he gave the same freedom to his students (and Max made plenty of use of that). When you did catch him, he was always genuinely present and fully engaged in the discussion, not continually glancing at his email inbox or phone. Terry doesn't use social media, and other unavoidable tasks, such as email, he tries to batch as much as possible. And he has always had a talent for avoiding any unnecessary admin work. "I put the onus on whoever is bringing me the paperwork," he says. We can all learn from this. The next time someone tries to add busywork to your to-do list, ask yourself if there's a way to make that person do the work themselves. You'll benefit both from the immediate time off you get, as well as the more long-term effect of building a reputation that stops people from distracting you with meaningless tasks.

Terry does all this very deliberately because for his actual work, the real deep thinking, he needs very long uninterrupted periods, ideally full days. "Even if I have three hours for something," he says, "the fact that it's too prescribed and I then have a meeting at the end of it makes the work less valuable. I work very hard to have chunks that are so long that the end doesn't affect me." Having a full day with nothing scheduled in his calendar allows him to enter a completely different mode of thinking. Unfortunately, as a professor leading a large research group and having teaching obligations, he found that blocking out entire days became less and less possible for him. Universities "are big bureaucracies with lots of inertia, it's challenging to block off time. It's just bits and pieces, and your teaching timetable isn't in your control."

But Terry recently managed to escape the "admin creep" of academia and is taking time off from his professorship. In 2017, together with some colleagues, he cofounded the quantum computing startup PsiQuantum (PsiQ for short), whose goal is to build the first commercial photonic quantum computer. As their website boldly proclaims, theirs will be "the first useful general purpose quantum computer." This might not mean much to you, but achieving this would be a big deal, leading to huge breakthroughs in pharmaceutical development, climate modeling, cryptography, and much more. And while the Palo Alto–based company is still fairly stealthy, mainly to avoid the distraction of marketing and unnecessary media attention ("Once you start that game, you've got to maintain it. It's just not worth the effort," says Terry), they have attracted some of the best physics and engineering talent from around the world and built a team of almost a hundred people.

You might imagine that running such a large company leads to even more admin creep than being an academic, but Terry and his colleagues built the company from the ground up around a culture and philosophy that avoids this. They allow people plenty of uninterrupted stretches of deep work and actual problem-solving. Tuesday mornings and Thursday afternoons are entirely reserved for deep work. "You're forbidden to schedule any meetings," Terry explains. They also have an open vacation policy that allows as many vacation days as you want, as long as it doesn't disturb things. Some of PsiQ's first hires were very experienced Silicon Valley engineers, and Terry jokes that they had to essentially reeducate them to make use of the holidays. He also sees a big difference in the use of the vacation policy between nationalities: "The Europeans use it more. We have to force the Americans." With a grin, Terry adds, "It's worked for us. If we end up being the first people who build a universal quantum computer, I can tell thousands of companies will copy us."

He also has a bit of a gripe with the productivity and biohacking community. "Here [in Silicon Valley] everyone is trying so hard to biohack themselves. More time trying to figure out what's your schedule on whatever thing you're taking when you could just get some shit done!" One of his favorite productivity tools is simply going for a run. In fact, he has two distinct modes of running, which he uses for specific purposes: There is a mind-clearing mode, which is when I run really hard on trails where I have to think about where I step. I don't meditate, I can't put 'nothing' in my head, but when I'm running like this, it's kind of the same. I'm concentrating just on the running and completely stop thinking about work. It's not possible to think of anything else, I'm just focused on my body and trying to get it to do something.

At other times, Terry makes a list of problems to think about before he sets out on the run:

In that case, I run much slower. The advantage of this kind of run is that it gets you away from distractions like your phone and your computer, but also from notebooks. The majority of my work and calculations have to be done in a notebook. But mentally, if I write something down, then my brain feels like, 'Okay, I don't have to store that anymore, I can just refer back to it.' But there are some things for which it's actually essential to try and keep the whole thing in your head. And you know, sometimes that's maths or physics, but it can be anything. On a run, you have no pen and paper, you can't write it down, you can't get lost in details. You just have to think, What is the narrative, what is the story, what am I trying to accomplish? You have to focus on the bigger picture.

For Terry, busyness and fragmentation of time are some of the biggest obstacles to deep thought: "Every person who has a normal job looks at academics and thinks those guys just laze around all the time. But that's actually crucial to doing creative work. Quite often, when I'm thinking, I get off my desk and lie on a beanbag, and it looks like I'm napping. But it's not like I'm trying to clear my mind. No, I want to think about something, with my eyes closed. And my brain is going even faster because it's not taking in any stimulus."

Maybe we should all just take a bit more time to lie with our eyes closed on a beanbag and let our mind get absorbed in deep thought. And no better way to do this than in solitude.

PRACTICE:

Run hard to empty your mind, or jog slowly to think through a problem without distractions.

If you need to clear your mind, go hard and challenge yourself so that you can't think about anything but the movement and sensations of your body. If you want to use the workout for productivity, set yourself some clear questions to contemplate in advance, and then use the time off from any distractions or helpful but constraining tools to get a macro view on the issue at hand, while you simultaneously do something good for your body. And if you are not a runner, just substitute your activity of choice.

SOLITUDE

Over two millennia ago, Aristotle already noted in his *Politics* that "man is by nature a social animal." From the very beginnings of our species, our social network was key to our survival: get kicked out of the tribe and you're tiger food. As a result, our thirst for social contact is about as fundamental as our thirst for water. Mankind wouldn't have survived its earliest days without it. Nor would it have developed civilization, science, art, or any of the other great achievements our modern life is built upon. Even our large brain size is often linked to our social nature and the use of language it requires.

Given all this, it is easy to get carried away and assume that being in the company of others is the most natural state for humans, and conversely, that time spent alone goes against our nature. "However," warns psychologist Adam Waytz, "enthusiasm over the social brain, social hormones, and social cognition must be tempered with evidence that being social is far from easy, automatic, or infinite. This is because our (social) brains, (social) hormones, and (social) cognition on which social processes rely must first be triggered before they do anything for us." Yes, we are social animals, but even our social nature needs the right environment, as well as the right balance, an ebb and flow between socializing and *solitude*.

"Isaac Newton craved it. So did Albert Einstein. Henry Cavendish and Paul Dirac positively exuded it. Silence, and its companion solitude, seems to be a recurring feature in the history of physics," writes Felicity Mellor in her piece "The Power of Silence" in the journal *Physics World*. But the current research landscape and academic environment offer very little of either one. Even the bastions of deep thought, the universities and institutes of advanced study of the world, are progressively becoming noisy factories of groupthink. Constant participation in committees, public outreach, review processes, and policy initiatives seem increasingly mandatory and unavoidable.

And Mellor sees this as a reason for concern: "Current research policy, in the UK at least, emphasizes silence's opposite.... There is a danger that in the midst of all this enforced interaction, an important precondition for creativity in physics could be lost." That precondition is solitude, the particular kind of silence that allows our minds to wander extensively, free from any external input or distraction.

Communication is necessary, and science has always been a group effort. But the amount of communication and the number of different channels have gotten out of control. Mellor doesn't dispute the importance of communication, but she calls for balance: "Communication, yes," she says, "but on the physicist's own terms, in the manner that suits each individual best." She worries that scientists have lost this control, backing it up with the example of Peter Higgs (of Higgs boson fame) who "recently claimed that he would not have been able to complete his Nobel-prize-winning work in the current research environment. The peace and quiet that he enjoyed in the 1960s is, he thinks, no longer a possibility." And many other Nobel laureates have echoed similar statements in recent years, acknowledging solitude's essential role in the development of their ideas and lamenting how we've come to devalue it.

Much research hints at the fact that collaboration and chance encounters, while certainly important to exchange vital information and spark new ideas, do not support deep thought and big creative breakthroughs. The bulk of almost any work needs to be done in isolation. Solitude has become a resource. And many of us are depleted of it.

Mellor concludes her article with a warning: "Delete the silences from speech, and one is left with incoherent babble. Delete the silences from scientific research and perhaps the result will be nothing but noise." We fully agree with Mellor, but think this phenomenon extends far beyond scientific research. It applies to any creative pursuit. True creative work and idea incubation happen when we get time to be alone with our thoughts.

ARTISTS WORK BEST ALONE

Most people don't consider themselves artists, but almost every knowledge worker relies on creativity and is, in some way, an artist, whether her artistic medium is code, business plans, or even human interaction. And artists, believes Apple cofounder Steve Wozniak, "work best alone where they can control an invention's design without a lot of other people designing it for marketing or some other committee." He encourages would-be innovators to "work alone. You're going to be best able to design revolutionary products and features if you're working on your own…. Not on a team." Solitude allows for uninhibited experimentation—there's no one there to see you screw up, question your wacky idea, or tell you how you should be doing things.

Thus, solitude also promotes originality. In his book *Solitude: In Pursuit of a Singular Life in a Crowded World*, Michael Harris argues that only in solitude, in the absence of external input, can we find our truly unique voice, our own way of creatively expressing ourselves. "We need to build new and stronger weirdo cocoons, in which to entertain our private selves," he urges us. Seek solitude, find out (and admit to yourself) what you are really into, and then let your mind indulge in it. With more time to yourself, you can shed the concerns and constraints that are holding back your full creative expression.

In our previous exploration of the creative process, we saw that balance of active (preparation, verification) and passive (incubation, illumination) aspects is key. An equally necessary balance exists between connection and solitude. We do need connection to get new stimuli and gather inspiration. But with these, we then need to retreat into our own mind, into our own weirdo cocoon, and make them our own. We need to let our mind observe them freely, unhindered by the constraints and (mis)directions of others' thoughts.

Unfortunately, this has become a daunting task for many. We have largely lost—and even rejected—the skill or experience of solitude.

Most of us think of it as identical to loneliness, since that's the only thing we know. But the two couldn't be more different. "Solitude," write psychologists Christopher R. Long and James R. Averill, "in contrast to loneliness, is often a positive state—one that may be sought rather than avoided." Or, as Harris puts it: "True solitude—as opposed to the failed solitude we call loneliness—is a fertile state, yet one we have a hard time accessing." Escaping the addictive pull of connectivity and giving our mind up to the gentle waves of solitude rather than loneliness has become increasingly difficult. But this also makes it increasingly valuable.

Constant input and connections keep us grounded in present reality, in the "what is." Only in solitude, free from inputs and distractions, does the mind wander far enough to make true breakthroughs and imagine the "what could be." "The power of the wandering mind," muses psychology professor Kalina Christoff, "is precisely the fact that it censors nothing. It can make connections you would never otherwise make." This is great for creativity, but a mind free of censorship and freely making distant connections can also take us places we would rather not go—which is part of the reason why solitude might seem scary to a large number of people. Self-reflection, particularly when we are not used to it, can be painful and scary. But embarking on this quest is worth the pain. Yes, it can reveal a void, especially if we feel like our life is lacking in meaning due to an underdeveloped leisure life, but it also shows us how to fill it. And besides, those darker alleys of the mind are often where creative gold (not to mention tremendous personal growth) is to be found if we just dare venture into them from time to time.

In *Solitude*, Harris points at the studies of psychiatrist Anthony Storr, who in the 1980s analyzed many great artists and realized that solitude played a large role in their creative process. Harris also refers to Mihaly Csikszentmihalyi, the famous Hungarian American psychologist who identified and popularized the idea of flow states, and who similarly found in 1994 that teenagers who can't stand being alone have lower creative abilities. Harris speculates that "only in solitude could those youths develop the creative habits—journaling, doodling, daydreaming—that lead to original work." Or as Johann Wolfgang von Goethe is said to have put it, "One can be instructed in society, one is inspired only in solitude." We need the mental freedom that only solitude can provide, and we need it for more than just a few minutes at a time. "A frantic, distracted mind may be broadly characterized as 'wandering,'" muses Harris, "but one requires a luxury of empty time before the mind can be expected to engender fresh insights. True wandering requires a long leash." And what better place for a long leash than the great outdoors?

Traditionally nature was always strongly associated with solitude. Nowhere else is it easier to get lost in our own minds than far away from the bustling cities and hyperconnected offices. It was in nature, on the solitary shores of Walden pond, that Henry David Thoreau wrote, "I love to be alone. I never found the companion that was so companionable as solitude." And not only is the solitude of nature highly companionable, it's also good for our brain. A study by Stanford scientists found that even just a 90-minute solitary walk in nature can significantly reduce levels of rumination and the risk for mental illness. The simple act of going on a stroll outside provides us with enough solitude to notably boost our mental health.

Part of being in solitude is the idea of getting lost, whether that's in our own mind, or literally on a walk out in the woods. Today we often cling to technological tools like Google Maps to help us stay on the right path, but the more we rely on them, the more we are numbing our awareness. Being lost, and even somewhat uncomfortable, is an important part of the experience. It leads to growth and discovery. It gives way to awe and wonder. And that's often exactly what we need to make impactful creative breakthroughs.

ED "WOODY" ALLEN (A.K.A. ETHERWOOD)

British Music Producer, Singer-Songwriter, and DJ

"I was trying to force myself into the studio, but I wasn't pleased with anything, so I thought it would be best to take a break and try [to] do little bits when I felt inspired."

"I went out to Finland for ten days about a year ago and stayed in this little cottage in the middle of nowhere on my own—it was literally so reflective. Most of the album was written in that short time."

Somewhere in the Finish wilderness, sitting by himself in a sauna, "a proper wood sauna with a stove, not electric or steam," Woody is fully unwinding from his busy life in London spent between his studio and the city's clubs, producing and performing under the name *Etherwood*. Here, all the city's stress and distractions fade away. After sitting in the sauna for a while, he jumps into some icy water right next to it—"It really helps to clear your head"—and sits on some rocks by the seaside, awaiting the sunset. It "was unbelievable. I have never seen anything like it before.... There was this time where I could see the stars reflecting in the sea. The whole thing was starlight, it was absolutely nuts!" At that moment, inspiration strikes, and he can hear a tune in his head. Not a fully polished tune, but an idea. He gets up and sprints back to his cottage, quickly writing and recording the piano line and adding some strings and a beat to glue it all together. This is how his track "Fire Lit Sky" came to life: "The color of the sky was constantly changing, so I wanted to capture that somehow in a tune, and 'Fire Lit Sky' does particularly sum up the journey of when I was there. The tune really means a lot to me."

And it was not just this one track. In fact, Woody wrote almost his entire third album, aptly titled *In Stillness*, in complete isolation in a little *mökki*, a Finish cottage. In early October 2016, he left the following post on his Facebook feed and just disappeared: "I escaped to Finland to stay in a *mökki* on an Island about an hour away from Helsinki and write music for two weeks. There's no one else here apart from the occasional moose and me. If you haven't heard from me by the end of October, then I love you all, and it's been fun." He wanted solitude and quiet, and he chose to disconnect completely. "When I was there, I literally didn't talk to anyone else except myself for nearly two weeks. It was a pretty mad feeling. Just the deer and swans, but I think they got a bit annoyed with me towards the end …"

Finland is known for its sauna culture, and Woody fully embraced it. Reflecting on writing the album: "A lot of those tunes were written in the sauna! Which is kind of strange when you think about it because I was sat there butt-naked writing an album in a steam room … You just get into a zone while you're inside and you become very relaxed with a clear head. Those are the times when the music starts coming to me. I start thinking of tunes when I'm feeling very comfortable and relaxed. For lots of producers, their tunes are triggered by deeper emotions like anger or love, but for me, it's just about that clarity of mind." We all have different triggers that get us into states of peak creativity and inspiration. What are your most powerful triggers? Whether they are strong emotions or complete serenity, try to create more space for them through deliberate use of time off.

Writing music in the Finnish wilderness had been one of

Woody's dreams for a long time: "Since I was young I've always wanted to go to Finland and literally just do what I did—find somewhere remote and write a load of music without there necessarily being any intention or pressure to create an album." Getting away from the pressure was crucial. After releasing his second album, he was struggling a bit. He wanted to work on new songs, but inspiration didn't come to him. "I wasn't feeling it and didn't want to just chuck something out there that didn't feel special." He was putting a lot of pressure on himself and spent a lot of time in his studio trying to force out new tracks. But the harder he tried, the more he felt stuck. Sound familiar? When he finally decided on his trip to Finland, he was determined to take a completely different approach.

He deliberately didn't set himself a goal. Writing the entire album there was never his plan. "I didn't want to put too much pressure on myself to come up with X amount of tunes before I left," he says. "There was no one else there. I was completely isolated, which is what appealed to me. When I arrived, I turned my phone off for a few days and just sat there taking in my surroundings." But precisely because of this, simply relaxing in isolation without any clear goal, surrounded by the vast expanse of beautiful nature rather than the confining walls of his studio, all the pressure that kept him from accessing his creativity disappeared, and ideas just came to him: "It felt so natural to me—as opposed to sitting down with a piano and spending all day writing different riffs." Thanks to this time off, he wrote an entire album in two weeks. He only had to finalize the tracks once he got back to London. Two weeks to write 15 tracks is an incredible achievement, and Woody managed to do it, not because of frantic busyness and forced focus (he had definitely tried that approach too before, but failed miserably), but because he allowed himself to relax. And the album, which turned into a big success, feels anything but rushed. Listening to it, you can almost imagine yourself sitting by your very own *mökki* and watching the sky slowly change color and the stars reflect off the sea.

Going on a creative retreat in the Finnish wilderness wasn't the only dream from his youth that he eventually turned into reality. In an interview back in 2015, he talked about another dream:

> Since I was a youngster there's only really one thing I've ever dreamt of owning or rather building. Some friends of mine had one of those ace old hippie Volkswagen campers that they used to take across Europe. I always thought 'imagine how boss it would be to have a studio in the back of that thing …!'… Nature plays a huge part in my music and sometimes it's tricky to capture the mood in a London flat at 3:30 pm on a Monday afternoon. I'd keep the windows of the van open the whole time for that natural ambiance and make an album influenced by the travels. A bit like an audio diary. It would be ace to hear how it turned out. I'm sure the reality of it would be more like creeping along a motorway hard shoulder, listening to the same cassette on loop, sweating out all over the leather seats, lonely and miserable in a van with barely enough juice to get the thing from Brixton to Camberwell, but a boy can dream, right?

And dream he did. Not too long after coming back from Finland, he got back to work. Despite the concerns voiced in 2015, he did exactly as he had envisioned as a kid and turned his mobile studio dream into a reality. He converted a camper van to fit his needs and has since been roaming the countrysides of Western Europe in pursuit of inspiration, freedom, and calm. This has already been fruitful, leading to his most recent EP, *Lost In The Right Direction*. Again, the experience is deeply embedded in the music, and listening to it, you can almost feel the freedom of aimlessly cruising through French hills and fields on a summer afternoon.

Maybe we should all allow ourselves to more often get lost in the right direction, finding answers and calmness in the beautifully soothing silence of nature. Quoting from "In Stillness," the title track of the album that came out of the Finland trip: "Surrounded by silence, I've uncovered the truth. The calmness around me has answered my youth." Let all our youths be answered!

PRACTICE:

Take a creative retreat in solitude

Get away from it all! If you don't feel the creative juices flowing, take time off and find a solitary place in nature like Woody's remote cottage in Finland for a creative retreat. Don't go there with too-high expectations of output; just let things naturally happen and create when you feel inspired to do so. Money is rarely an excuse here since finding solitude in nature (even a reasonably delightful cottage) is often cheaper than staying in a city, especially if you combine it with a solitary and minimalistic lifestyle. And it doesn't have to be an extended time either. Woody managed to write an entire album in less than two weeks, thanks to this method. Often, even a single day or a weekend out in nature can help you get unstuck and make creative breakthroughs that can fuel you for weeks.

THE COST OF CONNECTIVITY

If solitude is such a powerful tool for creativity and growth, why have we seemingly lost our ability to practice and appreciate it? A possible answer can once again be found in our earlier history discussion. Just like idle hands were believed to do the work of the devil, idle minds and daydreaming were seen as equally sinful by many Puritans. And once visible busyness was added to the picture, solitude and contemplation started to look even worse. After all, people need to see just how busy we are, and this doesn't happen in solitude.

Today, in a hyperconnected world, we are strongly incentivized to be as social (and even as loud) as possible—"If I CC the entire company to this email everyone will know how busy and important I am!"—and that makes solitude feel like a costly decision to make. But ultimately, by not taking time off for solitude, we're costing ourselves something much more expensive: our capacity to come up with big ideas and get meaningful work done.

Connectivity and the technologies that enable it are extremely valuable, but without the balancing force of solitude, we cannot make good use of the input they provide. Especially social media—this new technology that so directly speaks to our social urges and desire for connectivity might be the equivalent of fast food for our brain. Just like empty calories and binge eating leave us obese and physically unhealthy, the overabundant but shallow and fast-paced connections social media provides cause depression and yes, even loneliness, the very thing it is supposed to combat.

Cal Newport argues in his book *Digital Minimalism* that solitude doesn't require physical separation from others; it's a "subjective state in which your mind is free from input from other minds." Using this definition, even when we are physically alone, we might never experience solitude if we constantly get input from others via our connected devices. Not only has solitude become much harder to achieve, but it also feels much more wrong now than it used to, because our FOMO (fear of missing out) has been amplified. Never before has solitude been so distant from our usual way of operating.

Rather than relishing and seeking solitude, we stigmatize it, equating it with loneliness or reclusion. "There's a real taboo involved in solitude," laments Harris. We live in a world where we get negative remarks from friends if we don't immediately reply to messages, or turn down invitations for no good reason other than preferring to stay in. But especially because solitude has become such a rare commodity there is so much benefit—and competitive advantage—to be found if we can practice it.

During World War II, Dwight D. Eisenhower took frequent retreats to a secret cottage where he would spend his time playing golf and bridge, taking long walks, or reading cowboy novels, and where any talk of "work" (i.e., the war) was strictly forbidden. If the Supreme Commander of the Allied Forces at the height of WWII thinks the benefits of being disconnected and enjoying some solitude outweigh the potential risks, how bad can it possibly be for even the most senior executive, let alone the average knowledge worker further down the corporate hierarchy?

Not everyone requires the same amount of solitude to perform well, but particularly introverts can profit greatly from it. In her book *Quiet: The Power of Introverts in a World That Can't Stop Talking*, Susan Cain suggests the idea of finding "restorative niches," little pockets of solitude in our everyday lives. Not only do they provide time for solitary contemplation, they also allow our social muscles to recharge, and perform when it matters.

Glenn Gould, one of the most accomplished classical pianists of the 20th century, credited part of his success to the fact that he "always had a sort of intuition that for every hour you spend with other human beings you need X number of hours alone. Now, what X represents I don't really know, it might be two and seven-eights or seven and two-eights, but it's a substantial ratio." Ask yourself what your ideal number X is and if you are actually getting that amount of solitude. The key is being aware of your own preferences—and the cost associated with not respecting them. Being able to differentiate between what you truly want—and need—from what society wants for you. "The secret to life is to put yourself in the right lighting," writes Cain. "For some, it's a Broadway spotlight; for others, a lamplit desk."

Whichever side of this you fall onto, some amount of solitude should be part of what we all seek on a regular basis. And one of the simplest tools to get more solitude is the humble "no." Few people are better at using this simple word than Derek Sivers.

DEREK SIVERS

American Entrepreneur and Writer

"Nobody gives a novelist shit for writing alone. But an entrepreneur, programmer, or musician is expected to collaborate. I disagree, for me. I prefer the life of a novelist, whether I'm writing code, music, or systems."

"If you're not saying 'HELL YEAH!' about something, say 'no.'"

How many times have you found yourself in this situation? Someone asks for a piece of your time, for a favor, a social outing, or for your collaboration in what they genuinely believe is an interesting project. You're not totally convinced you should be doing it, but in the moment, saying "yes" is much easier than saying "no," and you don't want to disappoint. But then as the time comes closer, you start feeling *the dread*. You end up half-heartedly (and maybe also half-assedly) doing the work you're not particularly passionate about with people you may not necessarily like. Worse, your overcommitment to collaborations, social gatherings, and team projects does not allow you the quiet and creative independence to invest quality time, in calm solitude, into your own work. Your social muscles are constantly exhausted, you find no space for contemplation, and your creative output dries up.

Derek Sivers, founder and former president of pioneering online music distributor CD Baby, and author of *Anything You Want*, identified this problem for himself a long time ago, and has since built his life as an antidote to this problem, a calm fortress of solitude. When faced with any decision or commitment, he asks himself a simple question: How much do I want to do this? If it's not at least an 8 out of 10, it should be a no. "When you say no to most things," Sivers argues, "you leave room in your life to really throw yourself completely into that rare thing that makes you say 'HELL YEAH!' Every event you get invited to. Every request to start a new project. If you're not saying 'HELL YEAH!' about it, say 'no.' We're all busy. We've all taken on too much. Saying yes to less is the way out."

Sivers has perfected this way out for himself and uses it to deliberately cultivate solitude in his life—time for himself that he likes to invest in creating things. "I love to work alone 12 hours a day," he says. "I use the term 'work' because it's more understood, but really it's 'me time'—doing what I love. Writing, learning, improving, and creating. Whether it's creating music, websites, books, or companies, it's all just creating." And Sivers knows that to find your own creative voice, it's often best to work alone: "I prefer this as a solo pursuit. Being around other people drains me, and I don't want to compromise this side of my life. It's a very personal pursuit. It's not business—it's more like art. The rewards are internal." Sivers's form of time off might look like work to others, but that makes it no less valid. Time off is about intentionality. It's about not doing certain things to free up time for other things (or nothing at all). What these things are is up to every one of us to decide for ourselves.

Saying no to most things allows Sivers to dive very deep into his passions and pursue bigger objectives: "I've optimized my life for creating and learning. I've cut out most things from my life that most normal people do—(like hanging out or media consumption)—in pursuit of my bigger goal.... The word 'workaholic' would apply, except it's play, not work. It's completely intrinsic—just following my own interests. I've found what I love, and do it as much as possible." Through many hours of contemplation, he has identified his personal sweet spot, and he makes sure that he stays as close to it as possible.

Sivers fully embraces the fact that he is a pseudo-extrovert. He can definitely be around people. In fact, for most of his life, he was a professional musician and even worked as MC and ringleader of a circus for 10 years. But he knows exactly when he needs to retreat into solitude and recharge: "I have a social window of about 2-3 hours. After that, I'm drained, and want to be alone again." He does not feel guilty about this but uses it as the basis for his creative output. It allows him to go deep and focus intensely: "I single-task. I'm into only one thing at a time, focusing on it to completion, whether that takes hours, months, or even years." Besides his solitary work, Sivers spends up to three hours a day writing in his journal: "Reflecting, daydreaming, planning. Asking myself questions and trying different answers. It feels like all my learning happens here." Most of us probably don't spend this much time on learning and reflection in an entire month. But making just a bit more time for solitary mind wandering, even just a couple of minutes a day, can be a powerful tool to get some distance from the problems we are working on, see the bigger picture, and connect new dots.

The ability to stay focused on a single task is very important to Sivers, and he is skeptical about connected technology: "I don't use any apps on my phone, for this same reason. I don't want to depend on apps for productivity. Actually, I tend to avoid my phone, in general. I just use it for calling friends, or for GPS. No email. No social media. It sits in airplane mode much of the time, then I completely power it off an hour before bed, and turn it back on after I'm done writing in the morning. All of my current creative and learning goals can be achieved with these existing tools, so I avoid that time-sinking habit of looking for new ones." For the tech geeks out there, Sivers actually does all his writing in Vim (a super old-school command-line tool with literally zero distractions). You can't get much more disconnected than that while still using technology.

In recent years, Sivers found yet another reason to disconnect. In 2012 his son was born, and Sivers decided to essentially take a six-year sabbatical and make spending time with him a full-time job. "Since my son was born five years ago," Derek wrote in 2017, "I've spent at least thirty hours a week with him, just one-on-one, giving him my full attention." Derek is trying to cultivate a long attention span in his son: "Whatever he's doing right now, that's the most important thing. So I encourage him to keep doing it as long as possible. I never say, 'Come on! Let's go!' ... Nobody else can play with us like this. Everyone else gets so bored. Of course my adult mind wanders to all the other things we could be doing. But I let it go, and return to that present focus." And Sivers found that through spending time with his son in this way, his own rest ethic dramatically improved: "By cultivating his long attention span, I'm cultivating my own. By entering his world, I'm letting go of my own, like meditation. By broadening his inputs, I'm broadening my own."

We are all ambitious and want to get stuff done. But sometimes we have to realize that doing less is the way to achieve this. "Life can be improved by adding, or by subtracting," Sivers says. "The world pushes us to add because that benefits them. But the secret is to focus on subtracting. The adding mindset is deeply ingrained. It's easy to think I need something else. It's hard to look instead at what to remove." Sometimes, what we need to remove is frantic collaboration, excessive communication, and forced teamwork, and instead make time to work by ourselves, at our own pace and in our own way.

At other times, the thing we need to remove is simply effort and stress. Sivers observes that: "It's been amazing how often everything gets done just as well and just as fast, with what feels like half the effort. Which then makes me realize that half of my effort wasn't effort at all, but just unnecessary stress that made me feel like I was doing my best." In many cases, the extra stress or strain we put on ourselves isn't adding anything in terms of output—except visible busyness—and just burns us out.

Whatever we choose to remove, let's all try and say "no" more often, focus on the HELL YEAHs in our life, and reclaim our solitude to think deeply and create abundantly.

PRACTICE:

Do your work in solitude

In many professions we are led to believe that constant collaboration and communication are the ways to success. But Sivers and many other examples show that this is far from the truth. Resist the urge of the visible busyness built into collaboration, and instead get real work done in your own time. Try to live, like Sivers, "the life of a novelist." Use solitude as a tool—something you deliberately schedule in your calendar and defend with a polite "no"—to be more creative and productive and increase the depth and quality of your work.

COLLABORATIVE SOLITUDE

For many, the mention of solitude immediately conjures up the idea of loneliness and isolation. The rejection of companionship and engaging in antisocial behavior. But this couldn't be further from the truth. "The alternative to solitude was never companionship," writes Harris. "The alternative to solitude is loneliness." If we cannot find solitude, we will inevitably find loneliness, no matter how hard we try to drown it out with digital and social noise. Constant online companions and thousands of "friends" or followers don't fill our inner void. The lack of true and deep connection just amplifies it. The way out of loneliness is to embrace solitude. Relearning, as Harris puts it, "a certain practice, or alchemy, that turns loneliness into solitude, blank days into blank canvases."

Solitude does not have to be antisocial either; in fact, it can help us recalibrate our social senses and learn to be more empathetic. The solitude found in books is a great example of this. As Virginia Woolf said in a letter to Ethel Smyth, "The state of reading consists in the complete elimination of the ego." As we dive into the solitary world unfolding in our mind, we become one with the characters and the story. We live others' experiences and learn to see the world from their perspective. Through this solitary practice, we learn how to be social and develop our empathy.

Stepping away from a group or person allows us much more to reflect on our interaction with them, and appreciate our gratitude toward people. Harris mentions Eric Klinenberg, who in his book *Going Solo* "argues that our ability to be happily alone is actually a sign of strong social ties, not a lack thereof." Just think of a time you reunited with some really good old friends after a long time apart. You get this strong sense that in a way, nothing much has changed, and you appreciate each other even more. Even between lovers, real desire is only truly experienced in solitude. And the occasional distance helps us to process our own complex feelings, as well as those of our partner.

All too often in our relationships, romantic or otherwise, the new ways in which we communicate—frequent but shallow—leave us in some kind of grey zone that's neither solitude nor true connection. We should relearn to prioritize true conversation over mere connection and embrace both ends of the spectrum fully.

Business leaders should take note of this too. If they encourage—or worse, demand—too much collaboration within their team, they not only risk the team's creative potential by drowning everyone in idle chatter and information-oversharing, but they also weaken the bond between team members. Forced collaboration can breed resentment within a team and reduces each individual's own unique contributions. Even within a team effort, utilizing solitude as a resource, allowing each team member to come up with their own ideas and conclusions before bringing them to the collective, can be the key to success.

This book itself is a product of collaborative solitude. Franz Kafka apparently felt that "writing is utter solitude, the descent into the cold abyss of oneself." While Max and John wouldn't describe their process quite as drastically as Kafka, the bulk of the writing was still done by each individually in long stretches of solitary work, before finally joining the pieces together and weaving them into a seamless whole. They used technology—collaborative and connected technology—to do this remotely, with John in Texas and Max in Japan. But they used technology and communication methods on their terms, only as necessary, not constantly on and engaged.[4] With the right balance between solitude and collaboration, technology can facilitate great things.

So to boost your creativity and improve your connection with those around you, consider taking a rewarding journey into your own mind and spending some time in solitude, whether that's an extended solo trip into nature, or just an evening alone at home with the internet turned off. We're convinced that the initial discomfort you might experience will eventually give way to a blissful and rewarding experience.

---

[4]Besides the effective use of solitude in a team effort, this book also stands for the power and possibilities of remote collaboration in a connected age. As of publishing this book, John and Max have actually never met in real life. Their entire collaboration and friendship has, so far, been online. While it has been a very fruitful way of working, they hope to change this in the very near future.

FIRAS ZAHABI

Canadian Martial Artist, Coach, and Fitness Entrepreneur

"Consistency over intensity. Intensity can only be done every once in a while. There is a cost for going to your max. Nobody sprints every day."

Firas Zahabi isn't training just anyone off the street at his legendary Tristar Gym. This is where he prepared one of the greatest fighters in history, George St. Pierre—the former Ultimate Fighting Championship Middleweight and Welterweight Champion known for his epic nine title defenses. As St. Pierre's head coach, Zahabi knows what it takes to build up a world-renowned performer. Given that their sport is the modern version of gladiator fights, it's easy to imagine scenes of extraordinarily intense training where their workouts are all out, all the time. But Zahabi's approach is much different: "I am a big believer in never being sore. You should train, and the next day you should wake up feeling good."

When building the skills for world champion fighters like George St. Pierre, being mindful of and preventing overtraining is paramount. "Recovery is everything," Zahabi explains. "Stress plus recovery equals adaptation. Stress plus stress equals detraining and injury. If you

REFLECTION

Anyone who has followed the shows or writing of famous chefs like Gordon Ramsay or the late Anthony Bourdain is probably aware that the culinary industry is known for crazy working conditions—with 15-hour shifts and 80-hour weeks being completely normal. As Ramsay apparently once proclaimed, "If I relaxed, if I took my foot off the gas, I would probably die." Psychological as well as physical problems are the norm, few careers are very long, and addiction and substance abuse are common.

But in recent years, the attitude toward working hours has been changing in parts of the culinary world. Denmark's Noma, which was considered the world's best restaurant for many years, switched to four-day weeks after their reopening in 2018. Similarly, Ben Shewry of Melbourne's Attica switched to four-day weeks. They all had to raise their prices, but they saw that the quality they could produce as a result was so much higher that people were more than happy to pay the premium (and most of these restaurants had always been booked out for many months anyway).

While some restaurants scaled back their service time, one Scandinavian top restaurant took a slightly different approach to the problem. Swedish restaurant Fäviken, under the leadership of its owner and head chef Magnus Nilsson, decided not to reduce the restaurant's hours to give everyone more time, but instead to increase their staff count more than threefold from 12 to 37. As a result, each individual staff member's work time dropped from well over 80 hours per week on average to about 40-45 hours, with a strict maximum capped at 50 hours. Every employee also had to take five weeks of vacation per year, three of which had to be consecutive to allow for a real break and recovery. Nilsson wanted to induce a shift in his employees' mindset: "It's not as much about cutting down work time.... It's more about the importance of time off, ... and feeling at liberty to have time off."

None of these decisions were easy; they added significant financial and logistical burdens. But after putting in some deep thought, Nilsson and his team realized that this solution was the only way forward—and they found ways to make it work. Fäviken, which could seat up to 24 people per night, compensated for the extra cost by almost doubling its pricing from 175€ to 300€ per dinner. Given the improved quality and the jaw-dropping level of creativity coming out of Nilsson's kitchen every night, their guests were more than willing to pay the higher price.

While many other restaurants have been somewhat forced into embracing time off—some even getting in trouble with the authorities because of working hours way beyond legal limits— Nilsson and his leadership team at Fäviken realized by themselves that something had to change. They were all seeing signs of burnout—in themselves as well as the rest of the team—and none of them wanted to run the business five years from then, at least not in the way it was at that point. Taking a step back from the day-to-day madness in the kitchen, they realized they had to make a change even if it was risky; otherwise they'd have to close the restaurant eventually anyway. "It was really unfair that we were being pushed out of the business that we loved, that we are pretty good at," Nilsson notes, "simply because some other people long before us had constructed a system that was broken." This is a key insight that applies far beyond the culinary industry. Our society and culture have so many systems in place, constructed by a handful of people, often a long time ago, which we are now just perpetuating instead of questioning whether they make sense. In many cases, we don't even realize these systems exist because we are too busy running in circles within them. But it's worth taking the time to pause and reflect: In your industry or community, what are the assumptions and systems everyone believes in and relies on? Is it possible that some of them may be broken?

For Nilsson and his team, the results of challenging the status quo were profound. "I spend much more time with my family," he says, "which makes me a lot happier, which in turn makes me a lot better at my job.… I don't come into the restaurant anymore feeling like I have to be there. I come into the restaurant feeling like I really really want to be there. And it's fantastic!" Any craftsman and creative—and that's what most knowledge workers of the future will be—can benefit from such a change in attitude.

But even the most fantastic things come to an end. And that's okay. Accepting that even the best projects and experiences don't last forever, enjoying them while they last, and then letting them go gracefully is an important part of time off as well. In 2019, after 11 years of success, Nilsson decided to close Fäviken. "To run a place like Fäviken," he says in an interview with the *LA Times*, "the first thing you need to feel every single morning is excitement. One morning I just woke up, and for the first time in my whole life I didn't feel excited to go to work." That's when he realized Fäviken had to come to an end or else it would turn into a fake experience.

For over a decade, Nilsson and his staff had poured their entire passion into the restaurant, and they knew that continuing it with anything less would be a huge disservice to everyone involved. "In every strategic way, this is not a wise decision," Nilsson says. "But what's the reason that someone runs a restaurant like Fäviken? Because you want to; it's entirely driven by passion." And once the passion is gone, there is only one right decision to make. "I've always known that Fäviken was not going to be forever," Nilsson admits. "That's not really a revelation, because it applies to all restaurants and all businesses and really everything." Accepting this insight and having the strength to move on is something many of us could benefit from on a more regular basis. It requires good self-awareness and calm courage. It requires a deep understanding of your goals and priorities, and ultimately of yourself. And all of this can be found through taking time off for reflection.

EFFECTIVE ACTION REQUIRES QUIET REFLECTION

We all work hard during our time on (well, most of us do, anyway), but if we don't take time off from executing, we can lose sight of the bigger picture. It's essential that we step back from the work (and the working) to evaluate: Is this working? Am I creating something of value? What am I missing? To answer these questions honestly, and to ensure that we are heading in the right direction, we have to make time to pause and reflect.

"Follow effective action with quiet reflection," said Peter Drucker, one of the most celebrated business consultants to ever live. "From the quiet reflection will come even more effective action." Just like in the cycles of preparation and incubation and the ebb and flow of time off and time on, we require the right balance. "When we don't take time to ask these more strategic questions, we become a function of other people's agendas. We are left to react to the latest email and can become rudderless; blown about by every wind of corporate change," warns Greg McKeown, the author of *Essentialism*. And he encourages us to make such reflection a regular practice: "We can take a few hours every few months to think about the bigger picture questions: 'If I can only achieve three things over the next three months, what should they be?' and 'Where do I want to be five years from now?'" It seems we would do well to listen to these experts. Many of the people highlighted in this book made the most of their time thanks to frequent reflection.

Tony Stubblebine, a productivity coach and CEO of online coaching platform *Coach.me*, suggests making reflection a micro-habit using a technique he calls "interstitial journaling." He recommends that "during your day, journal every time you transition from one work project to another. Write a few sentences in your journal about what you just did, and then a few more sentences about what you're about to do." This approach has many benefits. Besides just acting as a small dose of regular reflection, interstitial journaling also helps our brain switch from one task to another. By putting our lingering thoughts on paper, we make it easier for our mind to stop thinking about the previous task and give our full attention to the next task. It also gives us a few moments to mentally prepare for what comes next. In Stubblebine's words, interstitial journaling "kills procrastination, empties our brain of the last project, and then gives us space to formulate an optimal strategy for our next project."

We get it, plowing ahead with work and busyness is often easier than pausing to reflect. We prefer doing over thinking and are afraid to sit still with our own thoughts. But this mental barrier gets lower and lower the more you practice reflection until you actually end up looking forward to those quiet moments alone with your thoughts and a notebook.

Authors, including us, will give you lots of (hopefully) great advice and directives to put into practice. It is easy to just passively absorb all of it and feel good about yourself for having read the advice, but never actually apply any of it to your own life. To avoid the same from happening with this book, we want to offer you this chapter as a way to train your reflection muscles.

We would like to invite you to gain more experience in the art of reflection, whether you are a novice or seasoned reflection pro. The following pages contain several profiles, each followed by a prompt to kick off or upgrade your reflection practice and prepare you to take effective action.

Writing down your thoughts helps you get them out of your head and makes reflection less daunting. So get out a notebook or feel free to write your answers directly in this book. We don't mind.

MARCUS AURELIUS AND THE STOICS

Roman Emperor and Philosopher (26 April 121–17 March 180)

"Nowhere can man find a quieter or more untroubled retreat than in his own soul."

"How much time he saves who does not look to see what his neighbor says or does or thinks."

"If you seek tranquility, do less. Or (more accurately) do what's essential. Do less, better. Because most of what we do or say is not essential. If you can eliminate it, you'll have more tranquility. Ask yourself every moment, 'Is this necessary?'" When he wrote these words into his private journal, which would later become the now-famous *Meditations*, Marcus Aurelius was emperor of the Roman Empire and arguably the most powerful man in the world. What's your excuse for being too busy?

Not only was Aurelius a Roman emperor—the last of the so-called Five Good Emperors—he was also one of the most prominent Stoic philosophers. Stoicism dates back all the way to Zeno of Citium, who founded the school in the third century BC, and Aurelius was its last great contributor. But most of his teachings were in fact never meant to be teachings at all—they were his own private musings, penned down in solitude and intended mostly for his own mind. The 12 books that make up what we know today as his *Meditations* were simply Aurelius's attempts at organizing his thoughts and making sense of the world around him, and formed part of his relentless striving to become a better person and more effective leader. While he certainly achieved this, his notes went much beyond his intentions. Today, his private reflections have become one of the most valuable—and surprisingly accessible—resources of Stoic thought.

At the heart of Stoicism is the art of acquiescence: if something is outside of your control, there is no point worrying about it. Just accept it and move on. This is not giving up. It's focusing on the things we can influence and not being distracted by useless anger or fear or trying to change the unchangeable.

When faced with adversity of any kind, be it an annoying colleague or something as serious as the loss of a loved one, the common reaction is some combination of anger, fear, disbelief, sorrow, confusion, and helplessness. We blame others or our environment for the misfortunes that befall us. But the only thing that really causes us pain and stands in our way is our own perception and approach to the problem. This is one of the core observations of Stoic philosophy. In the words of Epictetus, another prominent Stoic, "It is our attitude toward events, not events themselves, which we can control. Nothing is by its own nature calamitous—even death is terrible only if we fear it." Rather than being stunned by obstacles and suffering because of them, we can turn them into opportunities for growth and forward momentum. All we need is the right approach, the right personal philosophy. And no better way to develop such a personal philosophy than through quiet reflection, directing our thoughts inward.

The first step on the way to facing obstacles is training ourselves not to be subjective and reactive, but to have a calm and imperturbable mind instead. Stoicism is often mistakenly associated with a lack of emotion. But being emotional is fine. It's part of what makes us human. However, the problems arise when we react emotionally. We need to train ourselves to be calm and objectively reflect on the situation rather than blindly responding. While being aware of our emotions, we must not let them blindly guide our response or cloud our judgment of a situation. The aim is control and domestication of emotion, not its absence.

When faced with an obstacle, we should steady our nerves, revert to the present moment rather than having our mind race through all sorts of possible (or impossible) future scenarios, and focus on what lies within our control. Only then can we approach the situation undisturbed and see it for what it really is—which in many cases is not as bad as we imagined. There is a big but often underappreciated difference between observing and perceiving. One is objective and external, the other subjective and internal. Our aim is to reduce the gap between the two, making our perception more objective. Taking the time to journal, like Aurelius did on a regular basis, is a powerful tool to practice this. Getting our thoughts out of our head and onto the page helps us see them with fresh eyes and a more detached view. It allows us to make better decisions, and be a more effective, fair, and calm leader to others.

All this applies to how we approach time off. "A good person," taught the Stoic Seneca, "dyes events with his own color ... and turns whatever happens to his own benefit." With the right mindset, we can find time off in any kind of event, not just in the favorable ones. As Aurelius said, "Choose not to be harmed—and you won't feel harmed. Don't feel harmed, and you haven't been." Choose not to be busy, and you won't feel busy. Don't feel busy, and you aren't.

This way of thinking, as so many other ideas in Stoicism, lends itself well to a question that can be used as a starting point for reflection: How much of the stress and the lack of time off you experience is actually genuine, and how much are you creating yourself by worrying about your lack of time off or being annoyed at people trying to get a piece of your time? Many obstacles contain hidden opportunities or valuable lessons. The skill is to take any obstacle and flip it around, turning negatives into positives. All of this comes down to our attitude toward adversity. Problems are often precisely as bad as we think they are, because we naturally make them big.

But the solution can be extremely simple, as Aurelius reminds us: "The cucumber is bitter? Then throw it out. There are brambles in the path? Then go around. That's all you need to know." Don't get caught up in reactivity and the resulting stress and busyness. Stay calm, use reflection to assess the situation and your own response to it, and take only the action that is essential. Then move on and enjoy your resulting time off in tranquility.

The Stoics had a concept they referred to as the "Inner Citadel." It is the fortress within us that nothing from the outside can perturb. It is a trait that sets many great leaders apart from the rest. Crucially, it is not there from the beginning. No one is born with an Inner Citadel. We have to build it through introspection, and constantly reinforce it by reflecting on what is within our control. It is a concept that can be learned. Cultivating your Inner Citadel for tranquility and time off is equivalent to having a good rest ethic. Becoming impenetrable to the distractions and busyness the external world throws at us. If you can achieve this, it will reflect in every aspect of your life. As Ryan Holiday, a modern promoter of Stoic thought, writes, "How you do anything is how you do everything." How you approach your work reflects on how you take time off, and vice versa.

PRACTICE:

Find tranquility by focusing only on what's in your control

Try to cultivate your Inner Citadel as a fortress of time off and tranquility even in the most adverse situations. The next time you feel stressed, reflect on what factors you have control over and which ones are beyond your control. Don't waste any time worrying about the latter. Focus your actions and mental energy only on those things you can control, and you will find more tranquility and more time off. As Aurelius said, "Do less, better." But to know what to keep, and how to do it better, you need to pause and reflect.

REFLECTION:

- If you lost all of your material goods today, what are the things you could still be grateful for?
- How would you rebuild your life?
- In what ways could it actually be an opportunity in disguise?

SETH GODIN

American Author and Online Education Pioneer

"PROJECTS. A funny word to have used thirty years ago, but one that makes complete sense today. Thirty years ago, we were still fine-tuning our factories. Thirty years ago, everything was part of the assembly line. Today, though, we're in the project business. Just about all of us work on projects, and the one thing we give very little thought to is which projects should we do?"

Seth Godin is a prolific author and near-omnipresent voice in the marketing space. He has written dozens of best-selling books that have been translated into 35 languages, and for over a decade, he has published a new post every day on his blog. But, perhaps more impressively, Seth cooks dinner with his family nearly every night. If you find yourself thinking Godin must be one of the most productive people on the planet, you're in good company. It's hard to read his laundry list of accomplishments and observe what seems like a superhuman daily output and not wonder, "*How does he do it?*"

It's a fair question. Godin has the same amount of hours we do in a day, so how is he able to churn out best sellers, publish new writing daily, design and lead novel online learning platforms, stay deeply engaged with his hobbies like making artisanal chocolate, and, slow down to craft a slow meal with his family every night? And the answer is surprisingly simple: he is quick to say no and slow to say yes.

In his piece, "Do Less," Godin reminds us that "you can't have everything. Same thing is true with our business life. We can't have everything. We've tried, and it doesn't work. What we've discovered, though, is that leaving off that last business project not only makes our profits go up, it also can dramatically improve the rest of our life." For Godin, a bit of reflection coupled with a thoughtful "no thanks" is the key to turning out the meaningful, high-quality, even transformational content his audience craves. He understands that someone who says yes to almost everything, stretching themselves thin, is going to produce shallow work. Or they'll blow their deadline (failing to "ship" as he terms it). Or they'll burn out and produce no work at all. Say yes to just a few projects, and you end up with a portfolio of work that captures attention. Say yes to everything that comes your way, and you end up on the proverbial treadmill—running yourself ragged with little to show for your miles. Worse, you might have to say no to an awesome opportunity that comes your way because you are overcommitted from all the yes-saying. Or you're so wrapped up in the mediocre that you can't spot the great opportunities all around you.

Our illustrator, Mariya, personally grappled with this pressure to say yes to too many projects. She didn't want to say no to the work—or the money; she wanted to keep building out her portfolio and list of happy clients. She always thought that she should be happy to have an abundance of gigs and opportunities since many other illustrators don't have such chances. Busyness means you're successful, right? But deep down, Mariya knew something was wrong. Rather than the happiness that "should" come with consistent income and glowing testimonials, she mostly felt stress and pressure. Soon, Mariya had taken on too much and found herself taking the last train home from her studio, around midnight, almost every day. "In my head, I knew it wasn't right, I knew being busy isn't good, I knew I could say no, but I was trapped in the concept that 'this is right' and I couldn't get out," she recounts. "Even when people told me I could say no to some projects and make things better, that I've been working too much, I would say 'I know, but ...' And I think I even knew how foolish I sounded when I said that." But eventually, she hit pause and sat down for a quiet year-end reflection, which gave her the clarity and courage to put her feelings into action.

Mariya realized that she no longer found time to just draw for herself, sketching and experimenting. Worse, she had stopped truly enjoying drawing—a fact that really scared her, since drawing was such a fundamental aspect of her life. She also noticed that the quality of her work had suffered. All these realizations, a result of her honest reflection, made Mariya decide to scale back her workload moving forward. Her time, her happiness, and the quality and enjoyment of her craft were much more important than stacking up more clients. Like Godin, Mariya started turning down projects. Her reflection allowed her to "slowly put my foot out of the room I was trapped in." While she still struggles with saying no to work that comes her way, she has set herself a rule to be always at around 80 percent capacity (compared to 100 plus percent before) so that if a project she feels excited about (like this book) comes along, she has the space to say yes.

Saying no is not easy. But don't let that stop you. As *Essentialism* author and leadership consultant Greg McKeown writes, "Make your peace with the fact that saying 'no' often requires trading popularity for respect." It's a trade worth making. Saying no is one of the most powerful tools for acquiring time off, and all the benefits that come with it, and should be a central component of everyone's rest ethic.

In an interview with author Tim Ferriss, Godin critiqued the culture of busyness, saying, "You know super well that busy is a trap, and that busy is a myth," and urged his audience not to "play the busy card." Imagine if you implemented Seth's advice and, like Mariya did, deeply reflected on your client list and what's important to you. What would happen if you let go of the "draining" ones? Maybe consider the customers who pay late, who give you a hard time for not always being available, or those who have little interest in your bold ideas. If you let go of them, would your business improve? Letting go of some projects surely won't be easy, but once you take the difficult initial step, you will find that you can produce more high-quality work while still making time for the things you love. Next time a new project opportunity comes your way, take time to reflect before saying yes.

PRACTICE:

Find the right projects by making a "More of/Less of" list

Take out a piece of paper and draw a line down the middle. Reflect on your strengths and what matters most to you. On one half of the page, write what you want more of in your life. This could be more dinner parties with your family like Seth Godin, or it could be projects that feel exciting like Mariya. On the other half of the paper, write the items you'd like to trim down. This could be late-night email-answering or downer clients. When a new project comes your way, reflect on your list and determine where this opportunity fits. If it aligns with your "less of" list, consider saying no.

REFLECTION:

- Who, or what, gets the majority of your time? Your energy? Your focus?
- Are you giving the things you care about most the time they deserve? How could you redistribute (and reinvest) your resources?

MARIE KONDO

Japanese Organizing Consultant and Author

"Ask yourself this, often: Is what I'm doing connected to the kind of life that will spark joy for me? By thinking through this, the steps required to have that kind of life become clearer."

Physics is against us. The second law of thermodynamics states that entropy in the universe is ever increasing, that we are moving from order to chaos. In other words: clutter just builds up over time. We can fight back locally, restoring order to some of the chaos in our immediate vicinity, but that takes time and energy. And, particularly if we're busy and tired, time and energy are the last things we want to use more of—but decluttering might just be worth it, as it helps us get more time and energy back in the long run (and no, we're not suggesting that we can break the laws of thermodynamics and build a perpetuum mobile that runs on decluttering).

Marie Kondo, known for her best-selling books, including *The Life-Changing Magic of Tidying Up* and her Netflix show *Tidying*

Up with Marie Kondo, is the sworn enemy of clutter. At the heart of her process lies a single question: Does this "spark joy"? Her trademark KonMari Method starts with a firm commitment to tidying up. She then asks us to imagine our ideal lifestyles. What do we want our lives to look like? What are our priorities? Our values? Once we reflect on her questions, we can use them as a guiding principle for discarding things. Going through each object, category by category (clothes, kitchen utensils, books), we should ask ourselves if something "sparks joy," and if it supports our ideal lifestyle. If the answer is anything but a firm yes, we should discard the item. Take a moment to pause and appreciate the object, thanking it for the use you had for it in the past, but then be ruthless and don't hang on to it "just because."

While Kondo talks explicitly about the physical process of tidying up your home, we think you can apply the same method to your calendar with great success and, in doing so, create more space for time off. The process should be pretty much the same. Start out with reflection and introspection, asking yourself what parts of your calendar are on autopilot and not serving your creativity and joy. Then be ruthless with decluttering your calendar, getting rid of those existing engagements and making a firm resolution to keep these out of your calendar in the future. Just as Kondo recommends cleaning your house by object category, you might find it helpful to clean your calendar by time categories, such as "work," "family," or "social." Be clear about which events are taking time away from your creative pursuits. The key is to know what matters to you and why. If applied properly, this method can be very useful to achieve white space in your schedule. And if you really follow through with it, your time will be occupied entirely with things that spark joy.

Of course, assessing your priorities should not be something you do once and then be done with it forever. We all change and evolve, so keeping our self-understanding up to date with that is essential. This doesn't have to be too rigid, but we should make time at semiregular intervals to reflect. Marie practices this herself:

"I might reassess my priorities at the start of a new year or on my birthday, but it's not fixed like that. My husband and I will talk about where we're at now and ask ourselves, 'How much do we need to be working? How much time can we devote to family?' Right now, I'm focusing on work. I'm starting this new project. This is where I'm at now, so I'm looking ahead to making that happen. Until recently, though, I was putting all of my energy into family."

Kondo knows that regularly spending time on reflection can also be extremely valuable in its own right. "When I need to sort through my thoughts," she explains, "I take a blank sheet of paper and write down everything on my mind. I identify any tangled feelings, reasons for worry or anxiety, and clarify which issues I can and cannot control.... Recognizing that something is out of my control helps me calm down." And she also has another great recipe for calming down our mind: "When I am burnt out and need to unwind, I forget everything and wipe the floor. Keeping my hands busy helps my mind find stillness."

Keeping your hands busy, doing something physical rather than just interacting with a screen, is an immensely powerful form of active time off. It doesn't have to be something big. We can use small rituals to punctuate our days and find some calm and presence amidst the busyness. John will close his laptop and open up his notebook to doodle a drawing or write a short poem with his favorite pen. Max enjoys making coffee. Smelling and weighing the beans, grinding them, wetting the paper filter and adding the ground coffee, pouring over a first small amount of hot water and giving it a vigorous stir to initiate the beautiful bloom, and then slowly in a circular motion adding the remaining water over a couple of minutes, and watching as the water, as if by magic, transforms into a delicious black elixir. Kondo herself prefers tea: "I drink multiple cups of tea a day. So that will be my break. After I've accomplished a few things or start to feel tired, I'll get up and make another cup." These little rituals might take only ten minutes, but they can completely reset and ground your mind and give you new energy (and maybe caffeine) to tackle whatever joy-sparking activity is next on your calendar. Try to actively cultivate these rituals and use them as a strategic tool whenever you feel the need to clear your mind and reset.

PRACTICE:

Apply the KonMari Method to your calendar to create time off

We all have events on our calendar that are running on autopilot. Without reflecting on them, they will continue to stay there, and before you know it, your calendar has no space for time off. Make a detailed list of all the repetitive events that are filling your calendar. Segment them by category, such as "work," "family," and "social." Then with each event, ask yourself if it "sparks joy" and helps you get closer to your ideal quality of life, creative state, or personal definition of success. If one of the events doesn't, commit to discarding it from your calendar.

REFLECTION:

- Are you proud of how you spent your last three months?
- Why did you say yes to the things that don't bring you joy or align with the life you want?

SAINT THOMAS AQUINAS

Italian Catholic Priest and Philosopher (1225—7 March 1274)

"The essence of virtue consists in the good rather than in the difficult.... Not everything that is more difficult is necessarily more meritorious."

"It is necessary for the perfection of human society, that there should be men who devote their lives to contemplation."

For centuries, knowledge and faith had been inextricably linked in Christian Europe. When Thomas Aquinas was born in the early 13th century, most Christians were convinced that nonbelievers could not act rightly or make sound decisions because they lacked faith. The wisdom of the ancient world had been forgotten or deliberately ignored and discredited. But the young Aquinas would set out to change this.

    Born into a wealthy noble family in Italy, Aquinas ended up going to the newly established University of Naples, the world's first secular university. There he discovered the texts of the ancient Greeks and was deeply intrigued by their thoughts. Despite being very religious—he would go on to become a Catholic priest—Aquinas saw great value and truth in the Greeks' ideas. It was their texts, and the insights they provided, written by non-Christian thinkers and philosophers, that inspired him to make one of his greatest contributions to Western philosophy and modern thought. Buried deep in the many pages of his unfinished magnum opus, the comprehensive theological primer *Summa Theologica*, he explained that, contrary to his contemporaries, he believed that reason was one of God's greatest gifts to humanity, and that everyone could make use of this gift and do the right thing, Christian or not. As an article on The School of Life website put it, Aquinas "universalised intelligence and opened the Christian mind to the insights of all of humanity from across the ages and continents. The modern world, in so far as it insists that good ideas can come from any quarter regardless of creed or background, remains hugely in his debt."

Aquinas found Aristotle particularly inspiring, and just like Aristotle, he considered happiness a central concept in his thinking. Driven by a deep appreciation of happiness and joy, Aquinas saw love as the most fundamental human emotion and believed that it was love of some form—for someone or something—that compelled us to do things. Satisfying this love brings joy (and many other positive emotions), whereas not having it satisfied brings various negative emotions ranging from greed to despair. For Aquinas, to really love something meant to not (just) see it for its instrumental value, such as fulfilling our hedonic pleasures or a utilitarian purpose, but to love it for its own sake. While he supported seeking happiness on earth, he tied this happiness to faith and God. The ultimate love, and thus also the ultimate joy, he believed, can only be found there.

However, in a modern (and potentially secular) context, we can interpret his words as looking at the root of what we truly love, trying to discover our true motivators and then attempting to satisfy those. Probably, in many cases, we are chasing false goals or drowning our dissatisfaction in busyness because it is easier than pausing and taking the time to reflect on what we truly love (whether that is a person or group of people, an activity or occupation, or even a place). We should get clear on what we are really after (not the delusional story we tell ourselves, which leaves us even more dissatisfied) and then try to satisfy this yearning. Consider the projects you are working on right now—what are your true motivators behind them? How about your relationships? Are you driven by actual love, or just drifting with the flow because of a lack of clarity?

One modern religious scholar particularly inspired by Aquinas was Josef Pieper, whom we already encountered in our history discussion. Pieper frequently references Aquinas in his book *Leisure: The Basis of Culture*. In it he also proclaims that "the ability to be 'at leisure' is one of the basic powers of the human soul." As long as we attach a utilitarian goal to leisure, such as being refreshed for more work, we are missing out on its deepest benefits and joys. We are distracted from the essence of inner calm by focusing on external goals. Pieper talked about "God's intuitions"—what we might in a secular way see as creative "aha" moments—visiting men during times of true joy and leisure. Only in those calm and silent moments is our soul receptive enough. Even God rested on the seventh day of creation to contemplate and celebrate.

Aquinas and Pieper both encourage us to listen to our joy, cultivate it, celebrate it through leisure, and follow it as a guiding light. What joys, small or big, are serving as beacons of motivation, creativity, and happiness in your life? Are you paying enough attention to them?

PRACTICE:

Tap into the love and passion that motivate you

What are the root causes, the passions and yearnings, that really compel you to do things? As Aquinas knew, there are few better motivators than putting our time and effort in service of the people and things we love. Are you making full use of this, or do you half-heartedly work on things you don't really care about? How about the people you surround yourself with? Once you are clear on what you truly love, take as much time off from everything else as possible and focus it on your love in order to find joy, inspiration, and creativity.

REFLECTION:

- What tasks in your daily routine feel the most tedious?
- If you can't avoid or replace them, how could you approach them in a more playful way, adding little moments of joy into them?

We hope that these profiles and their accompanying reflection prompts offered you some meaningful pondering. The practice of reflection is a necessary break from all of our task execution. These kinds of reflections help us hit the reset button and spot the hidden issues that may be keeping us away from quality time off and finding success without the stress.

Reflection can feel like a serious practice, and it should be taken seriously. After all, it's important to take an honest and sincere look at our lives from time to time. But as with everything, the right balance is key. And after all this seriousness, it's time to lighten the mood again. We need to harmonize the seriousness of reflection with the lightness of play.

PLAY

Where do you think the most innovation is happening within a 20-mile radius of you?

It's a question we love to ask at dinner parties, and though the responses can be as unique as the locale and the people sitting around the table, a few responses crop up again and again: "the universities," "our local startup accelerators," or "my corporate innovation lab." We won't deny that good and innovative work is occurring at these venues, but even at the most forward-thinking institution, the scope of innovation is limited by funds, bureaucracy, or just a lack of imagination. There is, however, a place where innovation is truly boundless, often bending or exceeding the laws of nature.

Somewhere near you is a playground. Yes, a place with monkey bars, screaming kids, brilliant ideas, and anything-is-possible mindsets. Remember the freedom, the inventions, the deep joy and endless possibilities for adventure? Many of us have forgotten how it felt to race, whooping and hollering, into play, but it's not too late to rediscover its importance. On playgrounds, we encounter profound wisdom.

THE PLAYGROUND MENTALITY

John was walking through his neighborhood in Austin, Texas, en route to his favorite coffee shop, when his stroll was suddenly interrupted by a "Hey mister!" calling out to him from the other side of the chain-link fence to his left.

"Hey mister," it came again. "We have a question!" John couldn't help but smile as he glanced down at the four little humans looking up at him. All of them were around seven years old, enjoying recess on their school's playground. He cracked a smile and thought, "This should be good." He could remember the types of questions he asked as a boy; he just hoped theirs wasn't about farts.

One boy stepped closer to the fence. "We would like to know if you think it is a good idea if we could create a thermostat for the whole world?" John laughed inside but wanted to see where this curious crew was going with their idea. "Why?" he asked. "Are you planning to turn your school into a laboratory for creating a world thermostat?" But their reasoning was surprisingly valid. They wanted to be able to make the Texas summers less hot so they could grow avocados and see some of the spring animals year-round, not just in March and April. Before John could ask them more questions about their new venture, a teacher disrupted the conversation. Recess time was over. They had to "get back to their learning."

While enjoying his coffee moments later, John pondered on how imaginative these kids were. Their world thermostat idea might not be possible any time soon (again, these damn laws of thermodynamics …), but their vision definitely left him thinking about a grander picture for climate preservation technology. The enthusiasm, curiosity, and play that so many professionals lose connection with is the fuel behind these children's ideas.

In John's business coaching practice, he helps his clients quiet their adult mind in order to have teams play again. His "Child's Mind" workshops start with anecdotes like the global thermostat kids. He then invites his clients to be playful, just like those kids, who practice creation and ideation for its own sake rather than for vanity, results, or politics. Within this state of play they can focus solely on the activity at hand and discover a more open and unrestrained channel for ideas and creativity. Their anything-is-possible mindset is unlocked.

By the end of his workshops, each participant is showcasing new business ideas or designs driven by their playful, seven-year-old mindset. An engineer starts pitching his vision of creating enormous biodomes that would house outdoor nature schools. A chef begins drawing out a menu concept for a hiking expedition restaurant experience. The workshops transform a stale room of serious attendees to an adult playground of potential. The connection between innovation and play becomes undeniable.

After reflecting on the success of John's Child's-Mind workshops, we started thinking about the playground atmosphere and how easily children can turn any place into a playground. Give them a few moments to spare, and they are transforming airport terminals, waiting rooms, and restaurants into laboratories, excavation sites, or space stations. A playground is an environment for play—an essential context for imagination and exploration—and such an environment can exist anywhere. No jungle gym required. Can we adults also benefit from creating this shift in our environment?

There is a time and a place for holding on to our adult mind, but so much of our work deserves boundless creativity. If each person in a meeting room (virtual or physical) brings their child's mind to their creative work, they are better able to explore, tinker, and brainstorm without fear of sounding silly. To make the most of our creativity, we need to unlock our sense of playfulness again. And at the heart of being playful is allowing ourselves to leave behind our everyday concerns, past and future, and get fully absorbed in the present moment.

ALAN WATTS

British American Philosopher
(6 January 1915—16 November 1973)

"There is indeed such a thing as 'timing'—the art of mastering rhythm—but timing and hurrying are … mutually exclusive."

"We get such a kick out of looking forward to pleasures and rushing ahead to meet them that we can't slow down enough to enjoy them when they come. We are therefore a civilization which suffers from chronic disappointment—a formidable swarm of spoiled children smashing their toys."

Few people have done as much to popularize Eastern philosophy, particularly Zen, in the West as Alan Watts. Watts, who held a master's degree in theology and spent five years of his life as an Episcopal priest, had an unrivaled talent for finding commonalities among the world's diverse spiritual and religious practices and interpreting them in a modern and relatable way. By stripping away the mystic elements, he saw these practices as a powerful form of psychotherapy. His many books and recorded lectures, delivered in his unmistakable British accent, have touched the lives of millions.

One of the key ideas permeating Watts's work is the importance of being present, attuned to the current moment, and his concern that we are losing the ability to do so. We are increasingly living with our minds in the future, forgetting to be happy (or even notice) where we are now—we are so absorbed in what may lie ahead that we lose touch with what is real and right in front of us. "The future," Watts writes, "is made up of purely abstract and logical elements—inferences, guesses, deductions—it cannot be eaten, felt, smelled, seen, heard, or otherwise enjoyed. To pursue it is to pursue a constantly retreating phantom, and the faster you chase it, the faster it runs ahead." His words conjure the image of greyhounds zipping around the dog track, chasing a mechanical hare they'll never catch. What hare are you chasing?

Watts knew that one of the best ways to be present in the moment, and leave our past and future worries behind, is to be playful. In his book *Psychotherapy East and West*, he warns us that "everything that is done playfully, without ulterior motive and second thought, makes us feel guilty," which leads us to falsely use means to justify the ends: "we relax to improve our work; we worship God to improve our morals; we even get drunk in order to forget our worries." Instead, Watts believed, we should leave our guilt about play and leisure behind, and enjoy them as essential aspects of life. "Psychoanalysis in the West and the ways of liberation in the East," he suggests, "should enable us to see that the only effective way is to appeal to Eros [the pleasure principle], without which Logos—the sense of duty and reason—has no life." In other words, if you want to be effective in your work—and find meaning in it—you need to also appreciate pleasure and play. It may just be the thing that sets us apart as we automate more and more work with machines and algorithms.

Way ahead of his time, Watts anticipated the rise of AI and how it will become better than humans at many routine tasks. "The working inhabitants of a modern city spend their days in activities which largely boil down to counting and measuring," he notes, remarking that machines could perform such tasks far more efficiently than their human counterparts and wondering whether the human brain could end up obsolete. Watts warns that "if we are to continue to live for the future, and to make the chief work of the mind prediction and calculation, man must eventually become a parasitic appendage to a mass of clockwork." Some of us are already on the verge of this transition. It is time to take action.

If we don't want to become obsolete in a world with "mechanical and electrical computers of far greater speed and efficiency" than the human mind, Watts believed that we have to shift our focus from predicting the future to living in the current moment, honing our present-based instinct. "Working rightly, the brain is the highest form of 'instinctual wisdom,'" he notes, asserting that our brains can only do their job "when consciousness is doing what it is designed for: not writhing and whirling to get out of present experience, but being effortlessly aware of it." We will revisit this idea toward the end of the book and pick up Watts's argument, making the case that AI taking over more and more tedious routine work is not something to be feared but embraced. It frees us up to focus our mind on the things that are distinctly human, like creativity and empathy. But in order to benefit from this, we have to stop trying to compete with the machines in their game of busyness, and instead hone our rest ethic as a balancing element.

Watts urges us to lose our obsession with the clock and immerse ourselves in the world, to be more present, to feel a bit more Kairos and a little less Chronos. "Clock time," as he reminds us in *Does It Matter?: Essays on Man's Relation to Materiality*, is as real (or unreal) as the latitudinal and longitudinal lines crisscrossing our maps but not our planet, "merely a method of measurement held in common by all civilized societies." Adhere too closely to Chronos and his beeping, wailing array of timekeepers, and you can't be present. "If you are bewitched by the clock," Watts warns, "'Now' will be no more than the geometrical point at which the future becomes the past." He believed that presence was the antidote to an overdose of clock time: "If you sense and feel the world materially, you will discover that there never is, or was, or will be anything except the present."

And while being more "in the moment" has received significant attention in recent years, particularly within the personal development community, Alan considered the entire idea of self-improvement nonsensical: "I can only think seriously of trying to live up to an ideal, to improve myself, if I am split in two pieces. There must be a good 'I' who is going to improve the bad 'me.'" Such separation, he reasoned, would only worsen his issues, not improve them. Whether or not you agree with him, it's certainly true that many of us obsess over self-improvement, reading book after book and attending seminar after seminar, but are nonetheless unwilling to be still and reflect on who we really are. This investment in self-development isn't "growth"; it's a defense mechanism. While you're reading this book, we encourage you to put it down from time to time and reflect on how these ideas relate to your life and how you can implement them for yourself. Sometimes, in order to really improve ourselves, we need to take time off from self-improvement and simply be present with our thoughts.

PRACTICE:

Optimize your life for presence

When was the last time you allowed yourself to be fully absorbed in an activity, just like a child at play? Not thinking, just being? List any instances from the last year that come to mind. What did you do? When did you do it and where? Was an element of play involved? If applicable, what logistical circumstances (such as a babysitter or a long weekend) made it possible? Then look over your list and see if you can find patterns. What activities allowed you to be more present and playful? What circumstances promoted or hindered true presence? Once you have done this reflection, try to optimize for presence and playfulness.

WHAT KIND OF LIGHT ARE WE SHINING?

MoMA curator and coauthor of *Century of the Child: Growing by Design 1900–2000* Juliet Kinchin expressed that "children help us to mediate between the ideal and the real." Playgrounds are where children alter a physical place with imagination, and we believe that any physical space can be made playful with the right intention. At playgrounds, we will naturally find a more lantern-like consciousness, and adult workplaces like offices, retail stores, and factories are where we will discover spotlight-like consciousness.

You are probably thinking: "Wait, what does a lantern or a spotlight have to do with playgrounds and consciousness?"

Alison Gopnik, a professor of psychology at the University of California, Berkeley, TED speaker, and best-selling author, is one of the leading researchers in developmental psychology. She is particularly interested in the study of children's learning and the question of how cognition develops in children. In her book *The Philosophical Baby*, she describes children as having a "lantern consciousness" with which they explore and model the world around them. They take in their entire surroundings, like a lantern casting light in all directions. Their lack of focus is purposeful and allows them to more easily be in a state of joy and possibility. Their lantern consciousness is how they eventually make sense of everything, from social encounters to the physics of walking. Their mindset lights up everything around them. New connections are being made, and new corners are being turned.

Gopnik explains that the opposite of lantern consciousness is what we see in most adults, what she calls "spotlight consciousness." We adults are superb at lasering in on the task at hand, while missing out on a lot of exciting things going on around us. Like a spotlight, we fixate and illuminate only the things in our intended direction. This kind of consciousness limits us, especially our innovation and creativity.

Creativity is about connecting the dots, and playfulness allows us to find patterns and make those new connections. Connecting dots and creative play, for both children and adults, is essential to problem-solving, as well as cultivating a sense of possibility. As Gopnik notes, "a child's brain is extremely plastic, good for learning, not accomplishing," for "exploring, rather than exploiting." While our normal adult brain is an efficient decision-making machine relying on extensive experience, it often traps us in well-worn mental grooves and patterns and doesn't allow for the same exploration of far-fetched solutions and unhindered perception of new ideas. Looking back at our earlier exploration of creativity, it is almost as if the adult's mind is particularly suited to the conscious phases of initial preparation and ultimate verification, while a child's mind is much better at the unconscious stages of incubation and illumination.

And luckily, even as adults, we aren't permanently stuck with a spotlight consciousness. Regularly exposing ourselves to new and unfamiliar ideas and trying to see the world from someone else's perspective (maybe even someone we disagree with) are some of the best ways to temporarily flip into lantern mode. And lantern consciousness is also apparent in adults under the influence of psychedelics. When Gopnik first saw the results of a recent wave of studies on psychedelics' effects on the brain, she was astonished by just how similarly the brain of a young child and an adult on LSD seemed to function. "The short summary is, babies and children are basically tripping all the time."

Interestingly, from our own experience we can attest that scientists, particularly physicists, are a group of people that are very open to experiment with psychedelics and use them to deliberately explore their own minds and to discover solutions to problems they are working on hidden in their subconscious. One of the main ideas behind Max's PhD thesis (related to how the notion of time becomes fuzzy at the quantum scale) may or may not have come to him in a somewhat altered state of mind. Being able to grasp that your everyday view of the world, filtered through the highly biased (albeit in many cases highly useful) lens of the "sane" adult brain, is only one particular way of seeing the world is tremendously valuable when trying to get your head around concepts that lie far outside of everyday common sense and experience, such as fundamental physics.[5]

During many forms of time off, our mind and perspective are also more like a lantern. But if we are not mindful of it, we will burrow back into our familiar routines focused on schedules and deadlines, racing through our chosen mazes. We get cynical and serious. We might apply the same rigid spotlight mindset to our teammates when instead what we really need to get to a breakthrough is lantern thinking. We contract rather than expand our thinking and enforce the same mindset in those around us. But we just need to look at children playing for inspiration on how to do the opposite. As Gopnik says: "If you want to understand what an expanded consciousness looks like, all you have to do is have tea with a four-year-old."

---

[5]Note that while we are very excited about the creative, medical, and therapeutic possibilities of psychedelics, we DO NOT advocate the use of psychedelics without the right guidance, supervision, and legal clearance.

ALICE WATERS

American Chef, Restaurateur, Activist, and Author

"You know, that's what I do every Sunday: I invite my friends over. I have food I got from the farmer's market. We don't know what we're going to cook, and we just figure it out. Then we all set the table and all clean up. It's really a moment in my week that I always look forward to."

We can learn two things from Alice Waters. One, granting time off in a time-sensitive industry helps foster more innovation and enthusiasm (as we also saw in the story of Fäviken). Two, taking time to cook and slowly enjoy a meal can help us return to our playfulness and humanity.

Waters, the owner of the famed restaurant Chez Panisse in Berkeley, California, doesn't start her days by checking emails or watching the news. Instead, you will find her watching over an open fire in a brick wall next to the dining room table. She uses the fire to toast bread before topping it with fresh hummus. She savors the warm meal along with a long-steeped cup of dark tea and the mild scent of burning wood. Enjoying food at this slow pace has been the core of her life's work. For Alice, food is both work and play—and cooking is an act of presence and boundless creativity.

Waters opened Chez Panisse in 1971 and defined what would come to be known as Californian cuisine. Decades (and countless accolades) later, she has been a pioneer and activist, building and leading movements to shift the American palate toward local, organic, and sustainably sourced food. Waters has tried to get Americans to rethink what they eat, promoting everything from the slow-food movement to providing more nutritious food in schools to refusing to include bluefin tuna on her menu. And through it all, her flagship restaurant, tucked into its cozy house on Shattuck Avenue, remains one of the most respected restaurants in the United States. Alice is innovative and harmonious with how she operates the restaurant. Rather than perpetually riding a fine line between burnout and inspiration, she delegates the workload in a way that is sustainable and decentralized. She makes time for presence and play.

"In the restaurant, café, and pastry, we have a two-chef system," she recounts. "It's hard for me to describe how valuable that is. It means you have a whole group of chefs who could take over in an emergency or if one person wants more time off. They also have time to be with their families and to research the food they're cooking. They can work days instead of nights. They can be home for dinner. And since we did that, the food has dramatically improved, because there's this healthy competition and collaboration that goes on. It really sparks the imagination." And when a host of talented cooks have the freedom to play with their food, magic happens. Chez Panisse's reputation for stellar, innovative, *playful* food is no accident.

You cannot force creativity, and you certainly cannot force play, but you can support a culture that helps cultivate it. And in that sense, we can learn a lot from Alice Waters and Chez Panisse. It's important to slow down and pare back to create the space to be creative, innovative, happy, and human. Create time off to play with your food.

PRACTICE:

Improvise a meal with your friends, family, or team

Go on an adventure to find a farmers' market for your ingredients. Rather than immediately jump to a recipe book, freestyle and let your creativity guide what the methods and composition of the dishes should be. Collaborate, laugh, and taste as you go. We highly recommend The Flavor Bible by Andrew Dornenburg and Karen A. Page for inspiration without a prescribed recipe. Alice Waters reminds us that "we want to be sitting around the table. We want to be smelling the fire. We want to be engaged with food in this way. I count on nature really becoming our teacher, too. She's been there since the beginning of civilization. So we have that in us all. And we've got to connect to it."

EMBRACING SILLY IDEAS

What happens when we deprive ourselves of play? Nothing good. Turns out, a steady practice of play is just as important as proper sleep and a balanced diet.

Dr. Stuart L. Brown has focused his time and attention on the importance of play within the human life cycle and explored the evolution of human and animal play. He has also run the National Institute for Play, a nonprofit committed to bringing the unrealized knowledge, practices, and benefits of play into public life. The consequences of an adult not getting enough play, according to Dr. Brown, include a "lack of vital life engagement; diminished optimism; stuck-in-a-rut feeling about life with little curiosity or exploratory imagination to alter their situation; [and] predilection to escapist temporary fixes." Worst of all, Brown adds one final hallmark of not getting enough play: "a personal sense of being life's victim rather than life's conqueror."

Looking around, these symptoms of a lack of play seem unfortunately quite familiar in the adult world. Some adults seem to consider playfulness to be little more than a sign of immaturity.

They may see playful behavior as nonsense and a waste of potentially "productive time." In the movie *Willy Wonka & the Chocolate Factory*, a dialogue in the film's screenplay counters this belief: After Mr. Wonka showcases the amazing Eggdicator, Mr. Salt criticizes it by saying, "It's a lot of nonsense." To which Mr. Wonka replies, "A little nonsense now and then is relished by the wisest men."

There is a lot of wisdom in Mr. Wonka's words. What some may perceive as nonsensical play can actually be the ultimate productivity— unrestricted, imaginative thinking leads to breakthroughs. Edward M. Hallowell, a psychiatrist who specializes in brain science, explains that many of our most celebrated creators made their discoveries in a state of play:

> Columbus was at play when it dawned on him that the world was round. Newton was at play in his mind when he saw the apple tree and suddenly conceived of the force of gravity. Watson and Crick were playing with possible shapes of the DNA molecule when they stumbled upon the double helix. Shakespeare played with iambic pentameter his whole life. Mozart barely lived a waking moment when he was not at play.

In innovation, we explore between the ideal and the real. We have observed that children on playgrounds foster a culture of flexibility, inclusiveness, and imagination. In this respect, they belong at the heart of utopian thought, and they inspire us to demand a different, better, brighter future. The group of kids presenting their World Thermostat to John on their playground were not being silly. They were brilliant. While they may still lack the rigor and analytical skills to take it to the next level, just having the idea in the first place puts them ahead of many adults. With the right mindset, silly ideas, even impossible ideas, can be the best starting point to come up with real breakthroughs. Thought experiments, hypothetical scenarios that often break the laws of physics or simplify the real world dramatically, like Einstein imagining himself sitting on a beam of light, have led to many leaps in science. These are examples of the scientific mind at play. The best scientists cherish and celebrate silly ideas.

Alison Gopnik, the developmental psychologist we encountered earlier, says, "It's not that children are little scientists—it's that scientists are big children. Scientists actually are the few people who, as adults, get to have this protected time when they can just explore, play, figure out what the world is like." And if you talk to scientists, especially the most accomplished ones, you'll notice that they might be the only profession where a large fraction of its practitioners openly admit that a lot of what they do is just a sophisticated form of play.

But regardless of our type of work, we can all be big children. We adults should learn from the playfulness of children. In our time of interesting environmental and socioeconomic challenges, play is a crucial practice for bridging the gap between the situation we currently find ourselves in and the better worlds we can imagine. We need to give ourselves time and space to play. As travel writer Rolf Potts remarks in his book *Vagabonding*, "If the clock appears to move faster than it did in sixth grade, it's only because we haven't actualized our power as adults to set our own recess schedule." In playfulness, time slows down. In playfulness, the irregular can occur. We aren't suggesting that you spend the rest of your life at a playground, but we could all benefit from occasionally bringing the playground mindset to our offices, living rooms, or workplaces.

Don't feel guilty about taking time off from your usual adult duties to play. It is contributing to your work. Consider the time as an investment in your innovation and overall happiness. What would happen if you went on a field trip with your team next week? What happens when you try to pitch your startup idea to a group of adventurous 10-year-olds? What happens if you and your friends go on a playdate? Aside from being joyful and entertaining, you will likely spot new possibilities that your adult routine defaults would never shine a light on.

Breaking your usual routine is one of the best ways to switch from spotlight to lantern mode, and to restore a sense of awe and wonder. Giving up your deeply ingrained habits and patterns is not easy in your usual environment, but it comes almost automatically if we change our surroundings. Traveling to a new culture and having to unlearn a lot of what we know is one of the surest ways to unlock our thinking, as we will explore shortly. But before we dive into the value of travel, let us meet someone who was a master of finding playfulness even in the simplest aspects of everyday life.

HERMANN HESSE

German Poet and Novelist (2 July 1877—9 August 1962)

"The high value put upon every minute of time, the idea of hurry-hurry as the most important objective of living, is unquestionably the most dangerous enemy of joy."

"The man who for the first time picks a small flower so that he can have it near him while he works has taken a step toward joy in life."

When we think of entertainment, the first things that spring to mind might be spectacular blockbuster movies, crazy nights out with friends at wild parties, or incredible adventure holidays in exotic locations. Whatever the activity, chances are it is something grand and dazzling. The bigger, the better. The more, the better.

The faster, the better. But while these activities certainly have their place, sustainable enjoyment and entertainment might lie closer to the opposite end of the spectrum.

Hermann Hesse was born and raised in a small town in southern Germany. His family was deeply religious, devoted Christians, but of a kind that was "not preached but lived." Many of his relatives, particularly his grandparents, had been missionaries and spent extensive time in India. This connection to Asia sparked an interest in Buddhist thought and philosophy in Hesse that would be evident in all his later works. He took a trip to India in 1911, and while the journey itself depressed him (largely due to the extreme poverty he witnessed), it had a deep and lasting influence. After trying a half-hearted apprenticeship as a clock mechanic and then becoming a bookseller, Hesse finally went on to establish himself as a respected writer. Some of his famous works include *Demian, Steppenwolf, The Glass Bead Game*, and one of Max's favorite novels, *Siddhartha*. He would also receive the 1946 Nobel Prize in Literature "for his inspired writings which, while growing in boldness and penetration, exemplify the classical humanitarian ideals and high qualities of style."

Already at the turn of the twentieth century, and without knowing the extreme extent another century would bring, Hesse came to see our fast-paced pursuit of entertainment as a deep and troubling issue. He felt that many of his contemporaries focused too much on work and busyness, and as a result, "live out their lives in a dull and loveless stupor." But it wasn't only the way in which people approached work where he saw an issue. He felt that entertainment was often approached with the same mindset: "Our ways of enjoying ourselves are hardly less irritating and nerve-racking than the pressure of our work. 'As much as possible, as fast as possible' is the motto. And so there is more and more entertainment and less and less joy."

Hesse might have been one of the first outspoken promoters of JOMO, the joy of missing out. Many of us are perpetually afraid of missing out on the next big thing, be that a new development in our field of work or a cool party all our friends are going to. But Hesse believed that missing out on such things can actually improve our quality of life, as well as the quality of our work. There is no need to follow every news article, see every new movie, immediately read and reply to every message we receive, or be aware of every development in our chosen field. In fact, those activities that give us a quick fix of feeling productive or entertained are often precisely the things that distract us from real productivity and joy. Instead of fearing what we are missing out on, we should celebrate the pleasure of having gained a little more time and mental space and courageously defend this decision.

While his specific examples may be somewhat outdated, it is remarkable how well the general sentiment of the following quote still applies today (just replace "theater" with "Netflix", and "publication" with the latest meme):

> In certain circles, [moderation] requires courage to miss a première. In wider circles, it takes courage not to have read a new publication several weeks after its appearance. In the widest circles of all, one is an object of ridicule if one has not read the daily paper. But I know people who feel no regret at exercising this courage. Let not the man who subscribes to a weekly theater series feel that he is losing something if he makes use of it only every other week. I guarantee: he will gain. Let anyone accustomed to looking at a great many pictures in an exhibition try just once, if he is still capable of it, spending an hour or more in front of a single masterpiece and content himself with that for the day. He will be the gainer by it. Let the omnivorous reader try the same sort of thing. Sometimes he will be annoyed at not being able to join in a conversation about some publication; occasionally, he will cause smiles. But soon he will know better and do the smiling himself. And let any man who cannot bring himself to use any other kind of restraint try to make a habit of going to bed at ten o'clock at least once a week. He will be amazed at how richly this small sacrifice of time and pleasure will be rewarded.

Occasionally restraining ourselves from enjoyment, taking time off from it, will make the times where we do indulge in it all the more joyful. Constant exposure to enjoyment (or anything really) just makes us dull to it. We forget how to be playful.

"The ability to cherish the 'little joy' is intimately connected with the habit of moderation," Hesse believed. "For this ability, originally natural to every man, presupposes certain things which in modern daily life have largely become obscured or lost, mainly a measure of cheerfulness, of love, and of poesy. These little joys ... are so inconspicuous and scattered so liberally throughout our daily lives that the dull minds of countless workers hardly notice them." We should all slow down a bit, stop our self-absorbed busyness, and actually take in all the fantastic details in our surroundings. "Gradually and without effort, the eye trains itself to transmit many small delights, to contemplate nature and the city streets, to appreciate the inexhaustible fun of daily life." True happiness can be so simple, we just have to take time to look for it. And those little joys are often the things that trigger our curiosity and spark new ideas and creativity in us. They revitalize our work.

Time off is all about being conscious of our time, and this includes being mindful of the little moments that can be filled with small joys. What Hesse suggests is essentially a microdosing of time off: "A stretch of sky, a garden wall overhung by green branches, a strong horse, a handsome dog, a group of children, a beautiful face—why should we be willing to be robbed of all this?" Yes, not everyone is in a position where they can take time off for an extended vacation, but Hesse's form of time off is accessible to everyone who is willing to take it. And we might first need to learn to appreciate these small moments anyway before we are truly ready to get the full benefits of extended time off. "My advice to the person suffering from lack of time and from apathy is this," Hesse writes. "Seek out each day as many as possible of the small joys, and thriftily save up the larger, more demanding pleasures for holidays and appropriate hours. It is the small joys first of all that are granted us for recreation, for daily relief and disburdenment, not the great ones."

PRACTICE:

Time Off Microdosing–Document something simple that brings a smile to your face

Are you so engrossed in your busyness and your addict-like entertainment consumption that you completely ignore the small joys—the true joys—of life? Today, make it your goal to pause at least three times and notice something simple that brings a smile to your face. Kids playing in the park, a pretty flower, someone smiling back at you, or the sound of the wind in the trees. Even better if you make a written note of each. Then repeat the same thing tomorrow. And the next day. Do it until this micro habit of time off becomes entirely natural for you, and you see the "inexhaustible fun of daily life" everywhere you look.

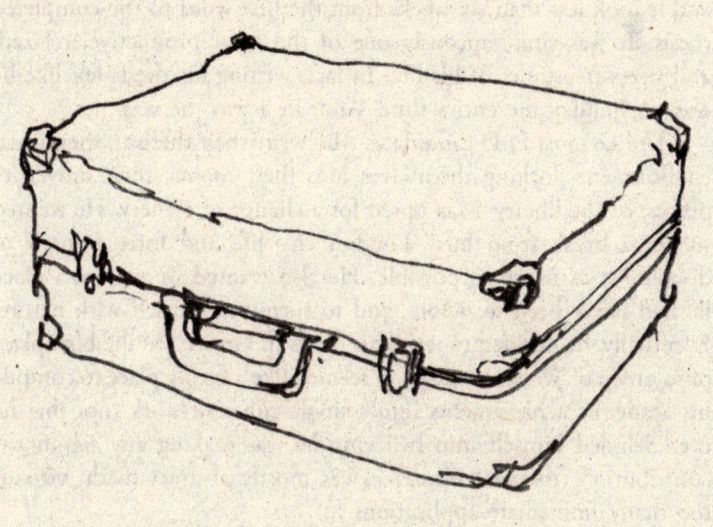

TRAVEL

Almost anyone with a PhD will tell you how much they hated writing their thesis, what a painful and excruciating process it was, how much they were stressed by the looming deadline, and how many months they toiled over it, writing a few words every day. But Max won't. He'll tell you it was a pretty enjoyable experience, and it took less than six weeks from the first word to the completed thesis. It was simultaneously one of the most productive, relaxed, and stress-free times of his life. In fact, writing his thesis felt like he was on holiday the entire time. And, in a way, he was.

Unlike most PhD candidates who write their thesis in their usual environment, locking themselves into their rooms, their university offices, or the library, Max opted for a change of scenery. He wanted to get a break from busy London city life and force himself to disconnect as much as possible. He also wanted to explore a place he had never been to before, and to surround himself with nature. Eventually, he decided to write his thesis in Greece. As the birthplace of so much of Western culture, it seemed like a fitting place to compile his academic achievements into a single coherent work (not that he ever deluded himself into believing he was making any significant contributions to that culture; it was mostly abstract math without too many immediate applications ...).

Max rented a small house in the mountains overlooking Ermoupoli, the port town of the small Greek island of Syros. It was a perfect mix of remoteness and beautiful natural scenery, while still providing fairly easy access to everyday necessities (and a decent internet connection). On a warm evening in mid-August 2016, carrying a suitcase stuffed with the many notebooks he had accumulated during his PhD, he arrived on Syros via ferry from Athens. At the port, he was immediately picked up and warmly welcomed by his wonderful landlords Betty and Yiannis, who not only made sure he felt at home on Syros but also introduced him to the local culture (and local *raki*).

After spending the first few days exploring the island, he quickly settled into a routine of contemplative solitude and deliberate rest, interspersed with short but highly focused writing sessions. Getting up around 9 or 10am, which was actually fairly early by his standards at the time (oh, the joys of being a PhD student), he would start his day meditating and stretching, before setting out for a short run in the mountains or riding the little scooter he had rented to one of the beautiful beaches for a quick swim. Afterward, he would leisurely make a nice big breakfast, which was usually followed by an hour or so of reading. Only after this, in the early afternoon, he would have his first 60-to-90-minute block of writing for the day, often in a small cafe in town. Despite only writing for a short time, his morning routine had put him in a state of calm focus, and the words usually flowed freely. At no point during this time did Max experience anything akin to writer's block. Having gotten some writing done, and maybe also having had a light lunch at the cafe he was writing in, he would usually head back home for a nap, which allowed his brain to process what he'd written. Then he went out exploring the island a bit more, doing grocery shopping, going for a swim, walking along the beach, or doing some more reading. All activities that didn't involve consciously thinking about "work." Inspired by Henry David Thoreau's *Walden*, which he was rereading at the time, Max spent many afternoons baking bread, a habit he really enjoyed (and still does today) not only for its delicious results but also for its meditative and reflective aspects.

Finally, he would have his second writing session of the day, followed again by plenty of time for undistracted thought. He often used this time to work on some other side projects, like teaching himself about AI and deep learning, a topic he was just getting into during that time but that would later become his main career. He took a leisurely approach to it, without any need for results or worrying about company deliverables, allowing himself to learn through exploration as opposed to study.

Eventually, he would pour himself a glass of wine and sit down for one more late-night writing session. The wine's effect often started out as a creativity boost, but then gradually shifted to him getting easily distracted. That's when he knew it was time to wrap up for the day, maybe watch a movie and read some fiction to wind down (possibly with another glass or two of local wine), and finally get some good sleep.

This kind of routine is certainly not what most people would associate with peak productivity. After all, Max spent less than four hours a day actively "working." Yet it was precisely this leisurely schedule in an inspiring new environment that allowed him to write his thesis faster than anyone else he knew, while simultaneously having a wonderfully relaxing time and even completing some other side projects he had been stuck on for a while. His mind felt clearer and sharper than it had felt in a long time. For Max, those few weeks on Syros were the most productive and leisurely weeks he had ever experienced.

LEISURELY TRAVEL

Sure, there is tremendous enjoyment and value to be found in visiting the main tourist attractions of a place, relaxing on a beautiful beach with an exotic cocktail in hand, or doing a long road trip trying to cover as much ground as possible. But often the best kind of travel happens at a more relaxed pace. It's not an escape from the daily grind and work, but something that weaves directly into our everyday life and lets us truly explore a place—as well as our inner selves, which are revealed and amplified when stripped from their usual surroundings. We really encourage everyone to try something similar. Yes, depending on your circumstances, it might not be as easy to get an extended time off, but fortunately you don't have to go all the way to Greece to get these benefits.

If you can't afford a trip far away, you can travel to parts unknown near you. On a sunny Saturday afternoon, John decided to leave his phone at home and walk to a piece of Austin, Texas, that he didn't know. It was a section of the east side of town that has a dense concentration of Latin culture. After an hour's walk into this part of the city, John felt like he was in Mexico. The smell of fresh-baked *pan dulces*, the swirling, colorful murals painted on the sides of the buildings, and the tin *milagros* glittering in shop windows had him convinced he was in Guadalajara. He spoke small-talk Spanish to a few neighborhood locals, and he even enjoyed a few mezcals at a neighborhood cantina. The entire afternoon felt like a trip to Mexico. All he had to do was explore a part of the city that was entirely new to him. In one way, this felt even better than some of his faraway travels. Rather than trying to coordinate what hotel to stay at that night or prepare for the flight back home, John was an hour's walk away from his bed.

There is undoubtedly excitement in taking a long flight to a faraway destination. But when our schedules don't allow us to take that multiweek exotic getaway, there are parts unknown right in our backyards. Aside from the new culture exposure, you get to see new tones of your city. You can find the beautiful diversity in the city or town where you reside. Go shopping at a farmer's market across town, or see what you discover on foot. It is what we do when we travel abroad, just applied to where we already live. As Herman Melville wrote in *Moby Dick*, "It is not down in any map; true places never are."

Unfortunately, many people approach travel just as an antidote to their busy work life, a short sprint that ends up being just as hectic and overscheduled as their normal life. So many tourists rush from one landmark to another without really experiencing a place. And when we think of long-term travel, we often just imagine more of that. Or, on the other extreme, doing nothing at all. We might find ourselves dreaming of getting rich and then escaping to a tropical paradise. But we rarely ask what we'd actually do once there. As Rolf Potts writes in *Vagabonding: An Uncommon Guide to the Art of Long-Term World Travel*, even with just a small amount of money, "in all likelihood, your enthusiasm for sitting around smeared in cocoa butter will run out before your money does." The tropical paradise of our imagination is nothing more than a contrast to the stresses at home. Once those stresses are removed, this image of paradise will seem pretty boring and lose its strength.

Real travel is different from this. It does not have to be expensive and hectic, nor does it have to be mere relaxation that will soon turn into boredom (not that there's anything wrong with pure relaxation from time to time). While Potts specifically talks about long-term travel when he writes, "If there's one key concept to remember amid the excitement of your first days on the road, it's this: 'Slow down!,'" we believe that this equally applies to shorter forms of travel. Rather than treating travel as "just another accessory—a smooth-edged, encapsulated experience that we purchase the same way we buy clothing or furniture," we should slow down and seek out a depth of experience, rather than breadth. This does not mean we should, as many do, obsess about the difference of "tourist" versus "traveler." This obsession just leads us to fetishize travelers or try to "be" a traveler more than to actually simply experience our travels. "Instead of worrying about whether you're a tourist or a traveler," recommends Potts, "the secret to 'seeing' our surroundings on the road is simply to *keep things real*." Like a child at play, open your eyes, activate your lantern mindset, and be amazed and inspired by the world around you.

While traveling, even the most mundane things like getting groceries or riding a bus become exciting and filled with unfamiliar sights, sounds, and smells. They allow us to really live a place. And if we never slow down, we miss these joys. It may sound cliché, but it's true that the journey is the reward. In the words of Lao Tzu, "A good traveler has no fixed plan, and is not intent on arriving." At its core, Potts argues, travel is "about being a student of daily life." Every traveler who decided to skip a restaurant visit and go to the local grocery store or farmers' market instead to find ingredients for their own creation will know this. The unique smell of spices, the unfamiliar fruits and vegetables, the exotic fish and meat selection— entirely trivial and boring to the locals—all trigger intense curiosity and creative possibility through the eyes of the traveler.

If we practice it properly, we can take this mindset back from our trip, and become more aware of the details of the everyday life we left at home. Both in contrast to the new things we experience on the road, and also long after the trip is over. If we manage to bring the spirit of travel home with us, we can even experience our hometown as if it was a foreign and exotic place, just like John did on his walk through Austin. If we slow down and look at our surroundings through the curious eyes of the traveler, which are not too different from those of a child engrossed in play, even our daily commute or a stroll through the backyard can become a form of exciting travel. And we might spot creative breakthroughs and brilliant ideas that were right in front of us the entire time, we were just too busy to notice.

STEFAN SAGMEISTER

American Graphic Designer

"We spend about ... the first 25 years of our lives learning, then there is another 40 years that's really reserved for working. And then tacked on at the end of it are about 15 years for retirement. And I thought it might be helpful to basically cut off five of those retirement years and intersperse them in between those working years. That's clearly enjoyable for myself. But probably even more important is that the work that comes out of these years flows back into the company and into society at large, rather than just benefiting a grandchild or two."

Stefan Sagmeister is a man of wild ideas. He co-founded a design firm called Sagmeister & Walsh Inc. in New York City, where his unique approach to graphic design, storytelling, and typography got him noticed—and celebrated—immediately. He has since been able to combine his love for design and music by collaborating with prolific musicians. He has designed album covers for Lou Reed, OK Go, The Rolling Stones, David Byrne, Jay Z, and Aerosmith. But one of his wildest ideas came when he decided to close his design studio for an entire year to go on a sabbatical. After the initial seven years of growing the business, he pressed the pause button on his entire company.

It wasn't a choice he made lightly. "Our design studio was seven years old," he recalls, "the first internet boom in full swing and everybody was in the business of making lots of money. It just seemed unprofessional to close the studio for a year to try out things." His firm was receiving awards, and the booming economy from the birth of the internet had filled their company's inbox with opportunities. So why on earth would he turn the business off for a year? Simply put, Sagmeister had become bored because the work had become repetitive.

Two events pushed him to finally make the move. One day, he was giving a workshop at Cranbrook Art Academy, and he realized that something needed to change. He noticed that the students at the college could spend their entire day just experimenting. That was not the reality for Sagmeister anymore, and he craved those kinds of days back in art school. Next, Ed Fella, a graphic designer many considered the contemporary master of hand-drawn typography, came into the studio and showed Sagmeister notebooks filled with his freewheeling typographic experiments. "That did it," he recalls, "I settled on a date a year in advance, and I called up all my clients." Sagmeister went on sabbatical for an entire year to get back to his experimental ways. And from that day onward, he would take another year off every seven years.

So, was his first year-long sabbatical successful? Sagmeister reported on the TED stage: "I really got close to design again. I had fun. Financially, seen over the long term, it was actually successful. Because of the improved quality, we could ask for higher prices. And probably most importantly, basically everything we've done in the seven years following the first sabbatical came out of thinking of that one single year."

If you are a business owner reading this, the thought of taking a year off from your business probably fills you with anxiety. Sagmeister also had his worries: "I had all sorts of fears, mainly, 'Oh my god, we're going to lose all the clients, we're going to be forgotten, all that we've built in the first seven years will be gone and we'll have to start again,' and none of these fears materialized. We actually found our clients reacted with slight envy, you know, I want to do this, too, and none of my assumptions were true. Lou Reed even moved his release date so we could still do the album [c]over. There were basically no downsides and almost all upsides, including even the strangest things, like I felt there was a financial upside seen over the long term."

Over the years, Sagmeister has arranged three sabbaticals and he has evolved the company's operations in each sabbatical cycle:

> The first sabbatical was the most radical, where we really closed. At that point we had an answering machine that said "call us in a year." The second time was a little milder. We had one designer stay behind to at least answer the phone and finish up some long-term projects, and the third time was almost no interruption because Jessica [Sagmeister's cofounder] decided she didn't want to do a sabbatical, and the studio basically remained open, just with me missing. But I found that all three were completely viable business-wise, that my fears were the biggest the first time around.

If you are a company or a professional whose value is attached to being creative, have you given a thought to what sabbaticals might look like for you? How long could you press pause? What could you do? What experiments or art could you create? Sagmeister found that his sabbaticals led to his firm being more unique:

Because of the sabbaticals, we started to do more things that other design studios don't do, so we completely took ourselves out of this price game. It wasn't like we did the same stuff that other design studios did and clients would just go with the cheapest. So even financially it turned out to be successful, but of course, that was not the reason to do it. The biggest thing I got out of the sabbatical was that I could continue looking at design as a calling rather than a job. And that's a big deal because getting bored with the things that you do is a giant problem in most professions.

It is all too common that we get burned out and fall out of love with our creative work. You might not have a yearlong break in your cards, but your version of a sabbatical could help you fall back in love with your craft. Sagmeister confirms that it is an excellent remedy to when you have lost your passion for the work: "Milton Glaser once told me that his proudest achievement in over 50 years of being a designer is that he is still interested and feels engaged. I myself find ... sabbaticals to be the best cure."

Sagmeister decided to step away from Sagmeister & Walsh Inc., departing in 2019. What will he do next? We don't know the specifics, but we wager that sabbaticals will continue to be a part of his rest ethic.

PRACTICE:

Plan a sabbatical in three steps: #1 Commit. #2 Tell others. #3 Have a plan.

Creating your own sabbatical isn't necessarily easy, but we can take a few notes from Sagmeister on three crucial steps. First, when you decide to take extended time off, you need to commit to it. There will be so many demands on your time, but if you want to make it a reality, dedicate the real estate on your calendar ahead of time. Once you have it on the calendar, you can then set expectations with people who are important to you. By telling other people about your plan to take time off, it helps you hold yourself accountable for your break. Or, as Sagmeister put it, "I told as many people as possible so I couldn't chicken out." Last, time off without a plan will likely be a lot of wasted time. Sagmeister said that in some ways his first sabbatical was rather disastrous because he thought he should do it with no plans: "Without a plan, I reacted to little requests, and I became my own intern." So he suggests you make a list of things you are interested in during your sabbatical. Then put those into a hierarchy and schedule your sabbatical time accordingly.

JOURNEYS OF LEARNING AND SELF-DISCOVERY

"On the road," Potts writes, "you learn to improvise your days, take a second look at everything you see, and not obsess over your schedule." It gets us out of our usual surroundings, a reboot for our mental patterns that have become deeply ingrained by our daily routines. "There's no better opportunity to break old habits, face latent fears, and test out repressed facets of your personality," Potts says. Travel, just like a playground, allows us to redefine and reinvent ourselves. Potts continues: "If you wander with open eyes and simple curiosity, you'll discover … the simple feeling of possibility that hums from every direction as you move from place to place." And many of these possibilities are internal. Much of what we learn on the road is actually about ourselves. Travel and foreign surroundings amplify our own tendencies, providing ideal conditions for self-reflection. Both John and Max had some of the key insights and experiences that led them onto the quest for more time off—and ultimately to write this book—during a time of travel.

Learning, or (re-)engaging in hobbies, can be a great way to use the time on the road. And we shouldn't feel guilty because we "could do it anywhere," or might be missing out on sights or another hour of tanning at the beach. The altered context, as well as different mindsets, will make it a novel experience and help to uncover new wells of creativity. It snaps you out of your routines and makes you alert, both to the bus that almost hit you because you stepped onto a busy road, as well as to new ideas that are sometimes hiding in plain sight. "However you choose to enrich your experience of a place," suggests Potts, "always challenge yourself to try new things and keep learning."

Even working on the road can be a thoroughly enjoyable and insightful experience (and might be a simple necessity for sustained travel). Journalist Charles Kuralt believed that "if you really want to learn about a country, work there." Potts brings up "anti-sabbaticals," short bursts of work between travels that allow you to make enough money to keep traveling. Whether you aim for sustained long-term travel or just a short trip, it's hard to disagree with Potts when he writes that "the first step of vagabonding is simply a matter of making work serve your interests, instead of the other way round. Believe it or not, this is a radical departure from how most people view work and leisure." Far from being restricted to vagabonding, we think this should be the first step of almost anything we do.

One of the books Max enjoyed rereading during his weeks on Syros was *Zorba the Greek* by Nikos Kazantzakis. The titular character, Alexis Zorba, personifies a passion for life. He is full of vices and faults. But despite these, or maybe because of them, he is an incredible teacher, an unconventional sage, and an admirable role model. As Zorba says, "It's all because of doing things by halves, saying things by halves, that the world is in the mess it is in today. Do things properly by God! One good knock for each nail and you'll win through! God hates a halfdevil ten times more than an archdevil!" Take Zorba's words to heart. Don't take half-assed holidays and trips that last a few days, during which you keep checking your work email constantly. Fully disconnect and work on that passion project you wanted to complete for so long. And give yourselves ample time to relax and recharge. And from time to time, screw all that work and just focus entirely on time off. Go ahead and indulge in a few vices. Your life will be all the richer. Don't consider this time wasted or unproductive. It is just as crucial to the creative process as the time you spend consciously working. Work less to get more done. You will be surprised by the creative and productive power you will discover within yourself. And the positive effects will last much longer than the trip itself, long after you have settled back into your normal life. As writer Pico Iyer observed, "We travel, in essence, to become young fools again—to slow down time and get taken in, and fall in love once more." Let's head out there and experience the world—near or far—with the eyes of the traveler. Let's rediscover and reinvent ourselves. Let's slow down time and fall in love with life again!

LUPITA NYONG'O

Kenyan-Mexican Actress

"Finishing an intensive project is kind of like having a hangover, where you're so used to a rigor of existence and then all of a sudden, there's none. I make the time because otherwise, I wouldn't survive."

Lupita Nyong'o played the role of Nakia in the Marvel Cinematic Universe superhero film *Black Panther* (2018). In the movie, her character is a brave spy protecting the fictional East African country of Wakanda. The film grossed over $1.3 billion worldwide and broke numerous box office records, including the highest-grossing film by a black director. It became the ninth-highest-grossing film of all time, the third-highest-grossing film in the US and Canada, and the second-highest-grossing film of 2018.

With the film's success, it seems evident that Nyong'o would be caught up in the hype celebrating a significant milestone in her acting career. Once the film wrapped, you might imagine her jumping from interview to interview, attending parties, or doubling down on talk shows to promote the movie. Or maybe leveraging the momentum by rushing to book another role for a film immediately. But instead, Lupita traveled away from the excitement to have a deliberate reset from the intense work that went into the film. Her destination, however, was far from an extravagant resort.

Soon after *Black Panther* was released, the day after her appearance at the Oscars, she flew to Texas to do a 10-day silent meditation retreat. Meditation was something that intimidated her, but a friend had convinced her to try it out. "It was a gift," she recounts. "I did it for my birthday. And it was the best gift because, the thing is, my job has two main parts. There's the acting, and there's the celebrity. And the celebrity involves a lot of giving. After talking so much, and just expend, expending, expending, to sit with myself and just listen. Our lives are so full of distractions; you go from one distraction to another."

The retreat provided a getaway from many distractions, and this connectivity detox was far from easy for Nyong'o. By attending the retreat, she had forfeited her phone, signed an oath to stay, and didn't have a vehicle: "I was constantly wanting to leave and then daring myself to take one more hour and another hour. And oh my God, it was crazy and beautiful, because, after the 10 days, it wasn't talking that I missed.... The heart of the program is about unclutching from attachments to pleasure and aversion, the idea that we attach to things that we love and to things we dislike. And our identities are built on assembling these things to basically write the stories of our lives, but learning to unclutch from that control makes it easier to live, to exist."

Has a friend told you recently that you seem like you need a break? Maybe you should listen. Those around us can often see us more clearly than we see ourselves. The friend who recommended that Nyong'o go to the retreat must have known that Nyong'o, now a celebrity, would genuinely benefit from releasing many of the pressures and identity hurdles of being famous.

After 10 days of a silent meditation retreat, what does someone do to integrate back into normal life? Again, Nyong'o's friend had a profound yet straightforward recommendation. She told Nyong'o to do herself a favor right after she got out of the retreat and listen to an album she loved:

> I listened to Kendrick Lamar, his album *Damn*. Usually, I listen to music and it's backdrop. But after that retreat, I was able to focus solely on that and for it to fill my existence in that moment. I listened to him on the flight back to New York. I loved the music, but rap sometimes comes at me too fast and I'm not really able to hear it fully. But this time, I heard every word Kendrick Lamar said. I heard the musicality. I heard instruments I'd never heard before. It was like clarity. And I was just, like, wow. I imagine that people sometimes get that from drugs. But it was really nice to get that just from spending time with myself.

Often, we see travel as something done with others. We want the company of our friends or family to share in the memory and sightseeing. There is nothing wrong with that (except for the times you indecisively debate on where the group should get dinner). But have you ever considered a trip alone with limited talking? Traveling this way can make a short domestic trip even feel like another world—it's less about the destination and more about the intention of really getting away. What if you made a playlist of your favorite albums and then walked around a new city or countryside that you have never visited? Maybe this is the celebration you need after completing good work.

PRACTICE:

Try out a silent retreat or listen to a song without multitasking

Nyong'o's silent retreat worked just as effectively as a trip to a foreign land. You don't have to go far to get a high-quality reset. You can treat yourself to a silent retreat after your next big project completes, or you could have a mini silent retreat today—maybe try an abridged version of not talking for a few hours before listening to music alone. Avoid the urge to multitask while you listen to your music. Just close your eyes or stare up at the trees while intently listening. This kind of immersion in a song might take you somewhere a plane ticket can't.

TECHNOLOGY

How many times have you been bored for just a few seconds, or waited in a queue at the supermarket or a cafe, and without even noticing, out of reflex, picked up your phone to check something you didn't care about and probably already had checked several times the last hour? There might be something new and exciting somewhere! A new like, comment, or mention. A new email, news article, or blog post. Anything. "My brain, I realized, wasn't just drifting. It was hungry. I yearned to check e-mail, click links, do some Googling. I wanted to be connected," muses Nicholas Carr in the introduction to his Pulitzer Prize–nominated book *The Shallows: What the Internet Is Doing to Our Brains*. We, too, have experienced this feeling many times, increasingly so in recent years, and it's a safe bet that you have as well. Our brains have become unable to sit still for more than a few seconds, to focus on a single task for long stretches of time, to process any information that can't be presented in a bite-sized snippet. How could they, when our attention is constantly being fragmented by all the distractions surrounding us? There is a simple, but not always easy, solution: take time off from technology. Unplug and disconnect!

While blaming technology for our fragmented attention is easy—and not entirely wrong—we have to dig deeper and consider the problem from a more nuanced perspective. Technology itself is not to blame. It is the way we use technology that's messed up. John and Max have both spent large parts of their careers working on creating new technologies and are still very positive about the possibilities and progress it offers. We wouldn't want to live without technology. The key is to use technology *in support* of what we want to do, to choose the right technologies and stay mindful of which ones to use, and how, and which to avoid. But this is easier said than done. The human brain wasn't designed for the constant onslaught of information that modern technology provides.

YOUR MIND ON TECHNOLOGY

The earliest "brains," starting all the way back from our single-celled ancestors, were nothing more than very simple machines turning perceptions into actions. A positive or negative environmental signal got perceived and processed, and then the corresponding action got initiated. There was no planning or goal setting, just pure reactivity. But as brains evolved and became more sophisticated, not only did our perceptions and actions become much more complex, but we also developed the ability to think ahead. Some argue that what makes us uniquely human is our ability to slip a pause into the perception-action cycle and let executive functions take the wheel. This allows us to choose our actions based on evaluation and decision, not just impulse and reflex (at least some of the time). Ingenuity and creativity never result from reactive behavior—they require us to pause and consider the bigger picture.

The interplay of the ancient bottom-up and more recent top-down processes is extremely complex. Unfortunately, it is also responsible for much of our recent struggles with attention and focus. As neuroscientist Adam Gazzaley and psychologist Larry Rosen point out in their book *The Distracted Mind*, the issue is not caused by modern technology, but a "fundamental vulnerability of our brain." Modern technology just happens to specifically trigger this vulnerability. It has not created the problem, but it has made it much, much worse.

Gazzaley and Rosen specifically call the problem "interference" and identify the two main processes behind it: "distractions from irrelevant information and interruptions by our attempts to simultaneously pursue multiple goals." The source for distractions and interruptions can be the same, but they are distinct in how we handle them, and each involves different brain mechanisms. But in both cases, the resulting interference can affect every part of our lives, from our mood and emotions all the way to our creativity and mental abilities. And usually, this effect is negative.

One of the most powerful tools we have in our mental arsenal is selective attention. It's this process that allows us to directly influence the perception-action cycle and deliberately set goals and act on them. But selective attention requires a high level of cognitive control. And compared to our complex goal-setting ability, our cognitive control, the way we "distribute, divide, and sustain attention," is actually quite primitive. While the prefrontal cortex, the part that is most responsible for cognitive control, has evolved more than any other part compared to our ancestors, it is still true that, as Gazzaley and Rosen note, "in many ways, we are ancient brains in a high-tech world." And one thing these ancient brains simply cannot do is multitask. On a neural level, we are not parallel processing, but network switching! "This act of switching," they write, "whether we make the decision to switch or not, diminishes our performance on a task." In a world of more and more interruptions, we are more and more likely to engage in task switching, whether we want to or not.

Unfortunately, task switching is selective attention's worst enemy. Two distinct processes are required for attention: focusing on one thing and ignoring all other things. These are not just opposites of the same, but two fundamentally distinct processes. Both are active and require resources from our brains. Surprisingly, experiments have shown that ignoring irrelevant information is even more important for remembering than our focus on the thing itself. And the part of our brain responsible for deciding whether to process or ignore instincts and reflex-based stimuli is particularly being pushed more and more to its limits. Early humans might have encountered a jaguar in a bush once a day. A hundred years ago, people might step on a street and have a car honk at them every few hours. But today, modern technology is bombarding us with potentially important "warning" triggers almost constantly. And the more we distribute our focus, the fewer benefits we gain from selective attention (if we can call it selective at all anymore). It's time to once again reclaim our attention and consciously take time off from distractions.

As cartoonist and educator Lynda Berry remarks, "The phone

gives us a lot, but it takes away three key elements of discovery: loneliness, uncertainty, and boredom. Those have always been where creative ideas come from." If we want to create, solve, impact, and do meaningful work, we need to reduce distractions, and find balance between our time on and time off from technology. Mind wandering—that solitary process so crucial to creativity—needs this downtime. Constant task switching and interruption allow our mind to wander only a few paces before being forcefully pulled back to their starting point. Instead of dragging our mind by the collar from one quick reaction to the next, we need to let it run free for extended periods of time.

But to do this requires good cognitive control, which can change all the time and depends on many factors, including stress, sleep, alcohol, and age, to name just a few. Particularly sleep deprivation, as we have encountered already, has one of the worst effects on sustained attention. And as cognitive control requires resources that get depleted, like a muscle that gets tired, the more we challenge it, the more we engage in multitasking and surround ourselves with distractions, the easier we make it to fall even deeper into this trap of scattered attention. The fact that our interaction with technology is becoming more and more multisensory, and as a result, even more attention grabbing, further worsens this issue. As a result, "we seem to have lost the ability to single task," Gazzaley and Rosen worry. "We have lost our awareness of what is necessary and what is simply reflexive responding as though prodded by a sharp stick." And the sharp sticks of the high-tech world are all but skewering our ancient brains.

DISTRACTION ENGINEERING

The fact that we ended up in this situation was not pure coincidence. To some extent, a lot of technology was carefully engineered to act this way. As Tristan Harris, the director and cofounder of the Center for Humane Technology, notes, big-tech companies are in a "race to the bottom of the brain stem." They employ droves of psychologists and clever product designers trying to make sure that their product is more attention grabbing than the next company's, get us to engage more often with their app, or makesus return more and more frequently to their website. Our attention is their ad revenue. By bypassing—or deliberately weakening—our cognitive control and appealing to our ancient instinct and reflexes, they want to get us hooked. And they are succeeding! How many times have you already checked your email, Facebook, or Instagram since starting this chapter? We challenge you to read the rest of it uninterrupted. Can you resist the tempting call of distraction?

Until the 21st century, we thought that only substances could cause real addiction. But over the last one or two decades, we have realized that behavioral addictions are just as real. One key force behind technology's addictive power is "intermittent positive reinforcement," rewards that are provided on a variable and unpredictable schedule. Studies have shown (and the experience of every casino owner or gambling addict has confirmed) that rewards delivered at random release much more dopamine than if the pattern was predictable. So every time we post something online, we are playing the lottery, waiting to see how many likes, comments, or followers we get. This element of randomness also explains our craving for checking our phones at the slightest hint of boredom. There might be something exciting waiting for us. Maybe. We won't know until we check!

In his book of the same name, Neil Postman defines "Technopoly" as a society in which there is almost no discussion of trade-offs of new technology. If it is new, it is good, and we should use it. He speaks of the deification of technology and the "Cult of the Internet." And many of us are living in this kind of technopoly, reinforcing it constantly. The instant messaging service Slack, which is widely used throughout organizations, proclaims through its tagline to be "Where work happens." But is it really? What kind of work? Could it be mostly shallow busywork? In his book *Deep Work*, Cal Newport laments that instead of performing the specialized tasks we were trained and hired to do, many knowledge workers have become nothing more than "human information routers." In some ways, Slack and other similar tools simply allow us to take visible busyness online, and it's part of why they are so popular and successful.

The developers behind these tools have the factor of novelty and our strong desire for visible busyness on their side. In a technopoly, questioning the new can be akin to heresy, or as Newport puts it, suggesting disconnectivity in an internet-centric age is like flag burning, "desecration, not debate." Yahoo's former CEO Marissa Mayer infamously banned employees from working from home because they didn't log in to check their emails often enough. How could they possibly be doing anything useful when they weren't visibly busy and connected?

A major force that encourages addiction is our drive for social approval. We are hardwired to crave it. When we were still living in small and close-knit tribal communities, it used to be imperative for our survival. Now, the like button provides instant access to social approval at any time, and we desperately crave this attention. This ancient drive also explains our urge to instantly respond to all messages or emails we receive. Again, we still have that deep-seated fear of becoming tiger food if we don't respond to the tribe's social prodding, and in some company cultures this is unfortunately not too far from the truth (figuratively, of course—unless you happen to work for some James Bond-style supervillain). Being fully aware of the science and our fundamental fears and cravings, developers carefully designed many technologies to capitalize on these addictive properties.

TRISTAN HARRIS

American Computer Scientist and Design Philosopher

"We want technology that cares about helping us spend our time, and our lives, well—not seducing us into the most screen time, always-on interruptions or distractions."

"The ultimate freedom is a free mind, and we need technology that's on our team to help us live, feel, think and act freely."

"When I was about five years old," recounts Tristan Harris, "my mom gave me a Macintosh LC II and I was hooked.… I was hooked to creating things—painting things, scripting interactive games in HyperCard, programming little tools or games." Many of us who are old enough to have experienced technology before smartphones and constant connectivity might have similar positive memories. But we can probably also relate with Harris as he continues, saying, "I feel constantly lured into distractions. I get sucked endlessly into email, distracting websites. I get bulldozed by interruptive text messages, back and forth scheduling, or find myself scrolling a website in a trance at 1am." What happened? "Why is our experience of the

Internet and computing going this way? Towards distraction, and away from empowerment?" Harris thinks he knows the answer: "It's because we live in an attention economy."

While most people might have an opinion on this topic, few are as well informed as Harris. He studied at the Stanford Persuasive Technology Lab and later applied his knowledge as a designer at Google (after his own company, Aperture, was acquired by them). But he quickly became concerned about the tactics employed by the designers trying to hack attention. He worried about where the technology industry as a whole was going: "The attention economy means that no matter what a technology company aims to create ... they win by getting people to spend time. What starts as an honest competition to make useful things that people spend time on, devolves into a race to the bottom of the brain stem to maximize the time we spend." Harris was outspoken about his concerns from the very beginning, which later led to him becoming a design ethicist at Google, tasked with steering design decisions in ethical and humane directions. When he eventually left Google, he became director and cofounder of the Center for Humane Technology and cofounder of the Time Well Spent movement. Today he is still at the forefront of fighting for more thoughtful design of technology. In a profile, *the Atlantic* magazine called Harris "the closest thing Silicon Valley has to a conscience."

It's easy to vilify big-tech companies, the likes of Facebook and Google, but most of them did not set out to create the attention economy we find ourselves in now. "No one profits when millions check their email and nothing's there," says Harris. "Neither did Apple and Google's designers want phones to work like slot machines. It emerged by accident." However, these companies now find their profits directly tied to catching our attention and, in many cases, will deliberately exploit our brains' vulnerability to get it. Harris argues that similar to "organic" labels in the food industry, we should introduce a "time well spent" label to certify software that helps us spend our time better instead of just competing for our attention: "We want technology that cares about helping us spend our time, and our lives, well—not seducing us into the most screen time, always-on interruptions or distractions." In other words, we want technology that fosters high-quality leisure and supports our rest ethic instead of eroding it.

Harris wants to stress that the Time Well Spent movement is not a movement against technology: "It is not a universal, normative view of how people should spend their time. It is not saying that screen time is bad, or that we should turn it all off. It is not saying that specific categories of apps (like social media or games) are bad." It is, however, a movement that encourages both consumers and developers to make more conscious choices about how they design and interact with technology.

Designers can be evasive when pressed on this issue, arguing that they simply provide the service, and if users want to use it nonstop and in a distracting and interrupting way, that's entirely their own choice. But that's an easy way out, and the reality is not that simple. If we create apps that deliberately hook people, we are at least partially responsible for these usage behaviors. It's time to acknowledge this responsibility and develop apps and services that empower people to spend their time in the best way possible. And as consumers, rather than taking the passive role, we should make conscious choices and reward only those apps with our attention that deserve and respect it, rather than waste it.

PRACTICE:

Assess whether the technologies you use deserve a "time well spent" label

As Harris points out, the game—at least currently—is rigged against us, and it's not (entirely) our fault that we get distracted by the litany of notifications competing for our attention. But that doesn't mean we should give up all responsibility. And we can put pressure on developers. So, go through all the services and apps you use and consciously think whether each of them would deserve a "time well spent" label. If not, get rid of them. Either find an alternative that respects your time more or accept that you probably didn't need this particular service in the first place.

FORAGING FOR INFORMATION

The foraging behavior of animals has been studied for centuries, and we have come up with mathematical models and theories that describe and explain optimal foraging behavior. The most prevalent model is the marginal value theorem (MVT), first proposed by evolutionary ecologist Eric Charnov in 1976. It assumes that resources occur in discrete patches, and describes when an animal should move on from the current source, which gets gradually depleted and offers diminishing returns. Essentially, an optimal forager moves on when the rate of return in the current source drops below the cost to make a move to the next source.

Gazzaley and Rosen argue that our information consumption is also a form of foraging. And the MVT can be applied to this as well. Deep down, we are information-seeking creatures. Just like hunger makes us gather food, we have an inherent drive that makes us seek out new information. Novelty triggers a sense of reward in our brain. Evolutionarily, this was a good force to help us explore new environments. And for most of our history, information resources were similar to food resources. They were scarce and came with a high cost of switching, even until fairly recently. The newspaper came once a day. Radio news aired every hour, and there were few channels available. And our direct personal encounters were limited unless we were willing to walk over to our neighbors, or even further, to strike up a new conversation. As a result, we truly made use of each resource and gave it its full attention. The cost of moving on was simply too high.

But now, on our smartphones with dozens of apps and the infinite depths of the internet at our fingertips, the cost of switching to a new information source has essentially come down to zero. It takes less than a second to switch apps, so we hop from one source to another, so fast that our attention can't even keep up with it. And it gets worse. In animal models, the optimal time to stay in a source is mainly influenced by external factors, such as how many resources remain in the current source or how far away the next source is. But our information foraging is also influenced by internal forces.

Anxiety and boredom especially cannot be ignored. Their influences can lead to even shorter times in a source than would be optimal. As a result, Gazzaley and Rosen worry that "too much important information is being 'left on the table.'"

The new factors provided by technology leave our information-foraging behavior far from optimal and have led us to a paradoxical situation. We have more information available to us than ever, yet our ability to absorb this information seems to be lower than ever. We are like little squirrels sitting on an ever-increasing pile of stashed acorns—saved articles, open browser tabs, endless group chats—but are somehow starving because we have lost the ability to digest those acorns. Our constant craving for information and optimization of information access has outpaced our own capacity to consume them. The pile is about to collapse, and it's threatening to drown us in a flood of information, rapidly eroding our remaining ability to be creative and get things done.

ATTENTION DEFICIT SOCIETY

We have already encountered the high cost of task switching and the toll it takes on creative mind wandering and selective attention. But the problem only gets worse. When switching between tasks, attention does not immediately follow. A residue of it remains on the previous task, and the effects of this are, in fact, devastating to our productivity, as Sophie Leroy notes in her aptly titled study "Why Is It So Hard to Do My Work?" on the challenge of attention residue when switching between work tasks. As Leroy describes, the effect is particularly bad if the distraction-creating task cannot be fully completed, such as glancing at an incoming email or Slack message without immediately answering it or resolving the issue raised. The mind is left with some attention on an unfinished task. And the more intense the attention residue, the worse the performance on subsequent tasks. When we switch between two tasks, we suffer both a time- delay as well as reduced performance on either task.

Even without immediate distractions, sustaining attention has its limitations, especially on "boring" low-stimulus tasks. And our threshold for boredom has dramatically gone down. As Gazzaley and Rosen remark, we "seem to have lost the ability to simply do nothing and endure boredom. This leaves little time for reflection, deep thinking, or even just simply sitting back and letting our random thoughts drive us places we might not have gone while immersed in direct thinking." We have all but banished the long-leashed mind wandering provided by extended solitude that is so crucial for creativity and ideation. The rapid reward cycles of modern media and apps specifically designed to catch us in their tight reward loops have fundamentally altered our boredom profiles, leading to a much quicker onset of boredom, more anxiety, and an ever-increasing fear of solitude.

In general, even excluding factors like exercise and eating habits, extensive media and technology use have been found to be clear predictors of ill health, physical and mental, in children and young adults. While younger generations estimate that they are better at multitasking—and engage in it more often—the cognitive effects are just as bad for them. Maybe even worse, considering they are in a stage of their life focused on learning and growth. Long uninterrupted stretches of concentration are essential for learning any new skill or wrapping our heads around complex concepts. Only deliberate, focused practice leads to the reinforcement of neural pathways, while distracted attention causes too many circuits firing simultaneously for any one of them to strengthen. Becoming a master of multitasking might feel like a superior skill, but in the long run, it is inferior (unless, that is, we practice it in the slow, deliberate, and distraction-free form of Tim Harford's slow-motion multitasking, or Søren Kierkegaard's crop rotation). Constant attention switching has a lasting negative impact on the brain. True deep work and deep thought become impossible.

HOW TO DISCONNECT AND PRACTICE DIGITAL MINIMALISM

When trying to reclaim our attention, we are, as Newport writes, "waging a David and Goliath battle against institutions that are both impossibly rich and intent on using this wealth to stop you from winning." But just like David, we can outsmart the Goliaths of Google, Facebook, and the like. There are two complementary approaches we can take to win the battle. We can change our brain to boost cognitive control, as well as change our behavior and environment to make distractions less likely.

The long-held notion that the adult brain is static and doesn't develop any further has now been completely discredited. Our brain retains its neuroplasticity throughout our entire life. So it is never too late to start improving our brain and boost cognitive control. The tools to do so are numerous and ever increasing. We are even on the brink of exciting new technologies, such as neurofeedback or transcranial magnetic stimulation (TMS), that directly (and noninvasively) stimulate nerve cells in our brain to enhance anything from sleep to mood, and cognitive control. But we don't have to rely solely on modern technology for this. There are also a number of old-school and low-tech options to improve our brain, many of which we have already encountered in earlier chapters.

Simply putting ourselves in new and unfamiliar situations and environments—for example, while traveling or at play—has been a proven way to stimulate brain plasticity. Mounting evidence is showing that a regular mindfulness practice—such as meditation or reflection—can directly improve our cognitive control. And so can the simple act of exposing ourselves to nature. Finally, one of the most well-studied enhancers of cognitive control—as well as overall mental and physical well-being—is exercise. All these forms of time off are thoroughly researched methods to boost our cognitive control and combat distraction. Noble leisure is arguably one of the best tools for staying mentally sharp.

If we combine this with modifying our behavior, we stand a good chance of breaking our chains of distraction. The first step here is to improve our metacognition, becoming aware of the problem—and acknowledging that we might suffer from it—and the high cost of task switching. We hope that reading this has already taken you there. Next, we need to develop what Newport calls a "philosophy of technology use," a set of rules for which technologies we allow into our lives and which we don't. We need to determine which digital tools we actually want to use, and not just blindly consume.

In *Digital Minimalism*, Newport urges us to "focus your online time on a small number of carefully selected and optimized activities that strongly support things you value, and then happily miss out on everything else." Like so much of time off, it is about being conscious about how we spend our time and attention. Every new tool or technology should be carefully evaluated, and only if it adds a lot of extra value—and it is up to us to define what value means—should we adopt it.

We often have this false perception that "general purpose" equals "productivity." But restricting capabilities available at any one time increases our focus and, as a result, our productivity. Even before modern technology, Henry David Thoreau already summed it up well in the classic *Walden* when he wrote that "the cost of a thing is the amount of what I will call life which is required to be exchanged for it, immediately or in the long run." Even if technology seems somewhat useful, it might require us to exchange more "life" for it than we will get back in return. How much life are you willing to exchange for that shiny new app you see in the app store?

Going a step further, most people only consider what technologies to adopt, but not how to use them. Social media can be a wonderful tool if used well, but it can also completely scatter our attention and make us miserable. One simple but powerful trick is to remove social media apps from your phone. You can still access them on your computer and get all their benefits, but without the constant distraction and availability, not to mention that many of the addictive features are specifically designed for the mobile experience. In general, anything that makes it more difficult for us to quickly switch attention is a good idea. Newport, who happens to be a computer science professor, says we should set up "computers that are general purpose in the long run but are effectively single purpose in any given moment."

The biggest culprit in making our computers multipurpose (as well as arguably one of the most amazing technologies if used right) is the internet. Using apps and tools like Freedom (which was involved in writing this book) that restrict internet access for set periods of time can be extremely effective—and surprisingly painful at the beginning, as we noticed, really showing us just how addicted we are to the internet. As any recovering addict will tell you, going cold turkey is extremely unpleasant and rarely successful in the long term, but if you build deliberate stretches of time off from technology, you can gradually recover your lost freedom.

It might initially be painful—and run counter to what we are used to and (think) is expected of us—but we can disconnect. We can turn off notifications. We can log out from our email accounts, Slack, and Facebook. We can even switch off our internet connection, put our phones in airplane mode, and turn off our devices entirely.

TIFFANY SHLAIN

American Entrepreneur and Filmmaker

"One day a week, we turn off the technology in our lives. It has been profoundly life-changing for us. It resets my soul each week. You end up doing all of the things you don't make the time to do when you have delicious screens in front of you."

When was the last time you navigated around a city with a physical map, handwritten notes, or printed directions? When was the last time you went 24 hours without interacting with any digital screens? For Tiffany Shlain, it was likely this past weekend.

For many years, Shlain and her family turn off all screens for one day a week for what she calls a "Tech Shabbat." Every Friday night, they unplug from all of their technologies and don't power them up again until 24 hours later. The practice of going nondigital for a full day gives her more quality time with her family and with herself. The weekly recalibration has also allowed her to not take technology for granted.

The notion of taking one day a week off from responsibilities and work is an old idea. The Shabbat is related to the concept of Sabbath and sabbatical. Sabbath is a day of religious observance and abstinence from work, celebrated by Jews from Friday evening to Saturday evening, and by most Christians on Sunday. In our always-connected world, it's an excellent time to take some inspiration from this religious practice and apply it to our technology relationships.

So how did her family start practicing the Tech Shabbat?

When she was first dating her partner, Ken Goldberg, he made it clear that he practiced Shabbat. He told Shlain that he doesn't work on Saturdays because it is Shabbat and that this day off is essential to him. She was intrigued, given that he was a highly respected robotics professor who seemed too busy to consistently take time off. Shlain herself founded The Webby Awards, a recognition for outstanding content on the internet, and as an entrepreneur and technology enthusiast had a hard time unplugging. Goldberg's deliberate practice was attractive to Shlain.

They eventually got married and had kids. Like most of us, they upgraded to smartphones and were soon engulfed by the addictive supercomputers in their pockets ready to feed them endless hours of information and enticing distractions.

In 2009, Shlain's father died and her daughter was born within days of each other. During this rare and deep time in life, she became sensitive to technology interrupting the present moment in some of the most important days of her life. During her grieving period, an organization she is a part of, called Reboot, did a National Day of Unplugging, a 24-hour respite from technology. When they asked her to join them, she was ready to explore more of life without devices: "So there I was, unmoored by losing one of my strongest connections, my father. I looked at the other people I loved deeply in my life and knew I had to do things differently if I wanted to live in a way I felt good about. We were ready to bring some presence back. The day that we participated in the National Day of Unplugging was so good and clean and present, we decided to make it a weekly practice."

Imagine a full 24-hour period without digital devices and screens. With newly open eyes, your own town or city can become a foreign country that you can explore. By not relying on your GPS, your inner explorer will pay attention to your surroundings more in order to set waypoints. When you can't do a Google search for somewhere to go, you are likely to ask a stranger or barista for recommendations. You can discover that the humans around you are actually some of the most amazing technology ever created!

Going offline takes a bit of preparation. Shlain prepares her friends and family to let them know they won't be digital for 24 hours. She sometimes prints or writes down their schedule, as well as phone numbers they might need. After the preparation is done, her family has a ritual of collectively turning off their devices at a specific time, or when the sun drops on Friday.

So what could you possibly do without screens for 24 hours? Shlain recommends reading a book, gardening, slow cooking a meal, visiting neighbors by foot, exploring and inventing games like a kid again, thinking through questions without being able to look up answers on the internet, or going on a really long date, as John did on his first Tech Shabbat.

During a podcast interview with Shlain, he was inspired to try out an official Tech Shabbat, so he and his girlfriend decided to give it a go. The one thing they both found to be incredible was how time seemed to slow down. They realized how all of our relationships could benefit from slowing down the moments we have together. Intentionally putting away the distracting devices for an extended amount of time is a sure way to foster more quality Time Off.

PRACTICE:

Do a micro Tech Shabbat

Most of us work with screens. But when was the last time you unplugged from the world of pixels to enjoy this other beautiful world that's out there? Yes, there is plenty of inspiration to be found online, but the majority of what you see online is a reference to something outside of the digital world. So give yourself some time to explore the original source, and discover new depths of experience and inspiration. Twenty-four hours without your devices sound too intense? Take baby steps and try an afternoon or morning Tech Shabbat. Rather than the 24-hour period between Friday night and Saturday night, go without devices after lunch or just for the morning. The time off from the screen will help you cultivate inspiration for when you log back on.

FILLING THE VOID

Improving our cognitive control and developing good habits around technology use are both important. Once we've done that, we might expose an underlying problem. We might discover that our addiction to technology was actually just a plaster that was covering up another issue. "For many people," Newport writes, "their compulsive phone use papers over a void created by a lack of a well-developed leisure life." Our lack of high-quality leisure "leaves a void that would be near unbearable if confronted, but that can be ignored with the help of digital noise." Again, we arrive at the problem of boredom due to us having forgotten how to really practice time off. As social psychologist Erich Fromm remarked, "Boredom is anxiety about absence of meaning in a person's activities or circumstances." We need to intentionally fill the newly created free time with meaning, or we risk quickly undoing our positive changes again and falling back to mindless technology use to avoid confronting the void. Now, maybe more than ever, do we need to return to Aristotle's noble leisure, to fill the void and give us a powerful—and meaningful—counterbalance to the ever-increasing pull of tempting distractions.

We can even use technology to do this. As Newport rightly says, "The internet is fueling a leisure renaissance of sorts by providing the average person more leisure options than ever before." And he urges us not to avoid anything digital per se, but simply to replace our prevalent state of passive consumption with more meaningful pursuits that facilitate high-quality leisure. He recommends that a lot of this should be tied to physical objects and skills in the real world or direct personal interactions. But the internet can be one of the best ways to develop such skills and learn new things. YouTube full of not just of cat videos, but also great instructional videos that teach skills we can apply in the real world. And as we get absorbed into a new hobby or skill, we dramatically decrease boredom and FOMO, which helps us stay focused on the pursuit, rather than engaging in constant task switching. In this way, by developing a more satisfying leisure life and cultivating our rest ethic, we directly improve the way we use technology.

And using technology in the right way, supported and balanced by time off and noble leisure, will be the competitive advantage of the companies, professionals, and creatives who will thrive in the future of work.

BRUNELLO CUCINELLI

Italian Fashion Entrepreneur

"Do you think that during the first five hours of the day you are the same as you are in the last five hours? No way. You're tired, and if you're tired, you stop listening, and the decisions you make are risky."

It is lunchtime in the town of Solomeo, Italy. At a cafe looking into the emerald hills of Umbria, relaxed people are enjoying a long family-style lunch. They are tearing apart warm bread, enjoying several courses of nourishing plates, and sipping wine. The sounds of chuckles and chatter are slightly louder than the beautiful Italian guitar playing in the background.

This description may sound like a scene from a dreamy summer vacation in Europe. However, it is just another daily lunch for the staff at Brunello Cucinelli, a fashion house well known for making luxury cashmere sweaters and over $450 million a year in revenues.

Cucinelli's staff thrive in a working culture that centers on human dignity and growing the soul rather than taking from it. Unlike many executives, Cucinelli isn't glued to his phone to check an overloaded email inbox. He refuses to let anyone at his company work around the clock. Rather than forwarding demanding emails to his team, he is likely thinking about how he will continue to preserve the cultural allowances the company offers to employees so they can learn new crafts and skills. He prioritizes a calm and creative workplace culture, because it ultimately pours into the beautiful fashion products they create. The company's code of ethics states that "'overall quality' is the result of each person's own internal quality.... The quality of life, emotional relations and the personal lives of workers are ... values to be safeguarded."

"If I make you overwork, I have stolen your soul," says Cucinelli. What would be possible when more leaders start to think about their workforce like this? Cucinelli's business practices are a good contrast to the purely number-driven, human-maximization mindset of many other leaders, and there is a lot to learn from a man whose business keeps growing at a healthy rate.

Otium! This Latin concept, being roughly translatable as the time off used to enjoy rest, contemplation, feasting, other leisurely endeavors, or simply the act of doing nothing, is at the heart of Brunello Cucinelli's personal philosophy. "In the winter on a Sunday afternoon, I can spend six hours in front of the fireplace, just looking at the flames and thinking. In the evening, I'm drunk with beautiful thoughts," he explains.

To Cucinelli, being away from work is an essential part of being better at work: "In this company, you cannot send emails after 5:30pm, when the company closes for the evening. The morning after, your rate of creativity is sky high." His style of leadership is treating people well. Fostering a beautiful culture is as crucial to Cucinelli as the timeless clothes his company crafts.

Cucinelli reminds us that "work, regardless of its nature and kind, should never encroach upon people's life, their rest, the time they need to find a balance between their soul and their body." Grazie, Cucinelli!

PRACTICE:

Lead others into a fair working life to unlock quality

What are you aiming for, quality or quantity? If increasing the quality of your work or workplace community is your goal—and let's be honest, that's the only way to not end up in a race to the bottom—you can learn from Cucinelli's leadership approach of protecting human dignity. Have you thought about when the workday is over for you and your team and then honor that? What kind of cultural allowance could you put in place so that your team feels supported in becoming more creative and interesting, rather than treating them like machines? By respecting your team's quality of life, you are also enabling the quality of your collective work to soar. It might not seem like a big thing, but becoming more conscious of your work habits will help you invest more otium into your culture.

THE FUTURE OF WORK

In March 2016, the computer science world was in shock. AlphaGo, an AI program developed by DeepMind Technologies, now a part of Google, beat the Korean grandmaster Lee Sedol four-to-one at the ancient strategy game of Go. At first glance, this victory might not be too surprising or particularly noteworthy to many people. After all, the chess grandmaster Garry Kasparov had been beaten by IBM's Deep Blue almost 20 years prior to that fateful Go match. However, the implications were quite different. At each turn of the game, chess has considerably fewer options and variations than Go. A sufficiently powerful computer can do an exhaustive search through the branching tree of possible chess moves and pick the best one. There was nothing particularly smart about Deep Blue; it was simply a very powerful computing machine using a brute-force search.

Go is different. It is played on a larger board, and with much simpler rules. But far from making it an easier game, this simplicity leads to a much higher emergent complexity. With fewer restrictions, the number of possible moves at each turn is far greater. After only the first two moves of a game, there are already 129,960 possible board variations, compared to just 400 in chess—and this difference keeps growing exponentially with every additional turn. In fact, the number of all possible variations on a Go board, a number with 171 digits, is vastly greater than the number of atoms in the entire universe (with our best estimate being at around a measly 80-digit figure). Even for the most powerful computer we can imagine, a brute-force search is out of the question. To beat Lee, AlphaGo had to genuinely outsmart him. Just like a human player, it had to decide which ideas to pursue in its "mind," and which to abandon. It required true artificial *intelligence*, not just the perceived intelligence of raw computing power executing predefined rules. And the fact that DeepMind had developed this kind of intelligence in their system, and done so many years sooner than most researchers had expected, shook the computer science (and Go) community.

One of the people responsible for this breakthrough was David Silver, principal research scientist at DeepMind and leader of the team behind AlphaGo. After the victory against Lee, rather than calling the problem solved, Silver and his team immediately tried to improve the AI even further. One follow-up version, which was both more powerful and more general (also being able to play other games like chess), was AlphaZero. And its origin story holds an important lesson for all of us. In an interview with Lex Fridman, Silver recalls: "I can tell you exactly the moment where the idea for AlphaZero occurred to me." It turns out, it was a moment of time off.

"It actually occurred to me on honeymoon," Silver explains. "I was in my most fully relaxed state, really enjoying myself, and just 'bing,' the algorithm for AlphaZero just appeared in its full form." Silver believes that it wasn't a coincidence that the idea came to him while at rest: "I think there's maybe a lesson there for researchers who are kind of too deeply embedded in their research and working 24/7 to try and come up with the next idea." We agree with Silver and believe his advice reaches beyond just the research community: to come up with big ideas in any domain, we need to step back from our work from time to time. Taking time off is how we'll stay competitive and relevant in a future where AI is not only besting us at some of our games but also in some of our jobs.

KAI-FU LEE

Taiwanese-born American AI Expert, Venture Capitalist, and Writer

"We certainly don't exist to do routine work. We perhaps exist to create. We perhaps exist to love."

"I take my vacations when my kids have time, not when I have time."

For much of his career, Kai-Fu Lee worked like a machine and prided himself on his relentless work ethic. He held a strong distaste for leisure and relaxation, seeing them as lazy vices, and it was common for Lee to have eighty-hour workweeks. He'd routinely wake at two in the morning to address his emails and respond to international colleagues, a signal to them that he was working diligently. And his achievements seemed to justify his efforts. In college, Lee developed Sphinx, the first-ever speaker-independent continuous speech recognition system. After that, he led AI developments at Apple, Microsoft, and Google before starting the venture capital fund now known as Sinovation Ventures.

Looking back at his habits, Lee admits his work ethic was maniacal: "For centuries, human beings have filled their days by working every waking hour, trading their time and sweat for money, shelter, and food," he reflects. "We've built deeply entrenched cultural belief systems and values around this exchange, and many of us have been conditioned to derive our sense of self-worth from the act of daily work. I'll readily admit that I was a willing victim of this workaholic brainwashing." For a long time, Lee put his work ethic ahead of his love for his family, but that would change in 2013, when doctors gave Lee months to live after a stage IV lymphoma diagnosis.

"I was suddenly faced with the real likelihood that I may have only a few months to live," Lee recalls. "During that time of ultimate uncertainty, I did a lot of thinking. I came to see how foolish it was to base my self-worth entirely on my accomplishments at work. My priorities were completely out of order. I neglected my family. My father had passed away. My mother had dementia and no longer recognized me. My daughters had grown up." Luckily Lee's cancer is now in remission, but during treatment, he had some transformative insights that can give us a glimpse at humanity's purpose in a world of AI—a world that Lee himself helped create.

In an interview with Andrew Zuckerman, Lee shared his thoughts: "I think my own illness made me think that during the Industrial Revolution we became programmed to work hard because the Industrial Revolution actually replaced artisan jobs with assembly line jobs." But as we have seen, this thinking did not stop at the Industrial Revolution, far outliving its applicability and leading Lee, and so many other people, down a path of obsessive busyness and overwork. "I had made myself into a machine," he realized. But it no longer had to be that way. AI could do the work meant for machines. And Lee is ardent that we will soon see machine learning and robotics create tens of trillions of dollars of wealth for mankind.

Tens of trillions of dollars. That is no trivial amount. This kind of technological progress is going to redesign economies across the globe while also remaking the employment landscape. These huge shifts are on the horizon, and as Lee points out, they will leave us with more time off than ever: "We're about to see many routine jobs being replaced so we have more free time on our hands." But how are we to reinvest this time?

"People are meant to do something else," says Lee. "Our specialty is in our creativity, our ability to deal strategically, our connections and compassion with other people, and our love. These are the things that I should do, and these are the things that I should help get other people to realize is what they should do. Not the routine work. Finding a way to let go of the routine work and finding what you love and embrace this creativity or compassion—I think therein lies humanity's hope of not only being able to survive AI and coexist with AI, but find a better definition or meaning for humanity going forward."

His brush with death gave Lee a fresh perspective on the very technology field he has worked so hard to improve. He believes an emphasis on love and creativity can apply to our relationship with artificial intelligence. In his book *AI Superpowers*, he reminds us that "we invent things. We celebrate creation. We're very creative about scientific process, about curing diseases, about writing books, writing movies, creative about telling stories, doing a brilliant job in marketing. This is our creativity that we should celebrate, and that's perhaps what makes us human." Lee also emphasizes that AI "will never be able to replace compassionate jobs." And he feels optimistic. Routine tasks "are not what makes us human. What makes us human is the capacity to love."

Given Lee's realization that human love and creativity will fuel our future in concert with smarter machines, he encourages all of us to imagine an abundant and enjoyable path forward for the future of work: "If we were to reconstruct the world from scratch, we'd be very happy human beings because we'd have machines do these repetitive and routine tasks. We can then elevate ourselves to be thinking, inventing, creating, socializing, having fun, and getting hobbies." And in many ways, this reconstruction of creative work is already happening. If Aristotle were alive today and could see our technological progress, we believe he would have viewed this exciting moment in time as humanity's opportunity to return to noble leisure.

The impact of AI is no longer a moonshot idea. Real commercial applications are being deployed today, and the future of work has the opportunity to be creative rather than cumbersome. Lee asserts that "what's here today is the super optimizers that can do a better job than humans in picking stocks, in making loans, in doing customer support, in doing telemarketing, in doing assembly line work, in doing assistance work, in doing broker's work, in doing paralegal work, and doing it better than humans. They're taking those over and freeing human time, allowing us to do what we really love and what we do best. That's the opportunity of a lifetime, not this dystopia of computers becoming superintelligent." Let's embrace this opportunity and cultivate our rest ethic now—investing in our creative potential and preparing ourselves for the post-AI job market.

PRACTICE:

Audit your creative skill set

Reflect on your work for a moment: Which parts of your job can be automated thanks to emerging technologies? Which require creativity? Now consider your skill set and where you invest more of your resources (time, effort, money). Is it in your creative and uniquely human talents, or your automatable ones? (Those who pride themselves on being an Excel whiz are likely taking a pause right now.) The creative work that you enjoy doing—some of it you may consider time off—is where you should double down. Start developing those areas now because creativity and human ingenuity will be the keys to having a thriving, impactful career in the age of AI.

HUMANS CAN THRIVE ALONGSIDE AI

Looking at the current job landscape, more and more people classify as knowledge workers—professionals whose line of work requires them to think and be creative rather than contribute value through manual, physical labor. And most knowledge workers are experts in their field, whether they acquired this expertise through higher education, direct practice, or a combination of the two. Yet knowledge workers typically spend only a fraction of their time using their expertise, doing what makes them an "expert," and instead devote the vast majority of their workday to tedious and repetitive routine tasks, like admin work or routing information (and no, no one is an expert in email or Slack). These are the tasks that are ripe for disruption, and ultimately replacement, by AI and other productivity and automation tools. Their days are almost numbered—and if we don't realign our careers toward the creative and human aspects of our expertise, ours might be too.

If what you do can easily be written down as a set of rules and instructions, you will be replaced—either by machines or by cheaper labor. It doesn't mean this work is easy; it just won't be as valuable in the future. So if we want to stay valuable, the smart play is to invest in the skills AI can't do. Deep learning, the most prominent current form of AI, is extremely powerful. But, at its core, it is really nothing more than a fancy type of statistical analysis of large amounts of data. Go and chess are what researchers call "perfect information games," situations where every detail of interest is known to the players, and in those scenarios, AI has everything it needs to spot the most successful patterns and win. But most of the real world doesn't have this luxury, especially in pursuits where human creativity and ingenuity are key. AI can do a lot, but it can't match our uniquely human ability to look outside the common patterns and readily available information. Truly creative ideas, by definition, always start off as statistical outliers. If we want to stay relevant, our goal should be to create such outliers.

We also have the innate ability to step back and reflect on what isn't working and do something about it. We can *unlearn*, accepting what no longer serves us and reinvent ourselves. Alan Kay, regarded as a pioneer in computer science, advised, "In some sense our ability to open the future will depend no[t] on how well we learn anymore but how well we are able to unlearn." Change has been a constant throughout history, but the rate of change is rapidly increasing. Unlearning allows you to embrace this change and take advantage of new opportunities and tools found within the next waves of technological progress.

To thrive alongside AI, you have to invest in learning how to learn rather than how to follow rules. You have to work outside the obvious constraints, make up your own rules, mix up the games you are playing, and connect the distant dots. You have to become comfortable with uncertainty and let your creativity guide you. Regardless of your discipline, you are going to have to learn the equivalent of improvisational jazz rather than follow the strict patterns of classical music.

Essentially, you have to be deeply human. From the industrial age assembly lines on, we've been taught to work like machines. Now, to thrive alongside the machines, we need to pass back the busyness baton and instead develop our uniquely human skills, traits, and talents. Fortunately, we already have them.

HUMANS CAN THINK BIG

In the wake of Lee Sedol's devastating defeat by AlphaGo, many Go players were dispirited. But after the initial shock had worn off, positive developments emerged out of the chaos. During the original five matches against Lee it had already become obvious that AlphaGo played very differently compared to human players. At times, the commentators were not sure whether the AI had made a fatal mistake or a brilliant move. All they could agree on was that no human master would have ever even considered the AI's move. But soon, human players started analyzing AlphaGo's play style, and used the AI as a powerful new training partner. In fact, the single victory Lee scored in the five matches against AlphaGo was based on a move, (which spectators later dubbed "God's Touch,") that he admitted would have never occurred to him had AlphaGo not put him against a wall with its unusual but very successful style and forced him to look for "super-human" moves himself. In the years since, many professional Go players found tremendous inspiration in the non-human play style, and used it to develop an even deeper understanding of the game.

Strategy is a core component of knowledge work. Creating and updating a strategy requires the ability to use divergent thinking (the skills to ideate and think big picture) and convergent thinking (the skills to drill down and hyper-focus). Our current AI applications and systems are excellent at convergent-style work. They are what experts call narrow AI, highly skilled at drilling down and focusing on a specific task but unable to extend their knowledge to even slightly unfamiliar tasks or situations. They can connect all the dots within narrow domains, but it is up to us humans, who have a natural gift at divergent thinking and the ability to zoom out and strategize, to connect the distant dots. Narrow AI will improve tremendously over the coming years, and most experts are skeptical about general AI in the near to mid future. It is—and very likely will be for a long time to come—up to us to think big. Our focus should be on how to make the most of the new tools' narrow focus, apply them in novel ways, and connect their results to come up with our own "God's Touch."

Those who succeed in this will do so by reflecting on the new possibilities of AI tools and strategizing on how to evolve, integrate, and translate them into new contexts. We are already seeing this today. DeepMind has taken some of the expertise it acquired through AlphaGo and other similar projects and applied it to diverse real-world problems like faster identification of eye diseases, optimizing Google's data center cooling to cut their energy consumption by 30%, and improving our understanding of protein folding in the human body.

Today's AI is an optimizer and an enabler. It cannot strategize, think across domains, use intuition to handle unfamiliar situations, or see the bigger picture. But we can. And we can use AI as a powerful tool to do these things—which are inherently human—much better than we ever could before.

HUMANS CAN EMPATHIZE

Have you ever felt that Alexa or Siri understood you had a rough day? Probably not. The seemingly simple act of understanding and sharing the feelings of others is fundamental to our interactions and relationships. From giving heartfelt advice to a friend to sharing a bond with a coworker, empathy is a skill deeply rooted in our evolutionary history. It's essential for collaboration and cooperation. And machines are terrible at it.

Emotions and circumstances are as unique as the people experiencing them. While it is possible for AI systems to tell the difference between a happy face and a sad face, this apparent "understanding" of human emotions, though impressive, is nothing but pattern matching based on visual cues and lots of example data. But human emotions are much more complicated than this. We can cry with joy, or smirk when we are frustrated. Again, it comes back to our ability to apply intuition despite limited information. Human relationships and interactions are messy. They are anything but perfect information games like chess and Go. We often don't even understand our own emotions, let alone those of others. And correctly labeling an emotion is one thing, but understanding its context and endless spectrum of nuances and then reacting to it appropriately requires something machines do not have: empathy. An approach based on statistics and big data will never be able to match our innate ability to empathize with one-of-a-kind individuals. Our emotional intuition allows us to comprehend and have compassion for things that AI systems have no concept of. But we can utilize AI to get even better at it.

By collaborating with new technologies—allowing them to do the mundane parts of our work—we can capitalize on our unique skills and do what we are best at. In a previous job, Max led the development of an AI-powered product that helped financial analysts generate insights from large amounts of news data. With the new tool, analysts managed to cut the time it took to search for relevant information by up to 90 percent. That's 90 percent less time wasted on a routine task that can now be reinvested in work that actually matters and truly utilizes their skill, creativity, and human connection. Rather than seeing AI as a competitor, these analysts embraced it as an effective collaborator to take their own work to the next level.

Let's take a look at medical professionals or lawyers, two other stereotypical examples of "expert professions." How much of their time is wasted on administrative work or tedious search tasks, and how little time is spent in consultation with individual patients, or deeply understanding a client and their case? A modern hospital can at times feel like a factory, with patients treated as standardized units being sent, as if on a conveyor belt, from one station to the next to receive a quick glance to make sure they fall within a certain tolerance window and then move on. Now imagine what this could look like if AI allowed these doctors to spend 90 percent less time on all the routine tasks, and reinvested this into face-to-face time with their patients (or simply to get some sleep rather than pulling 30-hour shifts). How might the standard of care rise when humans can do the work of humans because machines do the work of machines?

In the report on the 2020 edition of its annual roundtable on artificial intelligence, aptly titled "Artificial Intimacy," the Aspen Institute quotes Tom Gruber, former CTO, cofounder, and head of design of Siri: "A new role for AI would be to help us be our better selves collectively." The report also touches on the importance of unlearning and accepting ignorance, sharing MIT Professor Sherry Turkle's view that empathy "does not begin with 'I know how you feel.' It begins with the realization that you don't know how another feels." This realization, based on reflection and compassion, is something that requires human skills. But it can be enhanced through a collaboration with AI.

HUMANS CAN CURATE

While working on this book, Max was also a full-time member of Qosmo, a small Tokyo-based team working on computational creativity and applying AI to art, music, and design. Nao Tokui, Qosmo's CEO and Associate Professor of Computational Creativity at Keio University, likes to use a literary example to explain AI's impact and potential in the creative fields. The famous Argentine author Jorge Luis Borges, in his wonderful short story *The Library of Babel*, imagined an enormous library that contains every conceivable 410-page book—a book filled with 410 pages of nothing but "*a's*", one full of "*z's*", and every other possible combination in between. The vast majority of these books would be utter nonsense. But buried within this unimaginably large collection of books would also be stunning works of poetry, histories of countries true and imaginary, scientific papers with groundbreaking breakthroughs, your own biography past and future, and even this very book you are holding in your hands right now. The library contains everything that has ever been written or will ever be written (well, assuming it fits into 410 pages).[6] The problem is, these books are in completely random order.

Why is this story interesting or relevant in our context? It is relevant because we can imagine the equivalent of the Library of Babel in everything we create. There exists, even if just in our imagination, a library of all possible paintings, all possible software programs, all possible musical compositions, all possible business plans. When we create, we essentially stumble through this gargantuan library in search of the one piece that fits our needs. And this is where AI and deep learning come in. Probably no other tool in the history of mankind has allowed us to explore this library faster, and in a more deliberate way, than machine learning—and we are only at the very beginning of this journey. AI can help us surface what we want and bring some order into the library's chaos. However, it is still up to

---

[6]Estimating that each page has 30 lines, and each line contains 60 characters, a 410-page book would consist of 30 x 60 x 410 = 738,000 characters in total. Conservatively assuming the English alphabet with 26 letters (and not even distinguishing upper and lowercase), the digits 0 to 9, dots, question marks, and exclamation marks as the only punctuation, plus a space, gives 40 unique characters. This means that the total number of books in this library would be $40^{738,000}$, which is roughly 2 followed by 1.2 million zeros. If you're a writer and ever worried that everything interesting has already been written, think again, and keep this number in mind. And other artists, like painters or musicians, have even more creative freedom than the 40 or so characters available to the writer. Our creative possibilities are practically endless.

us to decide what to look for, and also what to keep once we find it. The AI might be a diligent and extremely helpful librarian, but we are the curators. We decide what is art and what is gibberish.

The introduction of Photoshop and other digital graphic design software did not suddenly make graphic designers obsolete—if anything it did the opposite. Those who decided to make the switch to the new tools found that they made a lot of processes *much* easier for them, and allowed them to navigate the space of possible designs much faster. The software didn't do the designing, nor did it decide what was good design. It only enabled the designer using it to explore more, and curate better.

AI is fundamentally no different from this. Like a painter studies his paintbrush and canvas and refines his strokes, or like a pianist studies the intricacies of her instrument and practices her technique, so too does a successful AI creator deeply study the system he is working with and the ways in which he needs to manipulate it in order to achieve precisely the creative outcomes he has in mind. AI and neural networks are not the creators. They are the pens, the brushes, the cameras, the violins, the chisels, etc. They are the tools. Due to their high complexity and novelty they may currently seem like magic, or even like autonomous designers, but in the end, they are mere utensils in the hands of us human creators.

Those of us who will embrace these tools, and collaborate with them by bringing our own human side to the table, will discover truly new ways of creative expression, be able to practice more empathy, and have more time to think big. AI is a new tool with tremendous potential. How we use it is up to us.

SOFT SKILLS WILL BE HARD CURRENCY

Camp counselors mentoring kids through playful outings that help them develop their skills; younger generations visiting aging communities to keep elders company; professionals gathering in a comfortable setting to open up about their mental health; or entire communities going out to plant trees in a once bland portion of a city.

All of these activities would traditionally just be called extracurricular or volunteer opportunities, but what they really are is noble leisure at its best—and their value will surge in the future of work. Rather than just volunteerism, this kind of human work is where we take care of each other, bring value to society, contribute a more positive energy to the world, and ultimately find meaning for ourselves. The youth becoming more emotionally intelligent, the elders being able to share their wisdom and feeling valued, people being less isolated and coming together, and nature thriving alongside modern society. Why wouldn't we be paid to enable all of this? Instead of "happy hour" being this tiny window of human connection that we escape to after a full day of traditional work, we will transform our extracurricular work into the many happy hours that fill our entire workday.

When working as Venture Partner at Animal Ventures (a technology firm specializing in supply-chain automation), John frequently advised Fortune 100 executives on how they could invest in the future of their workforce given the waves of automation impacting their industries. His advice was simple: train your people to be designers of ideas.

From huge corporations like Amazon or Apple to your local bakery or letterpress shop to freelancers operating online, every operation has a supply chain. And this can be broken down into roughly four aspects: designing, making, coordinating, and delivering. For example, an e-commerce startup selling plant-based clothing has to design their garments, make the clothing items from raw materials, coordinate the development of their inventory with multiple vendors, and ultimately deliver their niche product to the customer who pressed the "buy" button. A lawyer has to design her argument and perspective, draw up all the legal documents, coordinate with multiple sources and research partners, and deliver legal services for her clients. And with the rise of automation tools, three of these functions are being largely handed over to technology: the making, coordinating, and delivering are increasingly being managed by machines.

Let's imagine you are running the plant-based clothing startup mentioned above. Robots can now handle the making and manufacturing, machine-learning algorithms can coordinate and schedule the routing of materials and make predictions for all your supply chain partners, and drones and autonomous vehicles will soon be handling the final delivery of your product to the consumer.

But that leaves design. Jobs in which we "design" require very human qualities, like communication, empathy, creativity, strategic thinking in the face of uncertainty, questioning, and dreaming. Collectively, we often refer to these qualities as "soft skills," but don't let the name fool you; these soft skills will be the hard currency in the job market as AI and technology take over tasks more suited to machines.

As we have seen, most successful people contribute not through tedious, repetitive tasks but with their groundbreaking ideas and creativity; Bertrand Russell and Terry Rudolph are not known for submitting their grant applications in a timely manner, but for their contributions to philosophy and science. Beethoven, Tchaikovsky, and Etherwood are not delighting people with their music because they were masters of diligently copying the artists that came before them. Mike Mancias and Firas Zahabi did not become the outstanding coaches they are by following what every other coach was doing. Alice Waters and Magnus Nilsson are not world-class chefs because they are better at sourcing ingredients or scheduling their kitchen staff's shifts.

All of them contributed with their design work, their creativity, their playfulness and willingness to be silly, and their connection to other people. Yes, most of them have very clear "hard skills," but so do countless other people. What sets them apart is how they utilize their soft skills to make the most of their talents.

We hope that by now it has become abundantly clear that design work and incubation are fueled by the right use of time off in its many forms. So instead of getting mad at the automation coming our way, you should prepare to make the most of these sweeping changes on the horizon. If you take the right steps now and stop trying to work like a machine, you can have a unique advantage to position yourself as an ideal machine collaborator and thrive as this new landscape evolves. And leveling up your game requires you to reframe your relationship to work (and rest). Like David Silver, whose critical design insight on the AlphaZero algorithm came to him in a moment of relaxation, we need to recognize that time off and leisure are not just rewards for hard work.

In the future of work, time off will not be a "nice to have" or an attractive benefit that a generous employer provides to attract and keep talent. Our uniquely human capabilities, skills, and talents will be our key competitive advantages—and they are all enabled through the right use of time off. That makes time off as essential to our work as light and a Wi-Fi connection. We have a kind of intelligence that AI doesn't have, but we need the space to cultivate it. And it's up to us, as individuals but also as leaders, to create that space.

STEPHAN AARSTOL

American Entrepreneur and Writer

"The overall idea that workers are expected to endure 70 percent of their week so they can enjoy the other 30 percent? That's collective insanity."

"It's time we stopped drinking the busy Kool-Aid and started being more strategic with our time and decisions."

It's 1:30pm on a beautiful July day in sunny San Diego. While most other office workers in the city might be about to return to their email inboxes after lunch, settling in for the afternoon grind, the entire crew at Tower Paddle Boards is done for the day and heading to the beach to relax and enjoy themselves. It's not a company holiday or celebration. It's just a normal day in the office. Every summer from June to September, the company practices a five-hour workday, working only from 8:30am to 1:30pm, giving every employee plenty of time off to make the most of the season's extra daylight. As the company website proclaims, "Our workweek is better than most people's vacation weeks."

Stephan Aarstol, Tower's founder and CEO, believes firmly in the importance of time off and sees the five-hour workday as an essential part of his company's culture. In his book *The Five-Hour Workday: Live Differently, Unlock Productivity, and Find Happiness*, which outlines how he found success with a five-hour workday and how others can too, Aarstol makes the case for reconsidering our working hours, just like Henry Ford did a century ago for his factory workers. "The eight-hour workday was set up for the body, not the mind," he argues. And today's work world is dominated by the mind. So Aarstol and his company declared the eight-hour workday "outdated and largely irrelevant in today's highly productive knowledge work environment." The company implemented the five-hour workday instead.

Tower implemented its new policy across the entire company—including the physical store and the customer service department. Most business owners might expect such reduced availability would lead to disaster and customer outrage, but Aarstol had a different perspective: "Even in our instant-gratification society, being available all day isn't necessary. You just need to communicate when you are available." And it seems he was right. The months during which they practice the shortened workday, June to September, are actually their busiest months and account for 70 percent of their annual revenue. "Even though we're working part-time hours," Aarstol stresses, "this is not a part-time business." The five-day workweek is not permission to slack off and do less. Rather, the opposite is true. "You're getting the same or higher output in fewer hours. There is no loss to productivity, there are only gains."

The shorter work time requires focus and clarity. You have to develop what Aarstol calls a "production mindset," asking yourself what's essential and putting better processes in place. He believes most people don't spend enough of their work time thinking about how to work, instead of just working: "A five-hour workday offers baked-in time management by forcing workers to prioritize high-value activities." By creating artificial time constraints, you actually help unlock productivity enhancements because it forces you to reevaluate the way in which you do things. If this is done the right way, with both a good work ethic and the right rest ethic, Aarstol is confident that you can reduce your hours by 30 percent without diminishing your productivity: "Humans are not machines. Just because you're at your desk for eight hours doesn't mean you're being productive." He also points out another (often overlooked) factor: "Happiness boosts productivity. [And] fewer hours create scarcity." Besides this, Tower Paddle Boards' success speaks for itself. Tower was named the fastest-growing private company in San Diego in 2014 by the *San Diego Business Journal*, and investor Mark Cuban hailed it as one of his best investments on the show *Shark Tank*. In 2016, with only seven people working five hours a day, Tower made over $10M in revenue.

It is not only productivity on the job that rises when you have five-hour workdays. Entrepreneurship also flourishes in such a culture. And Aarstol believes that this is good for employees and employers alike. Tower not only tolerates but actively encourages and supports side projects and hobbies: "Like captains, entrepreneurs need to encourage their workers to experience the same sense of freedom by encouraging side gigs. Regrettably, however, too many employers try to keep their top talent from pursuing passion projects and attempting to hone their overall skill sets." The most talented people will work on their own stuff, anyway. But if we actively encourage it, everyone wins. For the employee, it leads to less financial pressure, more motivation, and increased creativity. And for the employer, if actively encouraged, it counterintuitively leads to higher retention. Not to mention the sheer experience and skill gained from entrepreneurial pursuits. Time off is a huge boost for entrepreneurship, volunteerism, community engagement, and the learning that accompanies them.

As with most forms of time off, the right balance and thoughtful intention are key. Aarstol is quick to admit that a five-hour workday does not always work. The reason the company is not practicing it year-round is that he noticed that people worked in a more solitary way when having to get stuff done. This is great for productivity, but it misses the camaraderies that are built from spending long hours together in the trenches of a "normal startup." So the rest of the year they stick to a more traditional 8:30am to 5:30pm schedule. And even during the summer months, things happen and people will have to put in long hours occasionally. But if this is an exception rather than the norm, it becomes much easier to do: "Just as with a 9-to-5 job, you have to recognize that there will be times when you want or need to work an extra-long day. But when you can leave the office at 1 p.m. to go surfing or pick your kids up from school, work isn't separate from life; it's all just living."

The shorter workday also doesn't suit everyone. So many of us have been trained to be lazy without even realizing because we were expected to stick around the office for eight or more hours, and some are unwilling to give up these old habits. To fit in at Tower, you need to be willing to break these habits, fully focusing on productivity when it matters and switching off when it doesn't. As an employer, Aarstol needs to be tough and show people that fewer hours does not mean less output. He has to teach a mindset of productivity, set clear expectations, and then follow through with them, even firing people when necessary. But he has more than enough talented people lining up who would be happy to embrace the new way of work. As Aarstol writes, "We do not have to accept what we've done in the past. We should not accept it."

> **PRACTICE:**
>
> **Enforce strict deadlines and develop systems to free up time**
>
> Try to set artificial deadlines and restrict the time you give yourself to complete a certain task, less time than you think is doable. Then work backward and figure out how you can still get it done in the allotted time. This forces you to think about how you work and put systems and processes into place. If you run a business, reflect on how you could implement a five-hour workday if you had to. And if you are really bold, follow Tower Paddle Boards' example and do it.

A CULTURE (RE)BUILT ON NOBLE LEISURE

To prepare for the future of work, we all need to assess our personal habits and behaviors, and refine our rest ethic. But beyond just ourselves, we need to approach this at a collective level. We need to look at the challenges—and opportunities—that present themselves in our societies, our communities, and our companies. Together, we must foster a culture built around the value of time off.

Humanity is facing many great challenges, from global warming and a widespread destruction of nature, to economic instability and social unrest. Responding to these challenges requires us to recognize that we are living in a new type of innovation-driven economy and that new global models and practices are needed to transition us smoothly into the future. The modern pace of technological change means that our systems of health, production, distribution, and energy (just to name a few) will be radically changed. Managing that change is no easy task, and we are all responsible.

In its 2018 agenda, the World Economic Forum urged us that "clinging to an outdated mindset and tinkering with our existing processes and institutions will not do. Rather, we need to redesign them from the ground up, so that we can capitalize on the new opportunities that await us while avoiding the kind of disruptions that we are witnessing today." We need to engage our playground mentality, be courageous to have silly ideas and imagine the "what-ifs," and allow ourselves the mental time and space to reflect on their implications and incubate on potential solutions. And we need to let go of outdated models and mindsets that no longer suit our modern world.

Many of the smartest knowledge workers have already realized this. Their goal is no longer to maximize their overall salary. Money for them is mostly only a resource to buy more time. So, instead, their key metric is salary per hour worked. And sadly, that is a fairly low number even in seemingly high-paying jobs. As a result, it's no wonder that some of the most talented people are leaving these jobs to pursue freelance work. In the world of freelancing, it is almost universally understood and accepted by both the freelancer and the clients that the only thing that matters is output, not the time spent on it. Somehow many traditional employers fiercely resist this insight. And as a result, these individuals who realize that they can get more done in less time if working on their own schedule choose a freelance career instead, and in the process often multiply not only their income but also the quality of work they provide. In the future of work, the relationship between productivity and leisure is no longer "either-or," it is "both-and."

Luckily, we see more and more leaders recognizing how overwork and a lack of time off hurt their business. And some of them are, like Stephan Aarstol, taking the initiative to make a difference. The founders of Basecamp and authors of *It Doesn't Have to Be Crazy at Work*, Jason Fried and David Heinemeier Hansson are longtime champions of ample time off within their company and have a helpful way for leaders to think about making their company more calm: "When you start to think about your company as a product, all sorts of new possibilities for improvement emerge. When you realize the way you work is malleable, you can start molding something new, something better. We work on our company as hard as we work on our products." Examine any company culture through this lens, and you can see that companies, just like software products, have bugs that need to be fixed. If you are aware of habits and expectations bugging your culture and leading to unnecessary stress, it's time to upgrade your company's cultural software.

Leaders like Aarstol, Fried, and Heinemeier Hansson are on the right path. But we need a broader cultural shift before their efforts can become truly effective. Some companies are introducing benefits like unlimited holidays and similar policies, but without the larger culture changing, many people are too afraid to make use of them or don't believe in them.

Especially in the US, open holiday policies often end up with people taking even less time off because consciously or subconsciously, they want to show how productive and hardworking they are. As a result, the well-intended policy might even become a new source of anxiety or burnout. "Forced" time off, such as company-wide holidays, might be the best way to approach this from the perspective of a manager in the current culture. Phrasing is crucial here. Instead of saying, "You don't have to read email after 7pm," it is much better to use "you're not allowed to read emails after 7pm." Same goes for saying, "You can take a holiday if you need to." The "if you need to" part makes it feel like an admission of weakness to take a break, and people won't do it.

Managers should take a serious interest in this issue. Burned-out people are not just suffering themselves; they also affect their coworkers, dragging everyone's motivation and productivity down with them. Rarely is there only a single case of burnout in a team environment—if one employee is struggling, others probably are too. We should really look at the underlying causes, especially as leaders and managers, to keep our team happy and creative.

"In the context of health and ecology," warns Jenny Odell in her book *How to Do Nothing*, "things that grow unchecked are often considered parasitic or cancerous. Yet we inhabit a culture that privileges novelty and growth over the cyclical and the regenerative.... We do not tend to see maintenance and care as productive." Entrepreneurs in particular have a tendency to get trapped in a growth mindset. While there are definitely times for growth and putting in the work, we also need to back off sometimes. As always, balance is key. It's why setting realistic goals and expectations is so essential. How else can we know what we are growing toward and when we've done enough?

We are all unique, and that's what makes us so valuable. The most successful collaborations are between people who complement each other and bring different skills, opinions, and ideas to the table. Yet most workplaces pretend that we all fit into the same model— another remnant of industrial-age thinking we seem to be reluctant to shake off despite the damage it is doing. "A good rule of thumb is that any environment that consistently leaves you feeling bad about who you are is the wrong environment," writes Laurie Helgoe in her book *Introvert Power: Why Your Inner Life Is Your Hidden Strength*. We should all become more conscious and ask ourselves if our (work) environment is helping or hindering us. If it is the latter, it might be time to either push back and try to reshape the environment, or find a new and more suitable one. When we have the flexibility to approach work in our own way, at our own pace, and in our own time, everyone gets a chance to unleash their full potential.

Unfortunately, we still live in a society where busyness, stress, and overwork are worn as a badge of honor, showing how accomplished and important we are. But as entrepreneurs, managers, and individuals, it's a dangerous and vicious cycle if we keep assuming that we are productive and effective only because we put in a crazy amount of hard work and long hours, grinding it out. All too often, we get stuck in mediocrity because we are afraid, or maybe just too lazy and comfortable, to question the status quo and the rules set by societal norms.

It doesn't have to be this way. We can rise out of mediocrity and fill our lives with success and meaning by building a culture of noble leisure. This culture will allow us to thrive in the future of work. But we don't have to wait for the future to come in order to reap tremendous results from such a culture. Before concluding this book, we want to share with you three more examples of people who have already found success by embracing these cultural shifts on personal, corporate, and societal levels.

PETE ADENEY
(A.K.A. MR. MONEY MUSTACHE)

American Retiree and Finance Blogger

"When people earn their freedom from money constraints, they usually don't stop working. Instead they start doing their best work. Looking at many of society's highest achievers right now, the world leaders and founders of the most productive companies, I see mostly people who have already made it. And yet are still working because it means something to them."

Ah, retirement. That sweet destination at the end of a long career. Finally, all the hard work is paying off and you can spend your time on the things you've always wanted to do. But do you really have to wait until your 60s or 70s to do so? A small but very active movement that calls itself FIRE—Financial Independence, Retire Early—thinks you don't. In fact, they believe you can retire *much* earlier, with most of your life still ahead of you. Maybe the most prominent voice within this movement is Pete Adeney, who writes a popular personal finance blog under the name Mr. Money Mustache.

Adeney himself retired in 2005 at age 30. And he did it without inheriting a fortune or making millions through a startup exit or some other singular event. Adeney was just a normal guy working a normal job. Before retiring, he and his wife were both software engineers, each averaging a yearly salary of just under $70K. What distinguished Pete and his wife from the average office worker, though, was that they lived frugally and saved aggressively, investing over half of their take-home pay into basic index funds and other conservative assets. By the time of their retirement, they had saved approximately $600,000 in investments, as well as owning a mortgage-free house worth around $200,000. These savings are enough to sustain Adeney and his family indefinitely.

A core tenet of the FIRE movement is the "4% Rule." Based on the fairly safe assumption that over the long run, index funds return on average 7 to 8 percent per year, Adeney and the FIRE community argue that 4 percent of your savings is a good safe withdrawal rate, "the maximum rate at which you can spend your retirement savings, such that you don't run out in your lifetime." The Adeney family always lived a very frugal life—but without feeling in want of anything. With total annual expenses not much above $25,000, they could happily sustain themselves within their safe withdrawal rate.

As many a recent retiree might tell you, what may seem like the pinnacle of time off, being completely free from work, can be quite a challenge if you don't fill the time with something new. Lying on the couch all day quickly loses its appeal—but according to Adeney, getting away from work isn't the point. It's more about working where you want and on what you want, freed from the concern of having to earn money with it. Adeney became much more active in his retirement. "I'm incapable of spending more than an hour on the couch or sitting at the beach," he writes. "During vacations, I have to find physical work projects to keep myself happily occupied. I've discovered that even one day of zero productivity is bad for me: if I stop doing things, I stop wanting to do things, and pretty soon I'm just lazing around on the couch or taking 11am naps. For me, inactivity leads to a depressive boredom."

One of Adeney's many activities now is teaching others "how we can all live a frugal yet Badass life of leisure" through his blog. But what he really enjoys is variety and getting his hands dirty, working on physical projects in the real world: "I never understood the joy of watching other people play sports, can't stand tourist attractions, don't sit on the beach unless there's a really big sandcastle that needs to be made.... If you leave me alone for a day ... I'll have a joyful time rotating between carpentry, weight training, writing, playing around with instruments in the music studio, making lists, and executing tasks from them." Most of Adeney's favorite activities are free or even generate money. They all revolve around creativity, making stuff, and solving problems.

Adeney promotes a new definition of retirement, one that isn't tied to old age and inactivity. You may even still do a job or start a business after you retire: "Early retirement, according to this new definition, does not mean quitting work, even while it may well mean quitting your job. It means opting out of the bullshit portion of your work. The commuting, the politics, the production of inferior products just because your boss has found a profitable niche to exploit." Instead, this new form of retirement allows us to produce what we are really passionate about, whether or not others find it useful. Rather than think of retirement as the opposite of work, we should ask ourselves the question: "How would you run your own life, with a continuing desire to create but no immediate need to make the next mortgage payment?" The answer to this question should be your new definition of retirement, and you can probably achieve it much earlier than you previously thought.

PRACTICE:

Assess your spending habits

Are you telling yourself that you would love to take some time off, but can't afford it? Does an early retirement sound good to you? Maybe it's time to reassess your spending habits. How much are your annual expenses? What are the essentials, and which nonessentials are tying you down the most? Do you want more things or more freedom? It's easy to get trapped in a cycle of aiming for more income, then spending more, and again aiming for the next pay raise. But with a bit of reflection and the right habits, it's actually more and more feasible to reach financial independence and (very) early retirement.

RICHARD BRANSON

English Entrepreneur, Investor, and Philanthropist

"It's archaic to assume that people do their best work at a desk. I have never worked from an office, preferring to combine working hard with spending time with my family."

"I'm lucky in being able to work wherever I am, at any time, and don't see work and play as separate—it's all living. I think this will be the case for more and more people in the future, to the benefit of businesses, countries and individuals. [...] If you trust people and treat them as adults, they will repay you by working effectively and efficiently."

Chances are you do not own a private island in the Caribbean or run a multinational business conglomerate spanning over 400 companies from banking to healthcare, and media to space tourism. So, at first glance, Sir Richard Branson, who owns Necker Island and founded the Virgin Group, might not seem like the most relatable person. But if you look beyond these "minor details," Branson is actually a very relatable guy. And despite his tremendous success and the demands of running a global suite of companies, he finds plenty of space for time off. He also promotes it among his employees and encourages other leaders to follow suit.

Branson likes to start his day early, getting up around 5am and getting in an exercise session right away, usually tennis or kite surfing. Family is extremely important to him, and after his workout, he has a leisurely breakfast with his family: "Exercise and family time put me in a great mind frame before getting down to business." And he concludes his day in a similarly social and relaxed way: "My day normally wraps up with a group dinner, where stories are shared and ideas are born. My bedtime is generally about 11pm." In between these grounding family times, that's where he runs his businesses.

Running multiple businesses on a global scale requires Branson to be connected a lot. So he embraced the possibilities of connected technologies, using their full potential to allow him a great amount of flexibility. And he makes sure to use them in a very deliberate manner, balancing their potential for distraction with plenty of quiet time for reflection, through journaling and note-taking: "Regardless of where I am or what I'm doing—perhaps with the exception of kitesurfing or swimming—I always have a notebook on hand. My secret 'life hack' has also been to write it down! I can't tell you where I'd be if I hadn't had a pen on hand to write down my ideas as soon as they came to me." Branson also dislikes too much formality and tries to keep his days as casual and active as possible: "I'm not a fan of formal meetings and would much prefer to lighten the mood with a shared meal, or if I'm pressed for time, a walking meeting." Journaling, shared meals, and exercise—these are the things a multibillionaire like Sir Richard finds time off in. Just an average guy, after all.

But one area in which Branson is anything but average (well, one of the many) is how he treats employees of the Virgin Group. He firmly believes in trusting his employees and allowing them to work wherever and whenever they think works best for them. "To successfully work with other people," he says, "you have to trust each other. A big part of this is trusting people to get their work done wherever they are, without supervision. It is the art of delegation, which has served Virgin and many other companies well over the years. We like to give people the freedom to work where they want, safe in the knowledge that they have the drive and expertise to perform excellently, whether they [are] at their desk or in their kitchen. Yours truly has never worked out of an office, and never will.... Working life isn't 9-5 any more. The world is connected. Companies that do not embrace this are missing a trick."

Branson's Virgin Group certainly isn't missing the trick. "Through a number of flexible working initiatives—like working from home, unlimited leave, integrated technology, and wellbeing in the workplace—we treat our employees like the capable adults they are," he writes. "We fully embrace flexible working at Virgin Management and believe giving people more options on how, when and where they work will only continue.... If we all work smarter, we won't have to work longer." Branson also believes that three or even four-day weekends might become more widespread and common in the not-too-distant future and that people will get paid more for working less time "so they can afford more leisure time." While he has some concerns with advances in technology causing job losses and the redistribution of work and leisure being "a difficult balancing act to get right," he is confident that it can be done properly. If we approach technology right and embrace it, we can get more done in less time, and enjoy more time to be creative and human.

Get the most out of your company's creativity, and your own, by letting people work when and where is best for them. By setting a strict working schedule (say 9-to-5), you are missing out on each person doing their best work because that window just doesn't work for everyone. Use the amazing tools and technologies available to offer real work flexibility—treating each person like the capable adult they are, letting them decide what their optimal balance of time on and time off looks like, allowing them to simply do their best work.

PRACTICE:

Embrace full flexibility

Every single one of us is unique, and that's what makes us so amazing and sets us apart from standardized, replaceable, and predictable machines. Rather than hiring an army of clones that all think and act alike (or worse, treat normal employees as if they were such clones), embrace your team's differences and enable everyone to bring their best and most creative self to your projects. Accept that there is no one-size-fits-all model. If you try to force one, you just limit everyone's creative potential and dilute trust. Instead, use technology to your advantage, allow your team to work asynchronously and remotely, and let everyone make the most of their uniquely human flexibility.

YOSHIE KOMURO AND SARAH ARAI

Japanese Work-Life Balance Consultants

"It's not your company that evaluates your life. It's your family!"

—Yoshie Komuro

"Try to imagine your ideal work and life. Then try to get closer to that. Imagine that when your children look up to you, they will think 'being an adult is a very nice thing'. I would like to encourage everybody to live a life where children can be hopeful and looking forward to becoming grown ups."

—Sarah Arai

Karoshi, the Japanese word for death by overwork. Coined in the 1970s and gradually gaining more and more relevance in the salaryman culture, the phenomenon recently reached a new peak (or rather abyss). After the suicide of a young office worker in 2015 and several other deaths were directly linked to overwork and its effects on mental and physical health, the public and the government finally took notice. A government study into the issue concluded that a staggering 20 percent of workers in Japan are at risk of *karoshi*. And even beyond the extreme of death, the impact of overwork on productivity, creativity, and life satisfaction is crippling the Japanese economy at large. But some people are determined to change this.

During her college years, Yoshie Komuro spent a year in the US, working as a babysitter for a single mom. What she experienced there left her stunned: the difference between American maternity leave and what she was used to in Japan. During childcare leave, the American mother used her time to study, and when she went back to work, she earned a raise and a promotion. For women in Japan at that time, having a child usually meant you had to give up your career completely. And the few who did rejoin the workforce were stuck in low-level positions. This experience inspired Komuro. Back in Japan, she joined cosmetics giant Shiseido after graduating and launched an internal venture project to support and encourage women returning to work. Her project was a big success, and in 2004 Nikkei named her Woman of the Year. Two years later, Komuro founded her own company, Work-Life Balance (WLB), to take her mission beyond Shiseido to a nationwide level.

Initially WLB focused on women's ability to raise children and build a family without having to give up their career. But Komuro realized that the root of the issue was deeper than this. She experienced the problem firsthand. When she and her husband had their first child, her husband would often come home from work at 2am, leaving her with most of the childcare burden. While she initially got angry at him, she quickly realized how tough his hard work was on him. Luckily, her husband managed to change his work style, and the couple are raising their two kids with an equal commitment from both parents—and the whole family flourished. This shift made her realize that "issues related to workers' mental health are also increasing in Japanese companies."

WLB's consulting work now targets all knowledge workers. workers. And a better work-life balance is desperately needed, especially for knowledge workers. "Unlike the manufacturing sector," says Komuro, "the productivity per hour among Japanese white-collar workers is extremely low. Work-life balance is essential for white-collar workers to foster their creativity, especially if they are moving to new types of industries." Despite its image, Japan has one of the lowest productivity levels in the world—nowhere else is visible busyness as common, accepted, and even expected. And the lack of private lives means that workers don't bring new ideas to the company. This leads to a negative cycle. The lack of ideas and creativity means workers try to make it up with even more hard work and longer hours, which leads to even less private life and less creativity. Fewer work hours, on the other hand, lead to more productive ways of working.

While the name of the company is Work-Life Balance, "it's not so much about balancing," explains Sarah Arai during a call with us, "but more about synergy. Work and life affect each other, negatively or positively, and the effect becomes synergetic." The idea that work and life must compete is a common misconception. "If you work too long," Arai says, "it means you don't have any life. Or if you spend too much time on your life, it means you are not working hard. But that's a misunderstanding. You can have both: rewarding work and satisfying life." Arai is one of the now over 30 consultants working at WLB. While she grew up almost entirely in Japan, her father is from New Zealand, and as a result she was exposed to many countries and ideas in her youth. Comparing the work situation of other countries to that in Japan, Arai thought "working in Japan is not a very attractive future for me. So I decided I'm going to work and live in other countries."

But while Arai was still at university, her mother passed away from cancer. Even though she had spent a lot of time with her mother, she still regretted that she hadn't spent more time with her. And she realized that, given the rapidly aging population as well as the current working culture, many other people in Japan will have the same regret. By chance, around the same time Arai came across a book that Komuro had written and felt "this is how Japan needs to change. If Japan changes like this, if adults can enjoy work and life, which means there are also more happy children, that's the Japan I want to live in." And rather than wait for it to happen, Arai decided to contribute to this change, eventually joining WLB as one of the company's earliest members.

Together, the team at WLB has helped over a thousand companies, from four-employee businesses all the way to multinational corporations with tens of thousands of employees. Despite the wide range of clients, their basic approach is generally the same. They start by asking the company to select several small groups, usually around 10 people per team, who work together closely on a daily basis. With each such team they then facilitate meetings, asking what the group's ideal style of work would look like and helping them define what they call the "goal image." This should be a very clear description of how they can enjoy their work and support each other, as well as how to spend more time with their families. Finally, Arai explains, "once they agree on their goal image, we help them tackle things step by step to get closer to this ideal goal image."

Initially, each change they implement might be small. Tidying up the workplace. Adding an email footer to inform people that they are trying to improve their work-life balance and are not sending emails late at night or on weekends. Or simply being nicer to each other. According to Arai, "In many Japanese companies people are so tired and often told that 'that's not how you're supposed to work' or 'this is what you have to do', they eventually stop thinking and get discouraged from coming up with new ideas and trying different things." And this is affecting productivity, creativity, and happiness. "Even if it's just small steps," she says, "if people can be empowered and encouraged to do what they think would be best for them, and the company, and the customers, the culture starts to change."

And small changes lead to a larger movement: as Arai explains, "When they see they can succeed at these small steps, they feel encouraged and empowered and they will be ready to focus on bigger challenges." Such bigger challenges might include changing the communication and collaboration style with particular customers to reduce both their burdens, as well as making the experience greater for the customer. Or they might go to upper management and try to make the company documentation or meeting policies more efficient. Again, each action is not too big, but once people get the sense that they can make a change and are allowed to voice their opinion, momentum gathers.

As these small groups change their behavior, often reducing their work hours by 30 percent, they feel more empowered and happier. And then they start to talk about it. As a result, their colleagues get jealous and want to implement what they are doing. The seed of time off has been planted. "Gradually, more small teams join the program, and over time this will transform the company," Arai notes. One key factor they've seen as important across all their clients is raising the quality of relationships: "If you have a better relationship with your teammates, the productivity will rise."

The key to productive teams is "psychological safety among teammates and balanced amount of communication within a team." Not a scenario in which one person talks and others are quiet. Everyone speaks up. And at WLB they practice what they preach, placing a high focus on the quality of relationships and psychological safety among people. They are very careful with how they communicate and create systems that encourage people to collaborate and support each other. They also hold regular meetings to reflect as a team how to work better, happier, and more effectively. Every morning, they start the day by scheduling their own work and then sharing it with their teammates in what they call 朝メール, morning mail. As a result, everyone knows who does what, when, and how things are going. "People can help each other, and fill in for each other if something comes up. If there are issues, we can support each other. And if we are successful, we can rejoice together."

Beyond just engaging with individual companies, WLB is trying to have a larger impact in society. Komuro's efforts have already contributed to changes in the Japanese legal system. In March 2019, Japan finally introduced a law capping overtime hours to 45 per month and 360 per year (with certain exceptions). These changes are gradually making Japanese society rethink their traditional working style. And while some of these issues might be uniquely Japanese, other countries are seeing similar demographic trends. Arai hopes that "the changes we are making in Japan right now can be a role model for other countries, especially for those in the period of demographic dividend, as they are likely to experience similar shifts in the demographic structure and in the market." Arai concludes by saying, "I just want people to be happier and enjoy their life. We have a lot to enjoy, so it's a waste if we are not enjoying our lives!" Let's follow Arai's advice and make the most of our work-life synergy, enjoying our time on and, of course, our time off.

PRACTICE:

Define your goal image

What would your ideal style of work and life look like? Reflect on this by yourself, and, if possible, also together with the team(s) you work with daily. Once you have defined this image for yourself and your team, you can work toward it, one small step at a time. In Arai's words, "Having a clear goal image, the ideal image of how you want to be working and how you want to be living, is very important. Only then can you see the difference to your current life. Once you know your goal image, you would know what you have to change."

BUILDING YOUR REST ETHIC

"Leisure is essential to civilization," proclaimed Bertrand Russell in 1932, and we hope you fully agree with him by now. But it is the second part of this quote where we should take particular note: "In former times leisure for the few was rendered possible only by the labors of the many. But their labors were valuable, not because work is good, but because leisure is good. And with modern technic it would be possible to distribute leisure justly without injury to civilization." Russell might have been a little ahead of his time, but now, about a century later, we find ourselves at a point at which AI can truly take over the "labors of the many." And thanks to this, for the first time in history, everyone will be able to join the leisure class. It's time to rebuild our society on Aristotle's ideal of noble leisure. And this time, everyone can take part in it.

We believe AI will not take away our jobs, nor will it threaten or weaken our human values. We'd argue that the opposite will be true. Yes, AI will disrupt the job landscape, but the jobs that will remain, as well as those that will be created, will center on human skills such as creativity and empathy. And these skills are not built on busyness, but on well-balanced cycles of fruitful work and nourishing rest.

We have been stressed out, burned out, and busy but unproductive for much too long. Worst of all we're not creative in the way that we could—and should—be. We've lost touch with the things that make us capable of huge impactful ideas. And if we don't change, we're either going to work ourselves to death or slip into irrelevance as the robots take over. Genuinely productive knowledge work is the opposite of busyness and requires a harder, more thoughtful approach. It requires taking time off seriously. And it's time that we, as individuals and as leaders, take notice of this.

Even when we recognize its importance, time off does not just magically materialize, especially if our current modus operandi is busyness. It's our responsibility to make time for it, and to defend it from the world's attempts to take it. This, somewhat counterintuitively, requires putting more thought into planning our leisure time and protecting it from encroaching work. It requires questioning assumptions and putting good processes in place. It requires building discipline supported by good routines and habits. Our rest ethic must be as strong as our work ethic.

In the future of work, a rest ethic means much more than a vacation policy or a weekend break. It is recognizing that we cannot and should not imitate the machines, but accept and embrace our need for downtime and detachment and take pride in the distinctly human skills they enable. Rather than looking at time off as a break away from work, see it as an essential part of work and our lives at large. Our strategy for creativity and big ideas is rooted in giving our thoughts time and space to incubate and wander. Our rest ethic is where we ultimately discover and unlock our deepest creative and human potential.

We believe that already, companies and individuals that focus on placing empathy and creativity, and the practices and habits that support them, at the core of their corporate or personal philosophy will thrive. And soon, it might be the only viable option. Busywork is easy to automate, and no one, no matter how many hours they put in and how much of their life they sacrifice, is going to outwork AI on these tasks. Creativity and empathy, on the other hand, will remain distinctly human for a long time to come. Those who understand these skills, as well as the new tools, will embrace AI not as an obstacle or adversary, but as an enabling technology to take their humanity to the next level.

What will empower them to do so will be a healthy approach to the rhythm of work and leisure, and the deliberate practice of time off. So we recommend that you start practicing right now.

You deserve your time off, you deserve your rest ethic, and you deserve to have both a high quality of life and high quality of work. We need new ways of working. We need a clean slate. We need big and bold ideas, to stay calm and work smarter. We need to return to Aristotle's noble leisure, creating more time off and filling it with meaningful pursuits. We need to become, together as a society, the leisure class that Bertrand Russell credits with all the major contributions to civilization. We need more leaders and creators like those we have encountered in this book. And it's up to all of us to join their ranks.

We need you, dear reader, to be the creative, impactful, empathetic, well-rested, and happy person to lead us into the future of work.

OUR STORY

JOHN FITCH

Coauthor

I have spent most of my career in technology startups. Venturing out, prototyping something from scratch, and seeing if people see value in it. When the iPhone was first released, I dropped everything I was doing to start designing software. I thought the only way to do it was through an obsessive work ethic. I guess you could say I'm a recovering workaholic.

Constant hustling, late-night hackathons, 80-hour workweeks, and every other software industry trope was my standard at a point in my life. My family, friends, and mentors would often comment that I deserved breaks or should actually enjoy the weekend by unplugging from work. I'd brush off their comments and keep my ass in the chair. They didn't know the secret I knew: *more work equals more success*. But they were seeing something I wasn't. And I didn't see it until I reached a breaking point.

In one week, when I was the most work obsessed, my long-term relationship of many years suddenly ended and a startup I had cofounded failed. At the time I was devastated, but I have now come to understand why it all came crashing down. I was working really really hard and nothing was working. I was addicted to busyness and my rest ethic didn't exist. In so many moments, throughout that chapter in my life, I wasn't there for the people who meant the most to me. I mean, I was there in person, but I was not present with them. Many times at various dinners, I was too busy keeping up with my email inbox. During my "vacations," I was thinking about the next feature for our app I could be working on. I was not really fostering relationships with anyone because I was in an obsessive relationship with always working.

But luckily, two longtime mentors changed it all for me. They reached out soon after my life meltdown and asked if I wanted to start up a new venture firm with them based in New York. I was ready for a new beginning, so I moved from Texas to the East Coast. We started the company off with a retreat. The purpose was to solidify a vision for the company before our first big projects. I obsessively wanted to only talk about the work and projects, but I was quickly overruled by the other two partners. They had other plans. We were going to spend the whole time discussing our work culture and our rest ethic. This was uncomfortable for me because I still had my bad habits of wanting to think only about work. But that way of being hadn't worked out so well for me, so I got on board.

After a weekend of long walks and conversations at a dinner table, we decided that the company culture would be centered on regular rest and reflection. If we couldn't do it, then we were not succeeding as a company. Our company values were things like not obsessing about how many hours we worked and to stay away from ASAP as our default deadline. Our most radical idea: everyone at the company would work on projects in periods of three months of incredible focus. After the three months, you took a month off to rest, reflect, recharge, and come back with a fresh perspective, and hopefully as a more interesting person. My inner workaholic was having a hard time believing that this was possible, but there was a part of me that was eager to give it a try. I guess having your world crash down around you can be pretty mind-opening.

After our first three-month software product build, our project team members took separate sabbaticals that lasted over a month. My business partners learned the value of living slow while walking 600 miles on the Camino de Santiago. Another teammate drove around Iceland and discovered its young, diverse geography. Personally, I explored Greece to study Mediterranean cooking and how to improve my quality of life through daily time off practices. A specific moment from my adventures, a conversation with a woman from the island of Ikaria, changed my entire perception of time off and leisure.

Ikaria is known as an island where people "forget to die," and it is common to run into someone who lives there who is over the age of 100. I was enjoying tea at a small restaurant overlooking the Aegean Sea. I sparked up a conversation with this nice lady from Ikaria. I was eager to understand her island's secrets to longevity. The kind and calm woman, who also happened to have a medical background, hit me with life-altering advice while we were waiting for our tables to be ready:

"*John,*" she said, "*you seem to care a lot about your agenda today. You see, in Ikaria, we value a relaxed pace of living that ignores watches and clocks. Because of this, we don't have a lot of stress hormones because we aren't strict about time. We don't control the coordination of other people, so why put so much stress on yourself by considering everyone's schedules? The universe laughs when we make plans. You can instead spend your time going deep in the things you do control, and be happy when you do get the chance to share time with others. Plus, I would imagine most of your best memories and ideas were from when you were not working.*"

She was right. Almost all of my big ideas did occur when I took the rare moments to unplug from my desk compared to the times I tried to force myself to be creative. After that conversation on my mini-sabbatical, I became a believer in time off.

I am now aware that my inbox and notifications are other people controlling my time and agenda. I know their intent isn't to make me unproductive, but I now focus on not letting that control my attention. I can choose to not be busy. I have unread messages in my inbox right now, and I will likely never get to most of them. It is okay because they aren't as important as the creative project I have chosen to focus on right now. I get more thinking time, and I am spending less time anxious on my phone. I am producing better, more profound work because of these changes. I am also happy to inform you that nothing is falling apart because of my unread messages.

After coming back from our sabbaticals, each one of us on the team had upgraded in several ways as an individual and we had collectively identified ways to run the company better. Our company's time off strategy also allowed us to decentralize our business operations. To still fulfill my responsibilities while I was away, I would offload my duties to several others on the team who were in their working cycle. While I was away, those team members would take ownership of my core job functions. When I returned from my time off, those job functions had been improved, and I had to relearn the smarter methods of working. Since those teammates had a fresh perspective while filling my job functions, they would identify ways to work smarter that I wasn't seeing—allowing us to evolve the organization through frequent upgrades to the way we worked. It prevented us from resting on our laurels and being stagnant. It allowed us to unlearn. Our intentional rest allowed us to do work we were deeply proud of.

Going from being someone obsessed with always working to being someone who now was a believer in the power of intentional rest, I started to wonder… was time off essential for other people too? I started researching the topic and started a podcast to have conversations with people to find out. After a few episodes and numerous hours of research, I realized that our company was not an anomaly, and there were a lot of people and cultures who also believed that being busy isn't the only way you accomplish what you want in life. And many don't see it at all as a way to accomplish anything. After broadcasting a dozen episodes of the Time Off podcast, many listeners suggested I write a book about time off, so the journey of this book began.

Two years after starting the book's outline, a lot has changed in our world. As I type this paragraph in April 2020 (one of the last tasks for this book), almost all of the world is sheltering due to the COVID-19 pandemic. We are still in the midst of the pandemic and don't yet know how it is all going to shake out. This, of course, has been a curse on many fronts, but I noticed something over the last month or so of being locked down that is a blessing. Many people have been forced into time off. On a daily basis when I go for a walk (keeping safe distances, of course!), I have seen and talked to people who are finally honoring their leisure. They are talking to their neighbors and taking time to enjoy a slow meal. They are thinking bigger about how we create a more sustainable and honorable healthcare system, rethink education, heal the environment, and create a modern economy that leapfrogs past our broken paradigms. All the while, I saw people going on walks who said they hadn't done it for years and that they had reflected on parts of the job that were no longer serving them. People have finally had a moment to pause and rethink their relationship to work and leisure. I have gone beyond hoping that my vision of the future of work is accurate to seeing many people connecting the dots themselves. Regardless of what unfolds with the pandemic, I feel optimistic. This event has shown us that we need moonshot-level ideas—and we need them now (some we needed yesterday).

So I helped write this book for anyone who is like my former workaholic self that said no to too many dinner parties, prioritized an inbox zero instead of enjoying his leisure time, and was working like a machine without getting much done. I hope that anyone reading this who is as overworked and overwhelmed as I was can not only see that you deserve to take a break, reflect, play, and recover, but that the world-changing project you are working so hard on will also benefit.

MAX FRENZEL

Coauthor

"Why the fuck do I feel so unproductive and uncreative?" It was August 2017 as I wrote these words in my notebook. I was sitting in my quiet room in an old guesthouse in the small town of Zao Onsen, overlooking the mountains of Yamagata Prefecture. I was on holiday, a slow trip on local trains through rural Japan. I live in fast-paced Tokyo and thought it might be nice to get a break for a few days, explore Japan a bit more, and get a fresh perspective. It wasn't an attempt to escape; I didn't feel like there was anything I wanted or needed to escape from. I thought everything was great. I love Tokyo, and I also thought I loved my job. Yet after a few days away from it all, it hit me. I realized that I had never felt less productive or creative. I also realized that I had never before felt more distracted and unable to focus. I started thinking back to my PhD days.

I did my PhD in Quantum Information Theory at Imperial College London under the supervision of David Jennings and Terry Rudolph. The fact that you are reading this right now is largely thanks to them and the time I spent there (or, more precisely, often didn't spend there). Their extremely hands-off approach and the complete freedom and trust they gave me allowed me to find my own working pace and style, and discover just how much you can get done by taking time off seriously. At the same time as doing my research in quantum physics, I also cofounded and ran a startup, worked several hours a week as a private tutor, trained for ultra-marathons (up to 15-plus hours of running a week during peak training time, not including other preparation and recovery activities), and somehow still found plenty of time to read widely, take naps and meditate daily, work on random creative projects, get drunk with friends (maybe a bit too frequently …), experiment in my kitchen with coffee and food, as well as experiment with my own body by means of various (ahem) "supplements" or unusual eating and sleeping patterns, and much more. Despite all this, very rarely did I feel stressed or busy. In fact, I rarely spent more than four hours a day actually engaged in work. But those hours I did spend were highly productive. However, reflecting during my time in the Japanese mountains, I realized that this was not my reality anymore.

What had changed? Why were things different? Despite doing an exciting job I thought I loved, working as a researcher at a small but rapidly growing AI startup, I realized just how unsatisfied I actually was. Days seemed to drag on seemingly without any real progress, even though I felt busier than ever and certainly spent more time engaged in "work" than ever. Inspiration didn't just come naturally anymore. In my free time, I didn't feel the same kind of motivation to pursue other interests as I used to. More than just uncreative and unproductive, I felt pretty boring compared to my old self.

All too often, we don't even realize how unsatisfying things are and how little we get done despite all the time we put in. We are too caught up in the everyday distractions to notice, too content with our "frantic, self-congratulatory busyness" as Tim Kreider points out in his wonderful essay "Lazy: A Manifesto." Most people are probably not even aware that they are operating at far from optimal. I am lucky enough to have experienced that it can be different. During my PhD days, I had the freedom to just disappear to another country for a couple of weeks whenever I felt like it, or let my physics research rest for several days if I didn't feel in the right mind for it and to focus my time on other pursuits or hobbies instead—and usually as a result come back to the research with lots of new ideas and motivation, quickly more than making up for the "wasted" time.

And still, despite having this experience and knowing how things could (or should?) be like, once I got into the routine of a busy job for a couple of months, I somehow forgot everything I had learned during those days, and it took a vacation far away from any distractions to notice for myself. Even after coming back from my vacation, I quickly settled back into my, by then, usual habits and daily routine and almost forgot about my realizations. But I gradually started being more aware of the issue. And instead of just giving up and quitting, or becoming satisfied with these new feelings (that voice saying, "Maybe I am just getting old?"), I started trying to figure out what the actual problems were and how they could be solved.

I started making changes, small and large, to try and get some of my PhD life back within the constraints of a "normal" office job. I reclaimed my mornings, starting my days with some deep work at home or in a cafe, rather than going straight to the office. And even once at the office, I would take more frequent breaks, go for long walks to think about ideas, or get some quiet time by working in another coffee shop. I also made it increasingly harder for people to reach me and get a piece of my time. And people started to respect that. My work was valuable, so most of my colleagues didn't care where or when I did it, and just assumed that even if they didn't see me some of the time, I was likely still working just as much as them.

This was also the time that I started writing about my experience, and my struggles to recover my previous style of working and my old levels of creativity and curiosity. The articles I wrote seemed to resonate with people, first close friends and increasingly also strangers on the internet, and I was encouraged to keep pushing, both in my writing as well as my efforts to reclaim my time off. Eventually this led to my collaboration with John, and the book you are now holding in your hands.

While I certainly made big improvements on my own rest ethic, my attempts to push wider cultural changes in my company were less successful, and eventually, a bit over a year after my insightful trip, I decided to quit. I didn't, however, give up on full-time employment. I joined Qosmo, a small team of digital creatives applying AI and other cutting-edge technologies to design, art, and music. Instead of working with large financial institutions or law firms trying to optimize their teams' performance, I was applying deep learning to create interesting pieces of music or live performances, devise novel and interactive works of art, or advise corporate partners on how to prepare their creative teams for an AI-enabled future. As a company, we were happy to be small. There was no goal to grow rapidly and exit spectacularly. The main goal was high-quality creative output and enriching peoples' lives, and there was an understanding that time off is a critical component in this. Just as we did not want to replace but augment and enhance human creativity with AI, we believed that leisure can similarly augment and enhance our ability to create. Hobbies, side projects, and other pursuits—such as this book—were not just tolerated, but actively encouraged because we understood that this kind of active and high-quality leisure will not only increase our happiness but also feed back into the work we do. To do interesting work, you have to live an interesting life!

I no longer believe that full-time employment and the kind of life I had as a PhD student are mutually exclusive. But they require the right kind of company culture, the right kind of leadership, and trust between everyone involved. Making sure that I work in such a culture, and actively creating it, has become a big priority for me. Thanks to this, my current daily routine is much closer again to what it used to be during my PhD times. The first thing I do after getting up is make a coffee and read for an hour. I love coffee, and this daily ritual of grinding the beans and brewing the perfect cup is really important to me (or maybe that's just me justifying a caffeine addiction …). I spend considerably more time working remotely than in an office, doing things on my own schedule and largely free from distractions, and using frequent changes of scenery (at home, in cafes, in nature) to find new inspiration when my ideas seem to run out. Moving between work locations, whether on a walk or by bike, has also helped me naturally integrate incubation into my everyday routine. I have also rediscovered my old passion for side projects and hobbies. Some of my current pursuits and obsessions include producing and performing electronic music, baking sourdough bread, growing mushrooms (no, not the magic kind), and staying active through running and CrossFit. Overall, I feel much more happy, creative, productive, and fulfilled again.

However, before concluding this story, I want to briefly talk about one of the potential pitfalls of time off. It turns out that time off is actually not that easy. It takes quite a bit of discipline, and a serious rest ethic. I painfully noticed that for myself at one point while we were writing this book. The freedom I got from work, as well as the freedom that you naturally have as a writer, together with a lack of clear planning and organization on my side, can lead to all of these things sort of blending into each other. Overall my days were quite relaxed, but I squeezed in some "casual work," be that working on the book or my main job, in any blank space in my schedule. Instead of having clear black and white spaces in the calendar, it all became a grey mush. Rather than using time off as a conscious tool, I let it vaguely diffuse through everything, and intermingle with work. While this is definitely much better than constantly "grinding it out," it's far from ideal—at one point, I felt almost burned out from my time off routine. I realized that I had to revisit my own advice about being conscious and deliberate about time off. Luckily, and in no small part due to studying and practicing the advice of the many amazing people who made it into this book, I quickly recovered my balance and became more deliberate about work and rest again. Time off is one of the most wonderful and powerful skills out there. But it is exactly that, a skill. It needs to be practiced and applied effectively.

As you can probably tell by my story, as well as the fact that I coauthored this book, I have spent a lot of time thinking about time off. I'm very confident in saying that most of the good things that happened in my life, most of my biggest achievements, did not happen in spite of me taking so much time off, but exactly because of all the leisure and the random adventures and pursuits they allowed me to follow.

I have been extremely fortunate to have experienced just how powerful the right kind of time off can be (and how disastrous the constant busyness is). And still, even I ended up forgetting this from time to time. I can only imagine how hard it is for people who were not in such a fortunate situation to have made this kind of experience, to really realize the power and importance of time off. But I truly hope that with this book we can help to show more people what is possible if you slow down from time to time and don't buy into the cult of busyness. Let's reclaim our time off and elevate leisure once again to one of the most noble and valuable things we can do with our lives.

MARIYA SUZUKI

Illustrator/Artist

I was getting a lot of client work and didn't know how to say no to any of it. In order to catch up, almost every morning I would go to my studio early to get started with the day's work, and not go home until the very last train around midnight. I felt stress and pressure, and it was easy to slip into a bad mood. But since many other illustrators struggle to get enough work, I felt like I should be extremely happy to have all these gigs and opportunities. I was being paid to do what I loved—drawing.

What I didn't realize was that while drawing was both my work and my hobby, the way I approached the two aspects and what I got out of it were entirely different. The illustrations I did for my work were to make clients happy, so I was constantly under pressure and worrying if the clients liked my illustrations. I would not venture too far out of the box or experiment with my style. Somehow, I had shaped my drawing style to fit the box, thinking that would make things easier for both me and for the clients, without realizing that this very choice I made would later take delight out of the act of drawing. The drawings I did in my free time, for no one other than myself, felt very different from that. Without any clear goal or purpose and none of the concerns about making "mistakes," these drawings became a source of relaxing self-expression, joyful discovery, and constant improvement. But with all the client work, at the end of the day there was neither the time nor the motivation left to just draw for myself. What was most natural to me—drawing in my sketchbook daily—was slowly but steadily disappearing. Like the sun gradually getting covered by clouds, or a smile fading into a sad face, so too were the color and joy slowly being removed from my life.

Once I realized that I wasn't enjoying drawing the same way I used to, near the end of 2018, I also found myself exhausted and unhappy. Drawing is what defines me, and the fact that I was no longer happy, despite drawing for a living, meant that something had to change. Granting myself some time off during New Year's, I noticed that something very ordinary, even boring at times, like spending a week with my parents, was so enjoyable and precious, and I felt refreshed afterward. I also started taking long walks, and now commute to my studio by foot nearly every day, almost a one-hour journey each way. Similarly, I started using my time for other activities like baking bread and crafting furniture for my studio, which made me happy. It was these little joys I found in my new lifestyle that helped me to realize the importance of time off.

I also started evaluating new projects in a different way. Before, I was trapped in the idea of having to accept all kinds of work, giving little thought to whether I'd really enjoy doing the work or not. But that's really important—what kind of work you are doing –if you want to keep enjoying and loving drawing. As I started to appreciate time off and found new hobbies, it allowed me to step back and give more thought to which work I wanted to do. It became quite clear: if I feel so much pressure and not a lot of joy, then the work is probably not for me. I am an illustrator, but first, I am an artist and I need to know what kind of artist I am. I still struggle with this. Still trying to figure out where I want to be as an artist. I don't know if I will ever figure it out completely. It's like a lifelong process because it's organic. But I think time off helps in this process.

So it was the perfect timing, and the perfect project, when John and Max approached me to work on the illustrations for this book. Not only could I reflect on and improve my own rest ethic with this and work on an exciting project I deeply cared about, I could also contribute to help others who are struggling with similar issues. I have seen the same, or even worse, problems in many people around me, especially in Japan. I believe it's a learning process, and each person has to find their own approach. I am working on finding mine.

ACKNOWLEDGMENTS

John owes a large group of people a meal or a drink for helping him foster the courage and energy to cowrite this book. First, to his family for showing him the beauty of farming, cooking, hosting a drawn-out meal, and spending time outdoors to recharge and gain a new perspective. Second, to the wide-ranging friends around the world who have been embodying this book before it was written. They are the people who have not lectured him about the importance of not always working, but have helped him step away from work and enjoy moments through taking him on hikes, forcing him into drum circles, ordering one more cocktail that he didn't need, challenging him to a midday workout, and encouraging him to live a simple life through the disciplined pursuit of less. Third, he would like to thank you, the reader, in advance for not only getting more out of life by taking time off but for creating more creative and interesting work because of it. We need you to not be burned out. Thank you for trying to change.

Max wants to thank his family, and particularly his mum Monika, for always unconditionally supporting him and allowing him to find his own path, free from any pressure to follow conventions or other people's ideas of success. Rather than pushing him to work harder, she would constantly ask if he is taking enough time off, be it from studying or later from work. Her love for books also rubbed off on Max and turned him into an avid reader from an early age. All these factors were essential in leading Max down the path that would ultimately lead to this book. Thank you!

Max also wants to thank his friend and fellow writer YuYang Huang. It was Yang who initially suggested that he should start writing down and sharing his thoughts, and who kept encouraging him to continue to do so. Acting as Max's accountability partner, she also made sure that he would stick to his commitments and ambitions. Above all, she has always been there to listen to his ramblings about the difficulties of writing, as well as life in general, and taught him how to be "a fucking bohemian writer."

Max also wants to thank all his other friends for their continued support and encouragement, and especially Shizuka Kamada for reminding him how to spend a lazy Saturday, and helping him stay sane during some of the tougher stretches of writing this book.

Mariya wants to thank John and Max for inviting her into this meaningful project and for, just in time, giving a name to what she had just put her foot in—time off. She is extremely grateful to her parents who have always shown her that she can pursue the life she desires and dreams. If it wasn't for them, her dream of becoming a professional illustrator might have disappeared along the way. She also wants to thank all of her cool friends who already practice time off in the most natural ways and guided her to see what she couldn't see in her most stressful days. She is grateful for always being surrounded by all the beautiful and patient people.

Together we want to thank our amazing editor Ann Maynard from Command+Z Content for turning our, at times, rambling, scattered, and long-winded ideas into the coherent and crisp narrative you now hold in your hands. We came to her with a rough (and very bulky) block of marble, and she guided us in chiseling away the edges to reveal the beautiful sculpture that was hidden underneath. And to our copyeditor Susan Cahill, for being our eagle eye, our comma-killer, our reference-hunter, and for reminding Max that "realize" is spelled with a "z."

Thanks to our designer Nikki Ellis for integrating Mariya's illustrations into the text in such a wonderful way, and also working with Mariya to design the gorgeous cover and interior. We really appreciate your patience with our long back-and-forth conversations and condensing all our ideas and inspirations into the final design.

To all our early test readers: Thank you so much for your support from the very beginning, when *Time Off* was barely more than a vague idea and a handful of short profile drafts. Your feedback, ideas, and, above all, enthusiasm and motivation made this book what it is today and kept us moving forward in times when we doubted ourselves and what we were trying to achieve. For this, a huge thank-you for gifting us your time and attention, Alyssa Estrada, Amanda Allen, Bill Davidson, Bogdan Teleaga, Carolina Canavati, David Topf, Erik Ours, Evelyn Chou, Faris Oweis, Gabby Jo Foster, Hayley Francis, James Baird, Jennifer Proescher, Mike Shaug, Moritz Graf, Natalia Wolff, Nick Walker, Niko Lanzuisi, Pablo Rendon, Sarah Rountree Schlessinger, Seth Williams, Shane O'Donnell, Shayna Dunitz, Shea Sulkin, Todd Spitz, Tomek Rutkowski, and Trevor Cobb. In particular, we want to thank Andrew Attard for his continued support and feedback that in some cases was more detailed than our draft itself. Your embrace of time off really inspired us. If you ever need test readers for a book draft yourself (and we hope you will), let us know!

Finally, we want to thank all the people whose stories made it into this book for inspiring us with their rest ethic, entertaining us with their fascinating stories, and showing us clear and actionable steps we can take to incorporate time off into our own lives. We are particularly grateful to those who took the time to talk to us in person, comment on early drafts, and give us valuable feedback. Thank you for being a part of this book, as well as pioneers of the time off movement! We hope that many of you reading this will follow their example.

BIBLIOGRAPHY

What is Time Off?

Aristotle. *Aristotle's Politics: Writings from the Complete Works: Politics, Economics, Constitution of Athens*. Edited by Jonathan Barnes and Melissa Lane. Princeton, NJ: Princeton University Press, 2017.

"Aristotle on Work vs. Leisure," The Noble Leisure Project. Accessed March 20, 2020. https://blogs.harvard.edu/nobleleisure/aristotle-on-work-vs-leisure/.

Fried, Jason, and David Heinemeier Hansson. *It Doesn't Have to Be Crazy at Work*. New York: Harper Business, 2018.

Miller, Bruce B. *Your Life in Rhythm: Less Stress, More Peace, Less Frustration, More Fulfillment, Less Discouragement, More Hope*. McKinney: TX Dadlin, 2016.

Minerd, Matthew. "Leisure: The Basis of Everything?" *Homiletic & Pastoral Review*, January 20, 2017. https://www.hprweb.com/2017/01/leisure-the-basis-of-everything/.

Newport, Cal. *Digital Minimalism: Choosing a Focused Life in a Noisy World*. New York: Penguin Business, 2020.

Oshin, Mayo. "Einstein's Most Effective Life Hack Wasn't about Productivity." Quartz at Work. Accessed March 20, 2020. https://qz.com/work/1494627/einstein-on-the-only-productivity-tip-youll-ever-need-to-know/.

Pieper, Josef. *Leisure: The Basis of Culture*. Indianapolis: Liberty Fund, 2010.

Russell, Bertrand. "In Praise of Idleness." *Harper's Magazine*, October 1932. https://harpers.org/archive/1932/10/in-praise-of-idleness/.

Sahlins, Marshall. "Hunter-Gatherers: Insights from a Golden Affluent Age." *Pacific Ecologist*, no. 18 (January 1, 2009): 3–9.

Sipiora, Phillip, and James S. Baumlin, eds. *Rhetoric and Kairos: Essays in History, Theory, and Praxis*. Albany, NY: SUNY Press, 2002.

Taleb, Nassim Nicholas. *The Bed of Procrustes: Philosophical and Practical Aphorisms*. Reprint edition. New York: Random House Trade Paperbacks, 2016.

Thompson, E. P. "Time, Work-Discipline, and Industrial Capitalism." *Past & Present*, no. 38 (1967): 56–97.

Time Off Throughout History

Aarstol, Stephan. *The Five-Hour Workday: Live Differently, Unlock Productivity, and Find Happiness*. Lioncrest Publishing, 2016.

"Bertrand Russell," Wikipedia. Last modified April 13, 2020. https://en.wikipedia.org/wiki/Bertrand_Russell.

"Burn-Out an 'Occupational Phenomenon': International Classification of Diseases," WHO. Accessed March 23, 2020. http://www.who.int/mental_health/evidence/burn-out/en/.

Davis, Pete, and Jon Staff. "People Fought for Time Off from Work, So Stop Working So Much." Fast Company, February 23, 2019. https://www.fastcompany.com/90309992/people-fought-for-time-off-from-work-so-stop-working-so-much.

Doukas, Dimitra, and E. Paul Durrenberger. "Gospel of Wealth, Gospel of Work: Counterhegemony in the U.S. Working Class." American Anthropologist 110, no. 2 (2008): 214–24.

"The 5-Day Week in the Ford Plants." Monthly Labor Review 23, no. 6 (December 1926): 1162–66.

Fogg, B. J. Persuasive Technology: Using Computers to Change What We Think and Do. San Francisco: Morgan Kaufmann, 2003. https://doi.org/10.1016/B978-1-55860-643-2.X5000-8.

Graeber, David. Bullshit Jobs: A Theory. New York: Simon & Schuster, 2018.

Huffington, Arianna. "Burnout Is Now Officially a Workplace Crisis." Thrive Global, June 3, 2019. https://thriveglobal.in/stories/burnout-is-now-officially-a-workplace-crisis/.

———. "Don't Call It a Vacation: Thrive Time Is the Key to Sustainable Success." Thrive Global, July 12, 2019. https://thriveglobal.com/stories/vacation-time-off-pto-prevent-stress-burnout-arianna-huffington/.

———. "Microsteps: The Big Idea That's Too Small to Fail, According to Science." Thrive Global, February 27, 2019. https://thriveglobal.com/stories/microsteps-big-idea-too-small-to-fail-healthy-habits-willpower/.

Katz, Emily Tess. "The Moment Arianna Knew She Had to Change Her Life." HuffPost, March 25, 2014. https://www.huffingtonpost.com/2014/03/25/arianna-huffington-fainting_n_5030365.html.

Newport, Cal. Deep Work: Rules for Focused Success in a Distracted World. New York: Grand Central Publishing, 2016.

"The Nobel Prize in Literature 1950," NobelPrize.org. Accessed March 21, 2020. https://www.nobelprize.org/prizes/literature/1950/summary/.

Petersen, Anne Helen. "How Millennials Became the Burnout Generation." BuzzFeed News, January 5, 2019. https://www.buzzfeednews.com/article/annehelenpetersen/millennials-burnout-generation-debt-work.

Russell, Bertrand. "In Praise of Idleness." Harper's Magazine, October 1932. https://harpers.org/archive/1932/10/in-praise-of-idleness/.

Saad, Linda. "The '40-Hour' Workweek Is Actually Longer—by Seven Hours." Gallup.com, August 29, 2014. https://news.gallup.com/poll/175286/hour-workweek-actually-longer-seven-hours.aspx.

Schroeder, Doris. Work Incentives and Welfare Provision: The "Pathological" Theory of Unemployment. Oxford and New York: Routledge, 2018.

Weber, Max. The Protestant Ethic and the Spirit of Capitalism. Edited by R. H. Tawney. Translated by Talcott Parsons. Mineola, NY: Dover Publications, 2003.

Creativity

Bennett, Arnold. *How to Live on 24 Hours a Day*. London: New Age Press, 1908.

Currey, Mason. *Daily Rituals: How Great Minds Make Time, Find Inspiration, and Get to Work*. New York: Picador, 2014.

Eiduson, Bernice T. "Scientists and Their Psychological World." *Engineering and Science* 26, no. 5 (February 1, 1963): 22–30.

Epstein, David. *Range: Why Generalists Triumph in a Specialized World*. New York: Riverhead Books, 2019.

Goldsmith, Margie. "Google A.I. Engineer/Rapper Wants Kids to Know It's Cool to Be a Genius." *Forbes*, January 21, 2019. https://www.forbes.com/sites/margiegoldsmith/2019/01/21/google-a-i-engineerrapper-wants-kids-to-know-its-cool-to-be-a-genius/.

Hallowell, Edward M. *CrazyBusy: Overstretched, Overbooked, and About to Snap! Strategies for Handling Your Fast-Paced Life*. New York: Ballantine Books, 2007.

Harford, Tim. "*A Powerful Way to Unleash Your Natural Creativity*." TED video, 2018. https://www.ted.com/talks/tim_harford_a_powerful_way_to_unleash_your_natural_creativity.

———. "Multi-Tasking: How to Survive in the 21st Century." *Financial Times*, September 3, 2015. https://www.ft.com/content/bbf1f84a-51c2-11e5-8642-453585f2cfcd.

Huxley, Aldous. The Divine Within: Selected Writings on Enlightenment. New York: Harper Perennial, 2013.

———. Music at Night and Other Essays. London: Flamingo, 1994.

Jacobsen, Annie. *The Pentagon's Brain: An Uncensored History of DARPA, America's Top-Secret Military Research Agency*. New York: Back Bay Books, 2016.

Kerst, Friedrich. *Beethoven: The Man and the Artist, As Revealed in His Own Words*. Edited by Henry Edward Krehbiel. New York: Dover Publications, 2011.

Koestler, Arthur. *Act of Creation*. New York: Macmillan Company, 1966.

Mejia, Zameena, and Mary Stevens. "This Engineer Was a Homeless Teen—Now He's a Rapper Who Also Works at Google." CNBC, January 8, 2019. https://www.cnbc.com/2019/01/04/google-engineer-went-from-homeless-to-rapper-and-ai-computer-scientist--.html.

Newport, Cal. *Deep Work: Rules for Focused Success in a Distracted World*. New York: Grand Central Publishing, 2016.

"The Nobel Prize in Physics 1964," NobelPrize.org. Accessed March 23, 2020. https://www.nobelprize.org/prizes/physics/1964/townes/facts/.

Rolland, Romain. *Beethoven the Creator*. Translated by Ernest Newman. New York: Garden City Publishing, 2007.

Tchaikovsky, Modeste. *The Life and Letters of Peter Ilich Tchaikovsky*. Edited by Rosa Newmarch. Honolulu, HI: University Press of the Pacific, 2004.

Tory, Brandon. "How Being an Apple and Google Engineer, and a Rapper, Are All

the Same. #Multidream." Medium, October 18, 2018. https://medium.com/@
brandontory/multidream-256d88cf8c3e.

———. "M U L T I D R E A M." brandontory. Accessed March 23, 2020. https://
www.brandontory.com/multidream.

Townes, Charles. Adventures of a Scientist: Conversation with Charles Townes.
Interview by Harry Kreisler, February 15, 2000. http://globetrotter.berkeley.edu/
people/Townes/townes-con0.html.

Wallas, Graham. *The Art of Thought*. London: Solis Press, 2014.

Rest

Bakker, Arnold B., Ana I. Sanz-Vergel, Alfredo Rodríguez-Muñoz, and Wido G.
M. Oerlemans. "The State Version of the Recovery Experience Questionnaire:
A Multilevel Confirmatory Factor Analysis." *European Journal of Work and
Organizational Psychology* 24, no. 3 (May 4, 2015): 350–59. https://doi.org/10.108
0/1359432X.2014.903242.

Bell, Eric Temple. *Men of Mathematics*. New York & London: Simon & Schuster,
1986.

Carr, Michelle. "How to Dream Like Salvador Dali." *Psychology Today*, February 20,
2015. https://www.psychologytoday.com/blog/dream-factory/201502/how-dream-
salvador-dali.

Ericsson, K. Anders, Ralf T. Krampe, and Clemens Tesch-Römer. "The Role of Deliberate
Practice in the Acquisition of Expert Performance." *Psychological Review* 100, no. 3
(1993): 363–406. https://doi.org/10.1037/0033-295X.100.3.363.

Frenzel, Max F., Bogdan Teleaga, and Asahi Ushio. "Latent Space Cartography:
Generalised Metric-Inspired Measures and Measure-Based Transformations for
Generative Models." *ArXiv:1902.02113 [Cs, Stat]*, February 6, 2019. http://arxiv.
org/abs/1902.02113.

Fried, Jason. "Workplace Experiments." Signal v. Noise by Basecamp, March 5, 2008.
https://signalvnoise.com/posts/893-workplace-experiments.

Immordino-Yang, Mary Helen, Joanna A. Christodoulou, and Vanessa Singh. "Rest Is
Not Idleness: Implications of the Brain's Default Mode for Human Development
and Education." *Perspectives on Psychological Science* 7, no. 4 (July 1, 2012): 352–64.
https://doi.org/10.1177/1745691612447308.

Kierkegaard, Soren. *The Concept of Anxiety*. Macon, GA: Mercer, 1985.

———. *Either/Or: A Fragment of Life*. Edited by Victor Eremita. Translated by Alastair
Hannay. London & New York: Penguin Classics, 1992.

Liu, Luke. "What Is Crop Rotation?" WorldAtlas, April 25, 2017. https://www.
worldatlas.com/articles/what-is-crop-rotation.html.

Pang, Alex Soojung-Kim. *Rest: Why You Get More Done When You Work Less*. New York:
Basic Books, 2018.

Pascal, Blaise. *Pensées*. Translated by A. J. Krailsheimer. Penguin Classics. London &
New York: Penguin Books, 1995.

Penfield, Wilder. *The Second Career and Other Essays and Addresses*. Boston: Little Brown, 1963.

Poincaré, Henri. *The Foundations of Science: Science and Hypothesis, the Value of Science, Science and Method*. Translated by George Bruce Halsted. New York: Science Press, 1929.

Raichle, Marcus E., Ann Mary MacLeod, Abraham Z. Snyder, William J. Powers, Debra A. Gusnard, and Gordon L. Shulman. "A Default Mode of Brain Function." *Proceedings of the National Academy of Sciences of the United States of America* 98, no. 2 (January 16, 2001): 676–82.

Servick, Kelly. "How Exercise Beefs Up the Brain." Science | AAAS, October 10, 2013. https://www.sciencemag.org/news/2013/10/how-exercise-beefs-brain.

Sonnentag, Sabine. "Psychological Detachment from Work during Leisure Time: The Benefits of Mentally Disengaging from Work." *Current Directions in Psychological Science* 21, no. 2 (April 1, 2012): 114–18. https://doi.org/10.1177/0963721411434979.

Westerborg, Dennis Van. *Quotes That Breathe*. Whimprint Books, 2016.

Sleep

Bezos, Jeff. "Why Getting 8 Hours of Sleep Is Good for Amazon Shareholders: Interview with Thrive Global." Medium, April 27, 2017. https://medium.com/thrive-global/jeff-bezos-sleep-amazon-19c617c59daa.

Cartwright, Rosalind D. *The Twenty–Four Hour Mind: The Role of Sleep and Dreaming in Our Emotional Lives*. Oxford: Oxford University Press, 2010.

Cooke, Rachel. "'Sleep Should Be Prescribed': What Those Late Nights Out Could Be Costing You." *The Observer*, September 24, 2017. https://www.theguardian.com/lifeandstyle/2017/sep/24/why-lack-of-sleep-health-worst-enemy-matthew-walker-why-we-sleep.

Domínguez, Fernando, Valentín Fuster, Juan Miguel Fernández-Alvira, Leticia Fernández-Friera, Beatriz López-Melgar, Ruth Blanco-Rojo, Antonio Fernández-Ortiz, et al. "Association of Sleep Duration and Quality with Subclinical Atherosclerosis." *Journal of the American College of Cardiology* 73, no. 2 (January 14, 2019): 134–44. https://doi.org/10.1016/j.jacc.2018.10.060.

Frenzel, Max. "The Effects of Caffeine, Alcohol, and Exercise on Sleep: Analyzing the Surprising Results." Medium, December 4, 2018. https://medium.com/better-humans/the-effects-of-caffeine-alcohol-and-exercise-on-sleep-analyzing-the-surprising-results-117330af2480.

Gritters, Jenni. "Why Strava's CEO Doesn't Work Evenings or Weekends." Medium, April 30, 2019. https://elemental.medium.com/why-stravas-ceo-doesn-t-work-evenings-or-weekends-a72093618711.

Irwin, M., J. McClintick, C. Costlow, M. Fortner, J. White, and J. C. Gillin. "Partial Night Sleep Deprivation Reduces Natural Killer and Cellular Immune Responses in Humans." *FASEB Journal: Official Publication of the Federation of American Societies for Experimental Biology* 10, no. 5 (April 1996): 643–53. https://doi.org/10.1096/fasebj.10.5.8621064.

James, LeBron, Mike Mancias, and Tim Ferriss. "LeBron James and His Top-Secret Trainer, Mike Mancias." *The Tim Ferriss Show*. September 27, 2018. https://tim.blog/2018/11/27/lebron-james-mike-mancias/.

Jensen, Tina Kold, Anna-Maria Andersson, Niels Erik Skakkebæk, Ulla Nordstrøm Joensen, Martin Blomberg Jensen, Tina Harmer Lassen, Loa Nordkap, et al. "Association of Sleep Disturbances with Reduced Semen Quality: A Cross-Sectional Study among 953 Healthy Young Danish Men." *American Journal of Epidemiology* 177, no. 10 (May 15, 2013): 1027–37. https://doi.org/10.1093/aje/kws420.

Mah, Cheri D., Kenneth E. Mah, Eric J. Kezirian, and William C. Dement. "The Effects of Sleep Extension on the Athletic Performance of Collegiate Basketball Players." *Sleep* 34, no. 7 (July 1, 2011): 943–50. https://doi.org/10.5665/SLEEP.1132.

Naska, Androniki, Eleni Oikonomou, Antonia Trichopoulou, Theodora Psaltopoulou, and Dimitrios Trichopoulos. "Siesta in Healthy Adults and Coronary Mortality in the General Population." *Archives of Internal Medicine* 167, no. 3 (February 12, 2007): 296–301. https://doi.org/10.1001/archinte.167.3.296.

Rea, Mark S., Mariana G. Figueiro, Katherine M. Sharkey, and Mary A. Carskadon. "Relationship of Morning Cortisol to Circadian Phase and Rising Time in Young Adults with Delayed Sleep Times." Clinical Study. *International Journal of Endocrinology*. Hindawi, 2012. https://doi.org/10.1155/2012/749460.

Sandhu, Amneet, Milan Seth, and Hitinder S. Gurm. "Daylight Savings Time and Myocardial Infarction." *Open Heart* 1, no. 1 (March 1, 2014). https://doi.org/10.1136/openhrt-2013-000019.

Shokri-Kojori, Ehsan, Gene-Jack Wang, Corinde E. Wiers, Sukru B. Demiral, Min Guo, Sung Won Kim, Elsa Lindgren, et al. "ß-Amyloid Accumulation in the Human Brain after One Night of Sleep Deprivation." *Proceedings of the National Academy of Sciences* 115, no. 17 (April 24, 2018): 4483–88. https://doi.org/10.1073/pnas.1721694115.

Walker, Matthew. "Proof the Secret of a Good Sex Life Is Sleeping Apart." *Daily Mail*, November 1, 2018.

———. "*Sleep Is Your Superpower*." TED video, April 2019. https://www.ted.com/talks/matt_walker_sleep_is_your_superpower.

———. *Why We Sleep: The New Science of Sleep and Dreams*. London: Penguin Books, 2018.

Exercise

Barba, Christine. "'Re-Sculpt' Your Brain with Exercise and Lower Dementia Risk by up to 90 Percent, Says Neuroscientist Wendy Suzuki." Being Patient, March 27, 2019. https://www.beingpatient.com/wendy-suzuki-exercise-brain/.

Pang, Alex Soojung-Kim. *Rest: Why You Get More Done When You Work Less*. New York: Basic Books, 2016.

PsiQuantum. "PsiQuantum." Accessed April 8, 2020. https://psiquantum.com/.

Servick, Kelly. "How Exercise Beefs Up the Brain." *Science*, October 10, 2013. https://www.sciencemag.org/news/2013/10/how-exercise-beefs-brain.

Suzuki, Wendy. "The Brain-Changing Benefits of Exercise." TED video. November 2017. https://www.ted.com/talks/wendy_suzuki_the_brain_changing_benefits_of_exercise/transcript.

Waitzkin, Josh. *The Art of Learning: An Inner Journey to Optimal Performance*. New York: Free Press, 2008.

Zahabi, Firas. "JRE MMA Show #32 with Firas Zahabi." *The Joe Rogan Experience Podcast*, June 19, 2018. https://www.youtube.com/watch?reload=9&v=xDsoWp743gM.

Solitude

Aristotle. *Aristotle's Politics: Writings from the Complete Works: Politics, Economics, Constitution of Athens*. Edited by Jonathan Barnes and Melissa Lane. Princeton, NJ: Princeton University Press, 2017.

Bratman, Gregory N., J. Paul Hamilton, Kevin S. Hahn, Gretchen C. Daily, and James J. Gross. "Nature Experience Reduces Rumination and Subgenual Prefrontal Cortex Activation." *Proceedings of the National Academy of Sciences of the United States of America* 112, no. 28 (July 14, 2015): 8567–72. https://doi.org/10.1073/pnas.1510459112.

Cain, Susan. *Quiet: The Power of Introverts in a World That Can't Stop Talking*. New York: Broadway Books, 2013.

Cott, Jonathan. *Conversations with Glenn Gould*. Chicago, IL: University of Chicago Press, 2005.

Dunbar, R. I. M. "The Social Brain: Mind, Language, and Society in Evolutionary Perspective." *Annual Review of Anthropology* 32, no. 1 (2003): 163–81. https://doi.org/10.1146/annurev.anthro.32.061002.093158.

Etherwood. "Etherwood's Facebook Page." Facebook, October 4, 2016. https://www.facebook.com/etherwood/photos/a.492668237465654/1154606401271831/?type=1&theater.

———. "Most Wanted: Etherwood Dreams of a Mobile VW Studio." fabric london, June 12, 2015. https://www.fabriclondon.com/blog/view/most-wanted-etherwood-dreams-of-a-mobile-vw-studio.

Flint, Kate. "Reading Uncommonly: Virginia Woolf and the Practice of Reading." *The Yearbook of English Studies* 26 (1996): 187–98. https://doi.org/10.2307/3508657.

Harris, Michael. "Need to Inspire Creativity? Give Daydreaming A Shot." Discover Magazine, May 16, 2017. https://www.discovermagazine.com/mind/need-to-inspire-creativity-give-daydreaming-a-shot.

———. *Solitude: In Pursuit of a Singular Life in a Crowded World*. New York: Thomas Dunne Books, 2017.

Hirst, Jake. "Etherwood Returns with New Music..." UKF, October 23, 2017. https://ukf.com/news/etherwood-returns-new-music/20578.

Hunt, Melissa G., Rachel Marx, Courtney Lipson, and Jordyn Young. "No More FOMO: Limiting Social Media Decreases Loneliness and Depression." *Journal of Social and Clinical Psychology* 37, no. 10 (November 8, 2018): 751–68. https://doi. org/10.1521/jscp.2018.37.10.751.

Klinenberg, Eric. *Going Solo: The Extraordinary Rise and Surprising Appeal of Living Alone*. London & New York: Penguin Books, 2013.

Long, Christopher R., and James R. Averill. "Solitude: An Exploration of Benefits of Being Alone." *Journal for the Theory of Social Behaviour* 33, no. 1 (2003): 21–44. https://doi.org/10.1111/1468-5914.00204.

Mellor, Felicity. "The Power of Silence." *Physics World*, April 3, 2014. https:// physicsworld.com/a/the-power-of-silence/.

Newport, Cal. *Digital Minimalism: Choosing a Focused Life in a Noisy World*. New York: Portfolio, 2019.

Sivers, Derek. "About." Derek Sivers. Accessed April 8, 2020. https://sivers.org/about.

———. "No 'yes.' Either 'HELL YEAH!' or 'No.'" Derek Sivers, August 26, 2009. https://sivers.org/hellyeah.

———. "Parenting: Who Is It Really For?" Derek Sivers, July 26, 2017. https://sivers. org/pa.

———. "Relax for the Same Result." Derek Sivers, October 2, 2015. https://sivers.org/ relax.

———. "Subtract." Derek Sivers, December 5, 2018. https://sivers.org/subtract.

———. "Workspiration with Derek Sivers." Workspiration, January 29, 2014. https:// workspiration.org/derek-sivers.

Thoreau, Henry David. *Walden*. Princeton, NJ: Princeton University Press, 2004.

Waytz, Adam. "2014: What Scientific Idea Is Ready for Retirement?: Humans Are By Nature Social Animals." Edge, 2014. https://www.edge.org/response-detail/25395.

Wozniak, Steve, and Gina Smith. *IWoz: Computer Geek to Cult Icon: How I Invented the Personal Computer, Co-Founded Apple, and Had Fun Doing It*. New York: W. W. Norton & Company, 2006.

Reflection

"A Stoic Response to Rejection." Daily Stoic. August 28, 2017. https://dailystoic.com/ stoic-response-rejection/.

Aquinas, Thomas. *The Summa Theologica of St. Thomas Aquinas*. Translated by Fathers of the English Dominican Province. New York: Christian Classics, 1981.

Aurelius, Marcus. *Meditations*. Translated by Martin Hammond. London: Penguin Classics, 2006.

Epictetus. *Discourses and Selected Writings*. Edited by Robert Dobbin. London: Penguin Classics, 2008.

Godin, Seth. "Do Less." Porchlight Books, August 24, 2004. https://www. porchlightbooks.com/blog/changethis/2004/Do-Less.

———. *Small Is the New Big: And 183 Other Riffs, Rants, and Remarkable Business Ideas*. New York: Portfolio, 2006.

Godin, Seth and Tim Ferriss. "How Seth Godin Manages His Life - Rules, Principles, and Obsessions." *The Tim Ferriss Show*, February 10, 2016. https://tim.blog/2016/02/10/seth-godin/.

Holiday, Ryan. *Obstacle Is the Way*. London: Profile Books, 2015.

Jenkins, Tom. "One of the World's Best Chefs Gives His Cooks Three Days Off a Week." Fine Dining Lovers, September 8, 2017. https://www.finedininglovers.com/article/one-worlds-best-chefs-gives-his-cooks-three-days-week.

Kondo, Marie. *The Life-Changing Magic of Tidying Up: The Japanese Art of Decluttering and Organizing*. Berkeley: Ten Speed Press, 2014.

———. "Marie's Top 5 Productivity Tips." KonMari: The Official Website of Marie Kondo, February 4, 2019. https://konmari.com/marie-kondo-productivity-tips/.

McKeown, Greg. "The Simplest Way to Avoid Wasting Time." Greg McKeown, October 2, 2014. https://gregmckeown.com/simplest-way-avoid-wasting-time/.

Milner, Rebecca. "How I Get It Done: Organizational Guru Marie Kondo." The Cut, March 6, 2018. https://www.thecut.com/2018/03/marie-kondo-lifechanging-magic-tidying-up-interview.html.

Nilsson, Magnus. "Magnus Nilsson Speaking at Food on the Edge 2017." Food on the Edge, February 1, 2018. https://www.youtube.com/watch?v=UOOa0Eqv6hs.

Pieper, Josef. *Leisure: The Basis of Culture*. San Francisco: Ignatius Press, 2009.

Scattergood, Amy. "The Story behind Why Magnus Nilsson Is Closing Fäviken." *Los Angeles Times*, May 6, 2019. https://www.latimes.com/food/la-fo-magnus-nilsson-faviken-restaurant-sweden-closing-20190506-story.html.

Stubblebine, Tony. "Replace Your To-Do List with Interstitial Journaling to Increase Productivity." Medium, September 8, 2017. https://medium.com/better-humans/replace-your-to-do-list-with-interstitial-journaling-to-increase-productivity-4e43109d15ef.

The School of Life. "Thomas Aquinas," November 13, 2014. https://www.theschooloflife.com/thebookoflife/the-great-philosophers-thomas-aquinas/.

Witts, Sophie. "Noma 2.0 to Reduce Opening Hours and Raise Prices to Reduce Staff Stress." Big Hospitality, November 15, 2017. https://www.bighospitality.co.uk/Article/2017/11/15/Noma-2.0-to-reduce-opening-hours-and-raise-prices-to-reduce-staff-stress.

Play

Beard, Alison. "Life's Work: An Interview with Alice Waters." *Harvard Business Review*, May 1, 2017. https://hbr.org/2017/05/alice-waters.

Brown, Stuart L. "Consequences of Play Deprivation." *Scholarpedia* 9, no. 5 (May 7, 2014): 30449. https://doi.org/10.4249/scholarpedia.30449.

Frenzel, Max F., David Jennings, and Terry Rudolph. "Quasi-autonomous Quantum Thermal Machines and Quantum to Classical Energy Flow." *New Journal of Physics* 18 (February 10, 2016): 023037. https://doi:10.1088/1367-2630/18/2/023037.

Gopnik, Alison. *The Philosophical Baby: What Children's Minds Tell Us about Truth,*

Love and the Meaning of Life. London: Bodley Head, 2009.

———. "*What Do Babies Think?*" TED video, July, 2011. https://www.ted.com/talks/alison_gopnik_what_do_babies_think.

Gopnik, Alison, Andrew N. Meltzoff, and Patricia K. Kuhl. *The Scientist in the Crib: What Early Learning Tells Us about the Mind*. New York: William Morrow Paperbacks, 1999.

Hallowell, Edward M. *Shine: Using Brain Science to Get the Best from Your People*. Harvard, MA: Harvard Business Press, 2011.

"Hermann Hesse—Facts." NobelPrize.org. Accessed April 10, 2020. https://www.nobelprize.org/prizes/literature/1946/hesse/facts/.

Hesse, Herman. *My Belief: Essays on Life and Art*. New York: Farrar, Straus & Giroux, 1974.

Hilbert, Matthias. *Hermann Hesse und sein Elternhaus - Zwischen Rebellion und Liebe: Eine biographische Spurensuche*. Stuttgart: Calwer Verlag GmbH, 2005.

Kinchin, Juliet, and Aidan O'Connor. *Century of the Child: Growing by Design 1900–2000*. New York: The Museum of Modern Art, New York, 2012.

Page, Karen, and Andrew Dornenburg. *The Flavor Bible: The Essential Guide to Culinary Creativity, Based on the Wisdom of America's Most Imaginative Chefs*. New York: Little, Brown and Company, 2008.

Pollan, Michael. *How to Change Your Mind: What the New Science of Psychedelics Teaches Us About Consciousness, Dying, Addiction, Depression, and Transcendence*. New York: Penguin Press, 2018.

Potts, Rolf. *Vagabonding: An Uncommon Guide to the Art of Long-Term World Travel*. New York: Villard Books, 2002.

Stuart, Mel. *Willy Wonka & the Chocolate Factory*. Paramount Pictures, 1971.

Waters, Alice. "Interview with Chef, Author and Slow Food Advocate Alice Waters." Julie Ann Wrigley Global Institute of Sustainability, March 20, 2019. https://sustainability.asu.edu/news/archive/interview-with-chef-author-and-slow-food-advocate-alice-waters.

Watts, Alan. *Does It Matter?: Essays on Man's Relation to Materiality*. Novato, CA: New World Library, 2010.

———. *Psychotherapy East and West*. Novato, CA: New World Library, 1989.

———. *Wisdom of Insecurity: A Message for an Age of Anxiety*. London: Rider, 1987.

Travel

Chambers, Veronica. "Lupita Nyong'o Talks *Us* Movie, *Black Panther*, and Working with Jordan Peele." *Marie Claire*, February 5, 2019. https://www.marieclaire.com/celebrity/a26102917/lupita-nyongo-us-interview-2019/.

Drew, Kimberly. "For the Love of Lupita Nyong'o." *Vanity Fair*, September 3, 2019. https://www.vanityfair.com/hollywood/2019/09/lupita-nyongo-cover-story.

Gayduk, Jane. "Beyond Stunts with Stefan Sagmeister." *Sixtysix Magazine*, July 10, 2019. https://sixtysixmag.com/stefan-sagmeister/.

Iyer, Pico. "Why We Travel." Salon, March 18, 2000. https://www.salon.com/2000/03/18/why/.

Kazantzakis, Nikos. *Zorba the Greek*. Translated by Peter Bien. New York: Simon & Schuster, 2014.

Kuralt, Charles. *A Life on the Road*. New York: Ballantine Publishing Group, 1990.

Melville, Herman. *Moby Dick*. Ware, Hertfordshire: Wordsworth Editions Ltd, 1993.

Potts, Rolf. *Vagabonding: An Uncommon Guide to the Art of Long-Term World Travel*. New York: Villard Books, 2002.

Sagmeister, Stefan. "Answers." Sagmeister Inc. Accessed April 13, 2020. http://sagmeister.com/answers/.

"The Power of Time Off." TED video, July 2009. https://www.ted.com/talks/stefan_sagmeister_the_power_of_time_off.

Tzu, Lao. *Tao Te Ching: A New English Version*. Translated by Stephen Mitchell. New York: Harper Perennial Modern Classics, 2006.

Technology

Bloomberg. "Brunello Cucinelli Insists on Balance at His Business." The Business of Fashion, November 5, 2015. https://www.businessoffashion.com/articles/news-analysis/italian-fashion-brunello-cucinelli.

Bosker, Bianca. "The Binge Breaker." *The Atlantic*, November 2016. https://www.theatlantic.com/magazine/archive/2016/11/the-binge-breaker/501122/.

Carr, Nicholas. *The Shallows: What the Internet Is Doing to Our Brains*. New York: W. W. Norton & Company, 2011.

"Center for Humane Technology: Realigning Technology with Humanity." Center for Humane Technology. Accessed April 13, 2020. https://humanetech.com/.

Charnov, Eric L. "Optimal Foraging, the Marginal Value Theorem." *Theoretical Population Biology* 9, no. 2 (April 1, 1976): 129–36. https://doi.org/10.1016/0040-5809(76)90040-X.

Cucinelli, Brunello. "A Fair Working Life." Brunello Cucinelli, June 12, 2012. https://www.brunellocucinelli.com/en/il-giusto-lavoro.html.

———. "Code of Ethics of Brunello Cucinelli," June 20, 2011. investor.brunellocucinelli.com/yep-content/media/Code_of_Ethics.pdf.

Fromm, Erich. *The Anatomy of Human Destructiveness*. New York: Holt Paperbacks, 1992.

Fuchs, Eberhard, and Gabriele Flügge. "Adult Neuroplasticity: More Than 40 Years of Research." *Neural Plasticity* 2014 (2014). https://doi.org/10.1155/2014/541870.

Gazzaley, Adam, and Larry D. Rosen. *The Distracted Mind: Ancient Brains in a High-Tech World*. Cambridge, MA: MIT Press, 2017.

Harris, Tristan. "Essays." Tristan Harris, May 19, 2016. https://www.tristanharris.com/essays.

———. "How Technology Is Hijacking Your Mind — from a Magician and Google Design Ethicist." Medium, October 16, 2019. https://medium.com/thrive-global/

how-technology-hijacks-peoples-minds-from-a-magician-and-google-s-design-ethicist-56d62ef5edf3.

———. "Is Technology Amplifying Human Potential, or Amusing Ourselves to Death?" Daily Good, June 17, 2015. http://www.dailygood.org/story/1063/is-technology-amplifying-human-potential-or-amusing-ourselves-to-death-/.

Kim, Tammy D., Gahae Hong, Jungyoon Kim, and Sujung Yoon. "Cognitive Enhancement in Neurological and Psychiatric Disorders Using Transcranial Magnetic Stimulation (TMS): A Review of Modalities, Potential Mechanisms and Future Implications." *Experimental Neurobiology* 28, no. 1 (February 2019): 1–16. https://doi.org/10.5607/en.2019.28.1.1.

Lendved, Nolan. "Lynda Barry at NASA: Drawing to Infinity and Beyond." Wisconsin Institute for Discovery, June 9, 2016. https://wid.wisc.edu/lynda-barry-at-nasa/.

Leroy, Sophie. "Why Is It So Hard to Do My Work? The Challenge of Attention Residue When Switching between Work Tasks." *Organizational Behavior and Human Decision Processes* 109, no. 2 (July 1, 2009): 168–81. https://doi.org/10.1016/j.obhdp.2009.04.002.

Li, Yunyun, Fang Liu, Qin Zhang, Xinghua Liu, and Ping Wei. "The Effect of Mindfulness Training on Proactive and Reactive Cognitive Control." *Frontiers in Psychology* 9 (June 20, 2018). https://doi.org/10.3389/fpsyg.2018.01002.

Malik, Om. "Brunello Cucinelli." On my Om, April 27, 2015. https://om.co/2015/04/27/brunello-cucinelli-2/.

Mandolesi, Laura, Francesca Gelfo, Laura Serra, Simone Montuori, Arianna Polverino, Giuseppe Curcio, and Giuseppe Sorrentino. "Environmental Factors Promoting Neural Plasticity: Insights from Animal and Human Studies." *Neural Plasticity* 2017 (2017). https://doi.org/10.1155/2017/7219461.

Mandolesi, Laura, Arianna Polverino, Simone Montuori, Francesca Foti, Giampaolo Ferraioli, Pierpaolo Sorrentino, and Giuseppe Sorrentino. "Effects of Physical Exercise on Cognitive Functioning and Wellbeing: Biological and Psychological Benefits." *Frontiers in Psychology* 9 (April 27, 2018). https://doi.org/10.3389/fpsyg.2018.00509.

Newport, Cal. *Deep Work: Rules for Focused Success in a Distracted World*. New York: Grand Central Publishing, 2016.

———. *Digital Minimalism: Choosing a Focused Life in a Noisy World*. New York: Portfolio, 2019.

Postman, Neil. *Technopoly: The Surrender of Culture to Technology*. New York: Vintage, 1993.

Rosen, L. D., A. F. Lim, J. Felt, L. M. Carrier, N. A. Cheever, J. M. Lara-Ruiz, J. S. Mendoza, and J. Rokkum. "Media and Technology Use Predicts Ill-Being among Children, Preteens and Teenagers Independent of the Negative Health Impacts of Exercise and Eating Habits." *Computers in Human Behavior* 35 (June 2014): 364–75. https://doi.org/10.1016/j.chb.2014.01.036.

Shlain, Tiffany. "Do Yourself a Favor: Unplug This Shabbat." The Forward, March 2,

2017. https://forward.com/scribe/364784/do-yourself-a-favor-unplug-this-shabbat/.

Shlain, Tiffany, and John Fitch. "Tech Shabbats with Tiffany Shlain." *Time Off*, June 10, 2018. https://anchor.fm/timeoff/episodes/Tech-Shabbats-With-Tiffany-Shlain-e1kcjd.

Skinner, B. F. *Science and Human Behavior*. Oxford, England: Macmillan, 1953.

Stenfors, Cecilia U. D., Stephen C. Van Hedger, Kathryn E. Schertz, Francisco A. C. Meyer, Karen E. L. Smith, Greg J. Norman, Stefan C. Bourrier, et al. "Positive Effects of Nature on Cognitive Performance across Multiple Experiments: Test Order but Not Affect Modulates the Cognitive Effects." *Frontiers in Psychology* 10 (2019). https://doi.org/10.3389/fpsyg.2019.01413.

Thoreau, Henry David. *Walden*. Princeton, NJ: Princeton University Press, 2004.

Zanto, Theodore P., and Adam Gazzaley. "Neural Suppression of Irrelevant Information Underlies Optimal Working Memory Performance." *The Journal of Neuroscience* 29, no. 10 (March 11, 2009): 3059–66. https://doi.org/10.1523/JNEUROSCI.4621-08.2009.

The Future of Work

Aarstol, Stephan. *The Five-Hour Workday: Live Differently, Unlock Productivity, and Find Happiness*. Lioncrest Publishing, 2016.

———. "How to Make a 5-Hour Workday Work for You." *Entrepreneur*, July 27, 2016. https://www.entrepreneur.com/article/279772.

———. "My Company Implemented a 5-Hour Workday — and the Results Have Been Astounding." Thrive Global, October 3, 2018. https://thriveglobal.com/stories/my-company-implemented-a-5-hour-workday-and-the-results-have-been-astounding/.

Adeney, Pete. "About." Mr. Money Mustache, April 27, 2014. https://www.mrmoneymustache.com/about/.

———. "The 4% Rule: The Easy Answer to 'How Much Do I Need for Retirement?'" Mr. Money Mustache, May 29, 2012. https://www.mrmoneymustache.com/2012/05/29/how-much-do-i-need-for-retirement/.

———. "Great News—Early Retirement Doesn't Mean You'll Stop Working." Mr. Money Mustache, April 16, 2015. https://www.mrmoneymustache.com/2015/04/15/great-news-early-retirement-doesnt-mean-youll-stop-working/.

———. "Seek Not to Be Entertained." Mr. Money Mustache, September 20, 2017. https://www.mrmoneymustache.com/2017/09/20/seek-not-to-be-entertained/.

Borges, Jorge Luis. *The Library of Babel*. Translated by Andrew Hurley. Boston: David R. Godine Publisher Inc, 2000.

Branson, Richard. "Flexible Working Is Smart Working." Text. Virgin, February 3, 2015. https://www.virgin.com/richard-branson/flexible-working-smart-working.

———. "Give People the Freedom of Where to Work." Text. Virgin, February 25, 2013. https://www.virgin.com/richard-branson/give-people-the-freedom-of-where-to-work.

———. "My (Usual) Daily Routine." Text. Virgin, April 7, 2017. https://www.virgin.com/richard-branson/my-usual-daily-routine.

———. "Proof That Flexible Working Works." Text. Virgin, April 26, 2019. https://www.virgin.com/richard-branson/proof-flexible-working-works.

———. "The Way We All Work Is Going to Change." Text. Virgin, December 12, 2018. https://www.virgin.com/richard-branson/way-we-all-work-going-change.

Fried, Jason, and David Heinemeier Hansson. *It Doesn't Have to Be Crazy at Work*. New York: Harper Business, 2018.

Fujimoto, Taro. "Work-Life Balance More Important Than Ever." Japan Today, March 9, 2009. https://japantoday.com/category/features/executive-impact/work-life-balance-more-important-than-ever.

Gloria, Kristine. "Artificial Intimacy: A Report on the 4th Annual Aspen Roundtable on Artificial Intelligence." The Aspen Institute, 2020. https://csreports.aspeninstitute.org/documents/AI2020.pdf.

Helgoe, Louise. *Introvert Power: Why Your Inner Life Is Your Hidden Strength*. Naperville, IL: Sourcebooks, 2013.

"Impact." Deepmind. Accessed April 22, 2020. https://deepmind.com/impact.

"Japan Debuts Legal Cap on Long Work Hours under Labor Reform Law, but for Now Only Big Firms Affected." *Japan Times*, April 1, 2019. https://www.japantimes.co.jp/news/2019/04/01/business/japan-debuts-legal-cap-long-work-hours-labor-reform-law-now-big-firms-affected/#.XdtM8S-Q3zI.

Kay, Alan C. "Predicting the Future." *Stanford Engineering* 1, no. 1 (Autumn 1989): 1–6.

Komuro, Yoshie. "Life Balance." TEDx Talks, June 29, 2012. https://www.youtube.com/watch?v=2Y4E2uCuJaE.

Kreider, Tim. *We Learn Nothing: Essays*. New York: Simon & Schuster, 2013.

Lee, Kai-Fu. *AI Superpowers: China, Silicon Valley, and the New World Order*. Boston: Houghton Mifflin Harcourt, 2018.

———. "Automation Will Force Us to Realize That We Are Not Defined by What We Do." Quartz, October 10, 2018. https://qz.com/1383648/automation-will-remind-us-that-we-are-not-defined-by-what-we-do/.

———. "We Are Here to Create." Edge. Accessed April 22, 2020. https://www.edge.org/conversation/kai_fu_lee-we-are-here-to-create.

Markoff, John. "Business Technology; Talking to Machines: Progress Is Speeded - The New York Times." *New York Times*, July 6, 1988. https://www.nytimes.com/1988/07/06/business/business-technology-talking-to-machines-progress-is-speeded.html.

Metz, Cade. "In Two Moves, AlphaGo and Lee Sedol Redefined the Future." *Wired*, March 16, 2016. https://www.wired.com/2016/03/two-moves-alphago-lee-sedol-redefined-future/.

Odell, Jenny. *How to Do Nothing: Resisting the Attention Economy*. Brooklyn, NY: Melville House, 2019.

Purtill, Corinne. "A Former Symbol of Silicon Valley's 'Crush It' Culture Now Regrets Working So Much." Quartz at Work, December 9, 2018. https://qz.com/work/1488217/a-former-symbol-of-silicon-valleys-crush-it-culture-now-regrets-working-so-much/.

Russell, Bertrand. "In Praise of Idleness." *Harper's Magazine*, October 1932. https://harpers.org/archive/1932/10/in-praise-of-idleness/.

Schawbel, Dan. "Shark Tank Roundtable —Their Best and Worst Deals." Forbes, June 4, 2012. https://www.forbes.com/sites/danschawbel/2012/06/04/shark-tank-roundtable-their-best-and-worst-deals/#6938437f9ca7.

Schwab, Klaus. "Globalization 4.0 - What Does It Mean?" World Economic Forum, November 5, 2018. https://www.weforum.org/agenda/2018/11/globalization-4-what-does-it-mean-how-it-will-benefit-everyone/.

Silver, David. "AlphaZero and Self Play (David Silver, DeepMind)." *AI Podcast*, April 4, 2020. https://www.youtube.com/watch?v=e77NkSjny H4&feature=youtu.be.

"Standup Paddle Boarding Careers at Tower." Tower Paddle Boards. Accessed April 22, 2020. https://www.towerpaddleboards.com/v/tower-careers.htm.

Tromp, John. "Counting Legal Positions in Go." John Tromp. Accessed April 22, 2020. https://tromp.github.io/go/legal.html.

Zuckerman, Andrew. "Kai-Fu Lee on the Power of A.I. to Transform Humanity." Time Sensitive. Accessed April 22, 2020. https://www.timesensitive.fm/episode/kai-fu-lee-power-artificial-intelligence-transform-humanity/.